PATH-WORKING AND THE TREE OF LIFE

Other Books by Ted Andrews

Animal Speak
Animal Speak Workbook
Animal Wise
The Art of Shapeshifting
Crystal Balls & Crystal Bowls
Dream Alchemy
Enchantment of the Faerie Realm
The Healer's Manual
How to Heal with Color
How to Meet and Work with Spirit Guides
How to See and Read the Aura
How to Uncover Your Past Lives
The Intercession of Spirits
Nature Speak
Psychic Protection
The Sacred Power in Your Name
Sacred Sounds
Secret Doors of the Qabala
Simplified Qabala Magic

TED ANDREWS

PATH-WORKING AND THE TREE OF LIFE

A Qabala Guide to
Empowerment & Intuition

LLEWELLYN
WOODBURY, MINNESOTA

Dragonhawk
Publishing

Note: The text for this edition is the originally published work. There are words and phrases included in this text that are outdated and no longer culturally acceptable.

First Printing
Originally published by Dragonhawk Publishing in 2009
First Llewellyn Publications Edition, 2026

Second Edition
First released under the title of *More Simplified Magic*

Cover design by Shira Atakpu
Cover art by Siolo Thompson

ISBN: 978-0-7387-8353-6

Library of Congress Cataloging-in-Publication Data
Copyright is registered with the Library of Congress
Registratrion Number: TX0004712231.

Llewellyn Publications
A Division of Llewellyn Worldwide Ltd.
2143 Wooddale Drive
Woodbury, MN 55125-2989
www.llewellyn.com

Printed in the United States of America

GPSR Representation:
UPI-2M PLUS d.o.o., Medulićeva 20, 10000 Zagreb, Croatia
matt.parsons@upi2mbooks.hr

To Kathy with Love

Table of Contents

Table of Contents

Part IV - The Holy of Holies

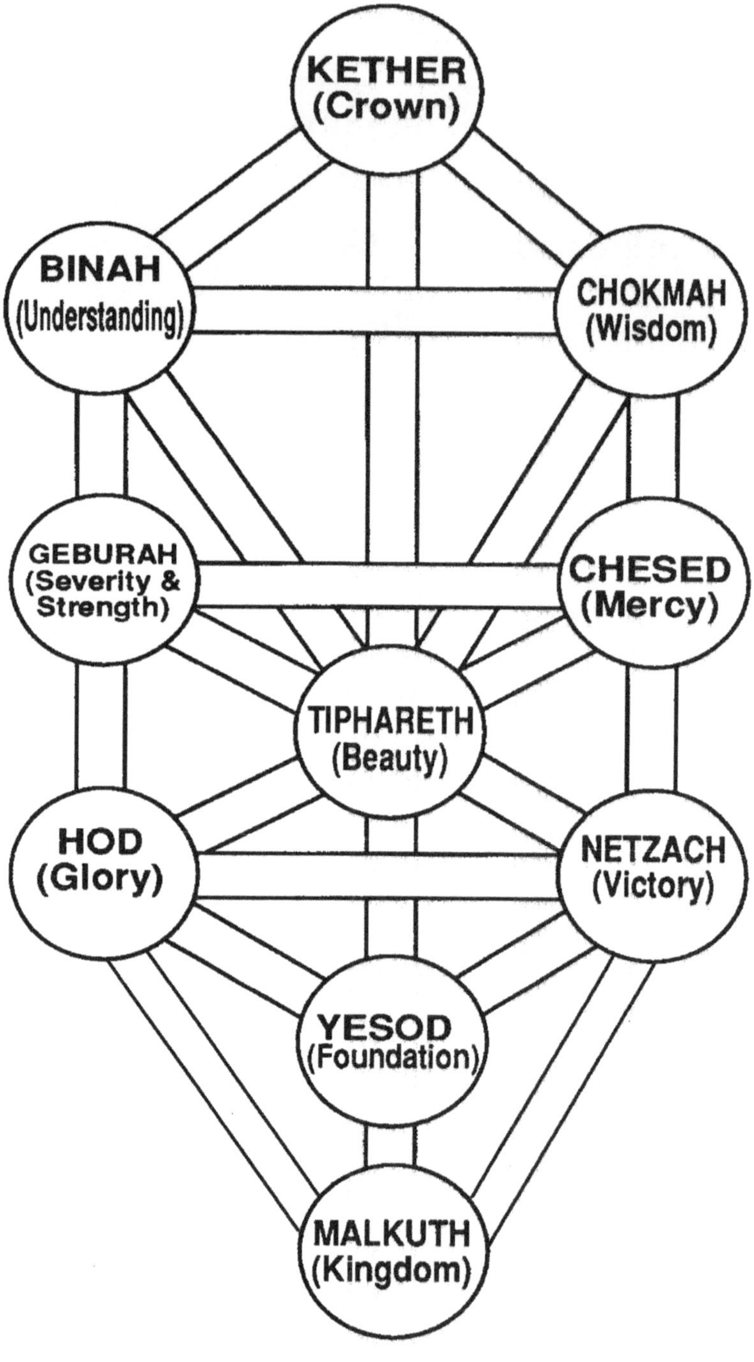
KETHER
(Crown)
BINAH
(Understanding)
CHOKMAH
(Wisdom)
GEBURAH
(Severity &
Strength)
CHESED
(Mercy)
TIPHARETH
(Beauty)
HOD
(Glory)
NETZACH
(Victory)
YESOD
(Foundation)
MALKUTH
(Kingdom)

Introduction

The Light Within

This is a magickal time to be living. It is a powerful, dynamic, growing time for both individuals and the planet. It is a time that many can use to bring ancient energies and myths to life within new scenarios. Because of increased awareness of other planes of life, opportunities to tap greater physical and spiritual resources surface daily - for the tearing down the old and building the new. It is a wonderfully exciting time of change, and if the changes are to be constructive, then a new understanding of life must arise with effective and beneficial methods for exploring it.

Today there is a greater revelation of the ancient mysteries than at any other time in history. The glamour and secrecy of esoteric traditions are dissolving. Opportunities to take higher initiations are available to all. These latter years of the 20th century have renewed interest in more compatible work with Nature, including work with the elemental and devic beings. There is increased blending of consciousness with and realization of higher beings and dimensions. Mysticism and spirituality are melding with psychology, physics, biology, engineering and other sciences. New sources of energy and new methods of healing are surfacing daily. All of these inspire greater interest in things beyond the tangible and visible.

If we are to take the fullest advantage of this wonderful time, we must reexamine some of the accepted paths and methods for unfolding higher consciousness. There are laws and principles that govern the raising of consciousness, not the least of which is personal responsibility. Unfortunately, we live in a "fast food" society. People like things quick and easy. They want to pull up to the drive-in window, get their stuff and drive on - even the psychic and spiritual stuff.

We live in a time that demands a fully conscious union with the spiritually creative, supersensible world. This cannot be fulfilled by mere clairvoyance or by demonstrations of psychic ability, for what is psychic is not always spiritual. What is occult or metaphysical is not always uplifting, and what is appealing is not always useful.

The purpose of spiritual studies is not psychic power, but the ability to look beyond the physical limitations, to learn the creative possibilities that exist within limitations while at the same time, transcending them. It's purpose is to help us rediscover the wonder, awe and power of the divine and to learn how that power reveals and reflects itself within us.

The qualities essential for accelerating our growth and spiritual evolution are innate, although this idea is often unrecognized or believed to be only for the realm of the "gifted few". Even when this innate ability is recognized, there is still needed an effective system or a means to release it. In our modern world, there are a myriad of individuals providing maps. How then are we to know which map to follow through the labyrinth of spiritual explorations?

The key is to remember that ultimately no one knows better for us than ourselves, and there is no one doing anything in the spiritual and metaphysical realm that we cannot also be doing in our own unique way. We must learn to take what we can from whatever source we can, work with it and adapt it into a method that works for us as individuals.

Then whatever system we use as a guide to explore other realms inside of us or outside of us should fulfill certain criteria. Such a system should be easily understood, and if based upon an older Mystery Tradition, it should be living and growing, adaptable to the modern world and to us within it. The system should be capable of awakening our inner potentials without overwhelming us in the process. Finally, it should enable us to experience the universal energies that fill and touch our lives daily.

The ancient mystical Qabala fulfills all of these criteria. It is a map that allows us to look into ourselves for our answers, for our magick and for our miracles. Not from books or from teachers - although they serve their purposes - but from the well of truth that lies within! Rather than searching for some light to shine down upon us, the Qabala guides us to the light within - to shine out from us! Only then does the path through the labyrinth of life become a path to the Holy Grail.

Part One:

The Mystical Qabala

"We need not be aware of the inner world. We do not realize its existence most of the time. But many people enter it - unfortunately without guides, confusing the outer with inner realities and inner with the outer - and generally lose their capacity to function competently in ordinary relations.

"This need not be so. The process of entering the other world from this world and returning to this world from the other world is as natural as death and giving birth or being born...

"Among physicians and priests there should be some who are guides, who can educt the person from this world and induct him to the other, to guide him in it and to lead him back again.

"One who enters the other world by breaking a shell - or through a door - through a partition - the curtains part or rise and a veil is lifted.

"The outer divorced from any illumination from the inner is in a state of darkness - is an age of darkness."

- *R.D. Laing*
"Politics of Experience"

Chapter One

Entering the Tree of Life

"...the Qabala opens up access to the occult, to the mysteries. It enables us to read sealed epistles and books and likewise the inner nature of man."

- Paracelsus

The mystical Qabala is one of the most ancient of all the mystery traditions. There exists much argument over its true origin, as does the origin of any oral teaching tradition. Qabala comes from the words *qibel* which means "to receive" or "that which is received", and it is aligned with those mystical teaching that were only passed down through word of mouth.

The Qabala is rich in powerful symbolism. Almost every major civilization has utilized aspects of the Qabala and its primary image, the Tree of Life. Most of what comes down to us today retains strong threads to the ancient Egyptian and Hebrew traditions. As will be seen, it is not necessary for us to be fluent in Egyptian or Hebrew or any of the ancient languages and traditions to understand and work with the Qabala.

At the heart of the Qabalistic teachings is the diagram of the Tree of Life. It is a diagram to the treasures of the universe - magickal and material. It is a symbol rich in rewards for those who have the keys to unlocking it. These keys are part of what this book will provide.

The Tree of Life diagram can be viewed from different perspectives. For our purposes, we will examine it from two. The first deals more with the philosophy and cosmology of the Qabala, while the second relates more to pragmatic applications. Most of our focused work will be connected to the second.

On one level, the Tree of Life symbol depicts how the universe was formed. The universe issued forth out of what is called *NOTHINGNESS*, some primal point from which we came and to which we will return. While we are in the physical we can know nothing about it, and thus it is called NOTHINGNESS.

The universe came forth out of the Nothingness and underwent nine stages of manifestation - nine stages of compacting, condensing and channeling of divine energy - to manifest in a tenth stage encompassing the entire material universe - all matter and life upon the earth. This can be compared to the process of condensing steam into water and then into ice. It is still two parts hydrogen and one part oxygen, but it has condensed into solid matter. The universe, including ourselves, is spiritual, divine energy that has densified into physical matter. This process of manifestation into material being is known as *The Path of the Flaming Sword.*

The Path of the Flaming Sword

There is much more to the Tree of Life than meets the eye. It reflects more than just the process that the universe underwent to come into being. It is also a map to the human mind. It is a map through the labyrinth of the subconscious. The subconscious mind controls over 90% of the body's functions, and it has many levels within it. Each level of the subconscious controls different physiological functions, different organs and different abilities.

Each of the ten stages or levels, known as a Sephira in the Qabala, represents a level of the subconscious mind - a

NOTHINGNESS—Primal Point from which we came and to which we return, beyond understanding.

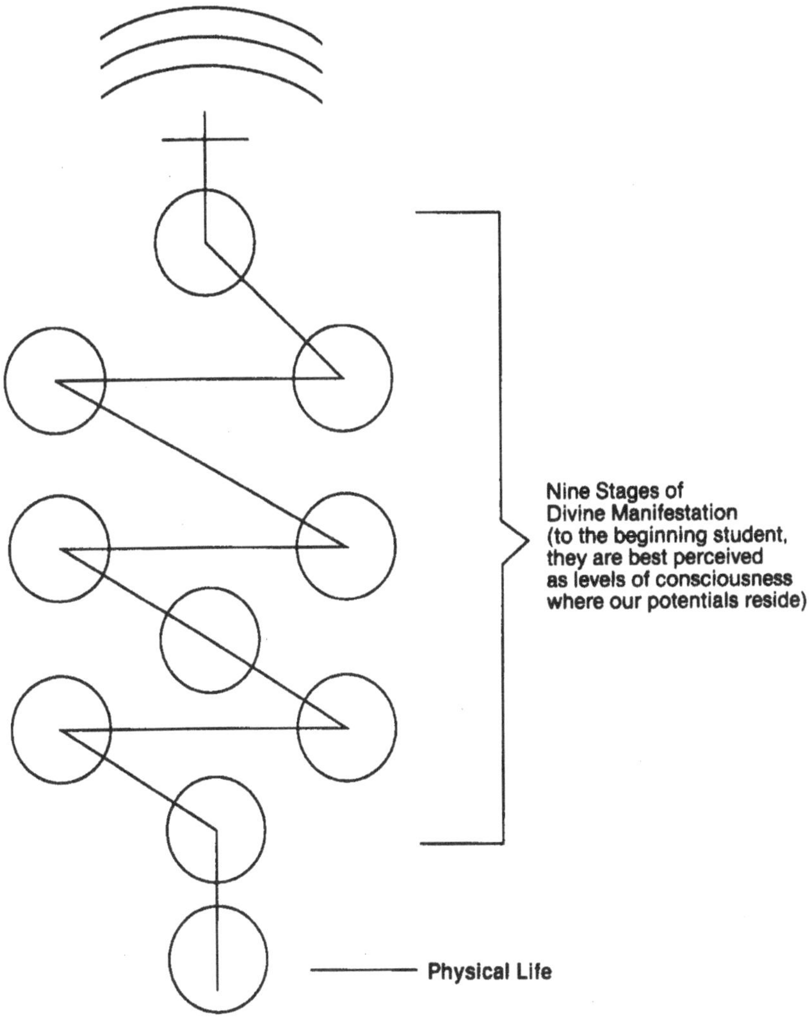

level of consciousness to which we have access. They are temples of the mind. Each temple or level of consciousness has its own gifts and its own unique benefits - from controlling physiological functions to stimulating artistic energies to communicating with animals and more. Through each level we can connect more fully and with a specific aspect of the Divine.

Through each level we can connect and communicate with a specific archangel and group of angelic beings. Through each level we can experience and understand specific astrological influences within our life.

Through work with the Tree of Life, we learn to consciously bridge our normal waking consciousness with the more subtle realms and temples of the subconscious mind. We learn to consciously awaken and manifest our most innate and forgotten abilities. Through the Tree we develop more tangible links to subtle and ethereal realms, dimensions, beings and energies once thought beyond our reach. And we learn to access them whenever we desire to whatever degree we desire!

In the Tree of Life, our normal waking consciousness is represented by the level known as MALKUTH (the kingdom of Earth). It is the seat of all of the other energies of the universe. We are the microcosm. We have all of the divine energies of the universe within us. The difficulty is finding practical and effective ways of manifesting them consciously within our daily lives. The difficulty is bridging and linking our normal consciousness with those more subtle levels. This is where the Qabala truly shines.

Associated with each level of the Tree of Life are specific correspondences. These correspondences include divine names, symbols, sounds, colors, fragrances, magical images and more. They serve as doorbells to each corresponding level of our subconscious mind, reflecting the energies and potentials inherent to within it. These energies and potentials become more available to us and our life if we access these temples of the mind appropriately. This is what the Qabala teaches.

Every civilization and religion had its magickal teachings. The phraseology may have differed and the symbols readapted, but only to conform to the needs of the time and the individuals. What is extraordinary, however, is that there are more similarities than differences in the methods used by ancient and secret traditions to change the consciousness of their students and practitioners. The Qabala encompasses most major magickal traditions. It incorporates, numerology, tarot, mythology, astrology, mystical linguistics, healing sciences, and so regardless of one's personal magickal heritage, the Qabala will add even greater depth and power.

The basic correspondences in the Tree of Life were explored in the predecessor to this volume – *Simplified Qabala Magic* (Llewellyn Publications). The following are brief reviews of these basic correspondences. Throughout the rest of the book, we will examine advanced techniques for using these correspondences to access and manifest our inner potentials more fully and more dynamically. That is when the magick of life begins to manifest!

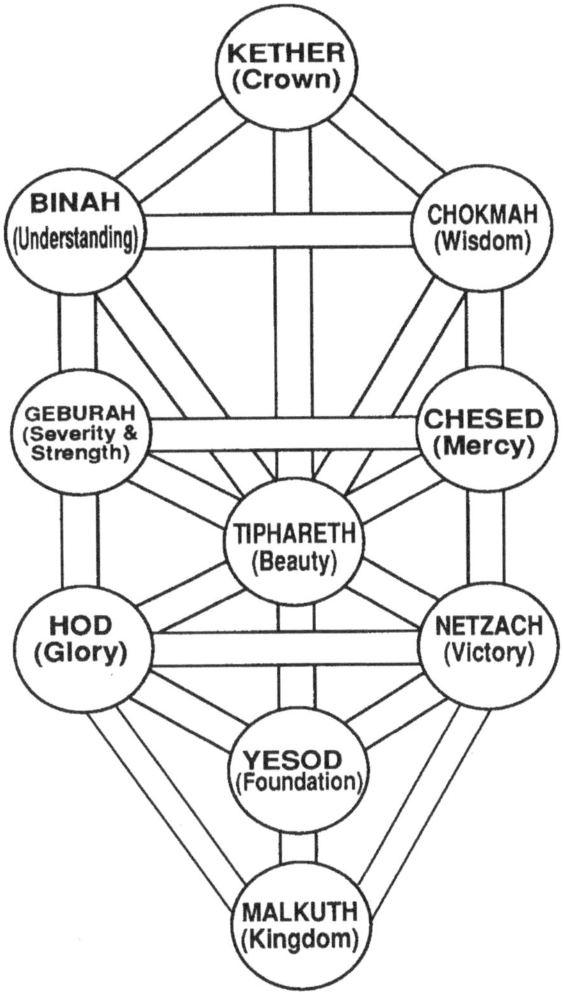

Malkuth

WHAT CAN BE ATTAINED THROUGH THIS TEMPLE OF THE MIND:

Greater ability to discriminate in life; overcoming of inertia; insight for all problems of physical health (self or others) and into all affairs of the home; greater self-discovery; contact with elemental life forms and beings of Nature; at deepest level, vision of Holy Guardian Angel; discovery of things hidden within the physical universe; prosperity & security.

Symbolized by the Magical Images & Gifts of:
baskets of grain, sacred oils, jewels & gems of the Earth

DIVINE FORCE AVAILABLE: Adonai Ha-Aretz - Lord of the Earth
(Most direct influence over physical/material affairs)

ARCHANGEL MOST ACCESSIBLE: Sandalphon - Angel of Prayer and Life
(Answers prayers; formation of life; intercedes w/Holy Spirit)

SPIRITS MOST ACCESSIBLE: Ashim - Blessed Souls
(Saints & angels assisting Sandalphon)

TOOLS & IMAGES TO HELP ACCESS THIS LEVEL OF THE MIND:

Colors:	Black, olive, russet and citrine
Fragrance:	Sandalwood, lemon, carnation
Meditation Stones:	Smoky Quartz
Astrology:	Earth
Magical Image of You:	Young maiden, crowned and throned

WEAKNESSES THAT HINDER MANIFESTING POTENTIALS:
laziness, greed, avarice, over- reactive, aggressive, recklessness

STRENGTHS THAT ASSIST MANIFESTING POTENTIALS:
discrimination, prosperity, common sense, physical energy, discernment

Yesod

WHAT CAN BE ATTAINED THROUGH THIS TEMPLE OF THE MIND:

Perception of rhythms of change; increased intuition & psychic abilities; dream consciousness; astral projection; true work with omens; strengthen emotional health; overcoming of idleness; at the deepest level, vision of the machinery of the universe (recognition of a divine plan at work).

Symbolized by the Magical Images & Gifts of:
silver winged slippers; mirror

DIVINE FORCE AVAILABLE: Shaddai El Chai -
Almighty Living God
(Aspect of divine recognized in all things)

ARCHANGEL MOST ACCESSIBLE: Gabriel -
Angel of Truth
(Guards gateways to other realms, instills hopes)

SPIRITS MOST ACCESSIBLE: Cherubim -
Beings of Light & Glory
(Keepers of celestial records)

TOOLS & IMAGES TO HELP ACCESS THIS LEVEL OF THE MIND:

Colors:	Violet; indigo
Fragrance:	Lavender, honeysuckle
Meditation Stones:	Amethyst
Astrology:	Moon
Magical Image of You:	Beautiful naked, strong man

WEAKNESSES THAT HINDER MANIFESTING POTENTIALS:
idleness; vanity; obsessive sex; impulsiveness; always a follower

STRENGTHS THAT ASSIST MANIFESTING POTENTIALS:
independence; spontaneity; dream study; conscious psychic development; self-awareness

Hod

WHAT CAN BE ATTAINED THROUGH THIS TEMPLE OF THE MIND:

Vision of truth; revelations of falsehood & deception; greater communication; knowledge of healing and magic; greater prosperity through increased knowledge; enhances any educational/scientific endeavor; at deepest level, a vision of the truth of our lives and truth in our lives.

Symbolized by the Magical Images & Gifts of:
Caduceus and staff

DIVINE FORCE AVAILABLE: Elohim Tzabaoth-
God of Wisdom & Harmony
(Divine overseeing of science, knowledge, evolution)

ARCHANGEL MOST ACCESSIBLE: Michael -
Angel of Balance, Protection
(Brings patience, protects against psychic dangers)

SPIRITS MOST ACCESSIBLE: Beni Elohim -
Divine Sons and Daughters
(Transmit divine consciousness & desire for the divine)

TOOLS & IMAGES TO HELP ACCESS THIS LEVEL OF THE MIND:

Colors:	Orange and peach
Fragrance:	Rosemary, frangipani, wisteria
Meditation Stones:	Citrine
Astrology:	Mercury
Magical Image of You:	Hermaphrodite

WEAKNESSES THAT HINDER HOD'S POTENTIALS:
deceit; impatience; dogmatism; over criticalness; separatism

STRENGTHS THAT ASSIST HOD'S POTENTIALS:
patience; practicality; knowledge; communication efforts; truthfulness

Netzach

WHAT CAN BE ATTAINED THROUGH THIS TEMPLE OF THE MIND:

Understanding of all relationships - especially love, unselfishness, artistic & creative inspiration, awakened sexuality, contact with Nature spirits (fairies & elves), awakened love and idealism, at the deepest level, a vision of our true beauty and that within others.

Symbolized by the Magical Images & Gifts of:
rose; wild flowers, sea shells

DIVINE FORCE AVAILABLE: Jehovah Tzabaoth - God of Hosts
(Divine assistance with proper expression of emotions)

ARCHANGEL MOST ACCESSIBLE: Haniel - Angel of Love and harmony
(Assists in artistic/creative endeavors)

SPIRITS MOST ACCESSIBLE: Elohim- Gods and Goddesses (of all traditions)
(Protectors of religion, beliefs; inspire right decisions)

TOOLS & IMAGES TO HELP ACCESS THIS LEVEL OF THE MIND:

Color:	Emerald and all greens
Fragrance:	Patchouli, rose, bayberry
Meditation Stones:	Malachite; emerald
Astrology:	Venus
Magical Image of You:	Beautiful, sensual, naked woman

WEAKNESSES THAT HINDER NETZACH'S POTENTIALS:
emotionalism; worry; envy; lust; impurity; possessiveness

STRENGTHS THAT ASSIST NETZACH'S POTENTIALS:
warmth; optimism; time in nature; creative activities; expressiveness

Tiphareth

WHAT CAN BE ATTAINED THROUGH THIS TEMPLE OF THE MIND:

Greater and higher sense of devotion; Christ consciousness; glory and fame; more energy for life and success; harmony to things of the heart; victory over adversity; access to the true energy of the rainbow; healing on all levels; miracles: at the deepest level, awakens vision of rewards of devotion to Great Work (the achieving of the Holy Grail).

Symbolized by the Magical Images & Gifts of:
crown that is too large

DIVINE FORCE AVAILABLE: Jehovah Aloah Va Daath - God of Knowledge
(Divine aspect that creates through the power of mind)

ARCHANGEL MOST ACCESSIBLE: Raphael - Angel of Brightness & Healing
(Ministers all healing energies, healer of the divine)

SPIRITS MOST ACCESSIBLE: Malachim - Virtues or Angelic Kings
(Bestow grace; guardian angels; workers of miracles)

TOOLS & IMAGES TO HELP ACCESS THIS LEVEL OF THE MIND:

Colors:	Golden yellows; pink
Fragrance:	Rose; jasmine; lily
Meditation Stones:	Rose quartz
Astrology:	Sun
Magical Image of You:	Majestic king; the child; a sacrificed god

WEAKNESSES THAT HINDER TIPHARETH'S POTENTIALS:
false pride; self doubt; insecurity; irreverence; blaming

STRENGTHS THAT ASSIST TIPHARETH'S POTENTIALS:
reverence; idealism; nurturing; compassion; devotion

Geburah

WHAT CAN BE ATTAINED THROUGH THIS TEMPLE OF THE MIND:

Vision of natural forces and how to use; overcoming cruelty and destruction; greater strength & courage; energy for tearing down old & building the new; critical judgment; insight into enemies and discord; at the deepest level, awakens vision of one's true strength & courage and how to manifest it.

Symbolized by the Magical Images & Gifts of:
sword, spear, armor, weapons

DIVINE FORCE AVAILABLE: Elohim Gibor - God Almighty
(Divine aspect that protects; eliminates old for new growth)

ARCHANGEL MOST ACCESSIBLE: Kamael - Angel of Strength & Courage
(Defends/protects the weak & wronged; fights dragons)

SPIRITS MOST ACCESSIBLE: Seraphim - The Flaming Ones
(Assist in stopping those who upset our lives)

TOOLS & IMAGES TO HELP ACCESS THIS LEVEL OF THE MIND:

Color:	Reds; Fire shades
Fragrance:	Cinnamon; tobacco; gardenia; cypress
Meditation Stone:	Garnet
Astrology:	Mars
Magical Image of You:	Mighty warrior; warrior in a chariot

WEAKNESSES THAT HINDER GEBURAH'S POTENTIALS:
anger; fear; cruelty; self doubt; manipulation; belligerence

STRENGTHS THAT ASSIST GEBURAH'S POTENTIALS:
confidence; critical judgment; initiative; activity; dealing with issues

Chesed

WHAT CAN BE ATTAINED THROUGH THIS TEMPLE OF THE MIND:

Increased abundance; opportunities for prosperity; justice to one's life; hearing and recognizing the inner spiritual call; awakens greater peace and mercy; new growth and movement; at the deepest level, awakens a vision of love and true power at its most spiritual level.

Symbolized by the Magical Images & Gifts of:
cornucopia of treasures, king's cup

DIVINE FORCE AVAILABLE: El - Divine, Mighty One
(Divine which reveals abundance, glory & grace of life)

ARCHANGEL MOST ACCESSIBLE: Tzadkiel - Angel of Mercy
(Protects teachers; guardian of east winds of manifestation)

SPIRITS MOST ACCESSIBLE: Chasmalim - Brilliant Ones
(Dominations; manifest /awaken majesty in our life)

TOOLS & IMAGES TO HELP ACCESS THIS LEVEL OF THE MIND:

Colors:	Blues; purples
Fragrances:	Bayberry; cedar; nutmeg
Meditation Stones:	Lapis Lazuli
Astrology:	Jupiter
Magical Image of You:	Mighty, crowned & throned ruler (king/queen)

WEAKNESSES THAT HINDER CHESED'S POTENTIALS:
hypocrisy; dogmatism; smugness; self-righteousness; false pride; bigotry

STRENGTHS THAT ASSIST CHESED'S POTENTIALS:
idealism; truth & loyalty; patience; devotion; endurance; committedness

Binah

WHAT CAN BE ATTAINED THROUGH THIS TEMPLE OF THE MIND:

Understanding & meaning of sorrows, sacrifices and burdens; all mother-type information; deeper relationship with Mother Nature; new birth; uncovering of secrets; at its deepest level, it awakens a vision of and understanding for the processes of birth and death.

Symbolized by the Magical Images & Gifts of:
robe of many colors, cloak of concealment, yoni

DIVINE FORCE AVAILABLE: Jehovah Elohim -
Perfection of Creation
(Divine aspect that gives understanding & new birth)

ARCHANGEL MOST ACCESSIBLE: Tzaphkiel -
Angel of Spiritual Strife against Evil
(brings understanding; eases sorrows; aids rebirth)

SPIRITS MOST ACCESSIBLE: Aralim -
Strong and Mighty Ones
(Give sustenance & understanding; guard Mother Earth)

TOOLS & IMAGES TO HELP ACCESS THIS LEVEL OF THE MIND:

Colors:	Black; all colors
Fragrances:	Eucalyptus; myrrh; chamomile; sage
Meditation Stones:	Obsidian; black tourmaline
Astrology:	Saturn
Magical Image of You:	Mature woman; matron; crone

WEAKNESSES THAT HINDER BINAH'S POTENTIALS:
impatience; greed; fear of future; unnecessary martyrdom; lack of confidentiality

STRENGTHS THAT ASSIST BINAH'S POTENTIALS:patience; silence; faithfulness; nurturing; discipline; strength of will

Chokmah

WHAT CAN BE ATTAINED THROUGH THIS TEMPLE OF THE MIND:

Greater initiative; opportunities for new undertakings; pure source of life-giving energy; any father-type information; realization of hidden abilities; revelations of things concealed; understanding of astrology and the influence of the stars; at its deepest level, it awakens a vision of the divine, face to face.

Symbolized by the Magical Images & Gifts of:
Scepter of power, staff, phallus

DIVINE FORCE AVAILABLE: Jah (Jehovah) -
Divine, Ideal Wisdom
(Divine that oversees the heavens influence upon us)

ARCHANGEL MOST ACCESSIBLE: Ratziel -
Angel of Hidden Knowledge & Concealment
(Teaches & reveals starry and hidden influences)

SPIRITS MOST ACCESSIBLE: Auphanim -
Whirling Forces
(Assist in visions of spiritual forces)

TOOLS & IMAGES TO HELP ACCESS THIS LEVEL OF THE MIND:

Colors:	Grays; fog & smoke tones
Fragrances:	Eucalyptus; musk; geranium
Meditation Stones:	Fluorite
Astrology:	Neptune
Magical Image of You:	Older, bearded male figure

WEAKNESSES THAT HINDER CHOKMAH'S POTENTIALS:
inefficiency; procrastination; envy; superstitious; fear of the future

STRENGTHS THAT ASSIST CHOKMAH'S POTENTIALS: initiative; devotion; study of stars; goal oriented; idealism

Kether

WHAT CAN BE ATTAINED THROUGH THIS TEMPLE OF THE MIND:

Creativity and artistic inspiration; revelations of endings and beginnings; opportunities and energies for change and transition; new insight into spiritual path; intensifying of any aspect of life or evolutionary path; Initiation of new life and opportunities; reveals what must be done to complete life's work and how to do it.

Symbolized by the Magical Images & Gifts of:
spinning top; spark of light; tinder box

DIVINE FORCE AVAILABLE: Eheieh - I Am That I Am
(Deepest spiritual aspect of divine we can experience)

ARCHANGEL MOST ACCESSIBLE: Metatron - King of Angels
(Links divine and humans; gifted human with Qabala)

SPIRITS MOST ACCESSIBLE: Chaioth ha-Qadesh - Holy Living Creatures
(Reveal love, light & fire in humans & nature)

TOOLS & IMAGES TO HELP ACCESS THIS LEVEL OF THE MIND:

Colors:	Brilliant white
Fragrances:	Frankincense; ambergris; sage
Meditation Stones:	Double terminated quartz; Herkimer diamond
Astrology:	Uranus
Magical Image of You:	Ancient, bearded king (seen only in profile)

WEAKNESSES THAT HINDER KETHER'S POTENTIALS:
excessive daydreaming; shame; self denial; unsympathetic; poor self image

STRENGTHS THAT ASSIST KETHER'S POTENTIALS:
creative imagination; sense of wonder ; embrace change; order

EXERCISE:

Planting the Tree of Life

Benefits:

- grounding
- empowering to all exercises
- awakens your inner magick

Awakening the Tree of Life and all of its inherent energies is essential to both the magical and mystical existence. It requires that we consciously stimulate our perceptions in both the physical and non-physical environments. This exercise is very powerful for awakening these new states of perception and for blossoming newer, stronger inner potentials. Some may consider this exercise just another form of sympathetic magic, but it is much more - especially when we consider its symbolic significance.

The tree is an ancient symbol. It represents things that grow. It represents fertility and life. To some, it is the world axis, and to others it is the world itself. Its roots are within the earth, and yet it reaches to the sky. It is a bridge between the heavens and the earth; the mediator between both worlds. This is most reflective of the Qabala and its application to our entire unfoldment process. Through it we work to bridge one level of our consciousness with the next, just as the tree bridges the heavens and the earth.

The tree, as the Tree of Knowledge, has been associated

with both Paradise and Hell. In Greek mythology the Golden Fleece hung upon a tree. The Christian cross was originally a tree, and Buddha found enlightenment while sitting beneath one. Druids recognized the energies and spirits of trees, while the Norse honored Yggdrasil, the Tree of Life. Every civilization and traditions has its stories, myths and mystical legends of trees.

Trees bear fruit from which we gain nourishment. They provide shade and shelter. The wood is essential to the building of homes, and it is also essential to the making of paper - a source for communication and knowledge. The leaves of many trees fall in the autumn only to re-emerge again in the spring, reflecting the continual change and growth - the dying only to be reborn. We rake the leaves in the autumn, gathering what has dropped to create mulch for future plantings. Trees also serve as barriers, often used as a windbreak or fence by farmers. They are boundaries, whether separating one piece of land from another or one world from another.

Trees have always been imbued with certain magickal and spiritual attributes. The superstition of "knocking on wood" originated as practice to ensure no spirits were in a tree before it was cut down and thus inadvertently upsetting the spirits. In German folklore, the kobolde were spirits inhabiting trees. When these trees were cut, a piece of the tree was carved into a figure so that the spirit would always have a place to live. These carvings were shut up in wooden boxes and brought inside of the house. Only the owner was permitted to open it, and if anyone else did, the result would be untold damage. Children were warned not to go near them, and jack-in-the-boxes were fashioned to scare kids and remind them not to touch the real boxes.

Most people are familiar with the family tree. This tree has its roots in our ancestors, both familial and spiritual. All that we are lies in the roots of the tree, and thus all of our ancestry can be awakened through the tree. There are exercises that we can do with the tree of life to reveal ancestors and past lives that have helped create and nurture the tree we are now.

A powerful process of awakening our own Tree of Life and all of its inherent energies can begin with a simple and fully conscious planting of an actual tree. This can be a tree for the outdoors or one that can grow inside. It must be an actual tree though. The kind of tree is individual. Each tree has its own energies and distinct properties. The list on the following pages can assist you in your choice, or you may wish to refer to an earlier work of mine, *Enchantment of the Faerie Realm.* Doing research on the tree, meditating upon it and deciding before purchasing or transplanting the tree is a way of preparing our internal soil. Our consciousness is being prepared for the awakening of the energies of life more fully.

By planting a tree we are performing an act of affirmation. We do not have to know all that this tree will reflect. That will unfold as it grows and we nurture it, but we should be somewhat aware of its significance and our goals. Do we want a fruit-bearing tree? Do we wish to bear a lot of fruit in our own life? If so, we must consider that most fruit trees have specific stages of growth, and only bear fruit seasonally. It doesn't mean there is no growth at the other times, but it may be less visible, less tangible.

We must learn as much about the tree as possible before choosing. We must also have some ideas of our own goals - immediate and long range. Then we can choose a tree that is more appropriate for our goals. Such decisions can be difficult, but there are simple things we can do to help ourselves. First, we must remember that we have all of the time in the world. Then we may find it easier to begin with the tree we have always felt closest to - our favorite. We could also go out into nature and meditate on which tree might be best. We should never choose a tree simply because we feel it may have more magickal associations. Those associations may not hold true or be as effective for us.

When we have chosen, we must plant the tree where we will see it everyday, a visible reminder that as it grows and blossoms, so will our own inner tree - *"As above, so below. As below, so above."* (Three initiates, *The Kybalion*. Chicago: Yogi Publications Society,

1940, p. 28.) This planting can be indoors or outdoors. If the tree is planted indoors, at some point we may wish to transplant it to the outdoors so that it can grow free and uninhibited. If so, we may wish to choose another tree for indoors.

The care of the tree is a potent part of this process. As we prune and water this tree, we should be aware that we are also pruning and watering our own inner tree, enabling it to take stronger root so that we can extend ourselves to the heavens.

The tree that we plant can be a wonderful way of empowering all of the exercises within this book or within any Qabalistic work. Before and after each exercise, we can take a few minutes and give conscious attention to the tree. Adding a little water before an exercise is a way of adding water to the aspect of the tree we will stimulate through the exercise. By taking a few minutes to reflect on the tree, what it represents and how much it has grown at the end of the exercise strengthens its overall effectiveness. It enhances our concentration and focus. Just as a tree planted on a hillside can prevent soil from eroding, this simple gesture prevents the energy awakened from eroding away or being dissipated.

At the end of the exercise, we can turn the soil around it or just place our hands within its dirt at its base. This is a way of grounding the energy we have accessed, and it helps to release it more tangibly and solidly within our physical life. Although it may seem silly to some or even mysterious to others, it is powerful and effective.

Inevitably there are some who will say, "I can't make anything grow. Every time I plant something, it dies!" The planting of the tree is a physical act to release change into our life. Death is always a companion to life, and it is change. It is part of the universal life cycle: life, death and rebirth. If we are unable to deal with this aspect, we will have trouble with all aspects of the Qabala. Trouble with this may be an indicator that the time is not right to work with the Qabala or that Qabalistic methods of unfoldment are not appropriate for the individual. Part of what the Qabala teaches is discrimination and discernment, and this must be applied to all aspects.

On the other hand, we must keep in mind that the tree is an outer reflection of an inner energy. If the tree dies, it does not foretell our own physical death. Most often it reflects that an aspect of us that is no longer vital has changed. Maybe the chosen tree was not the best to start with. Some people choose a tree because of its extensive magickal associations, but many trees are difficult to grow. Maybe the death of the tree only reflects attempts to undertake too much too soon.

With all work on the Qabala, we must start simply. We must allow the tree (inner and outer) to grow at the rate that is best for it. One of the tests that everyone must undergo periodically is the test of patience. The Qabala teaches that the growth cycle has its own unique rhythm for each of us. Forcing growth impairs judgment. Seeds need time to germinate, take root and then work their way up through the soil. Unfortunately, we live in a "fast food" society, and people wish to have their psychic and spiritual development quick and easy. They wish to pull up to the drive-through window, get their psychic unfoldment and then drive on. Often with the Qabala many assume that nothing is happening until they see the plant working its way out of the soil. The Qabala teaches us that things will happen in the time, manner and means that is best for us if we allow it.

If the tree does die, give it back to the earth. Thank the universe for its presence within your life - if only for a short period. Then get another tree. And another, if necessary. If we wish to truly bridge and unfold our highest capabilities, we must persist. *"Nothing in the world can take the place of persistence. Talent will not; nothing is more common than unsuccessful men with talent. Genius will not; unrewarded genius is almost a proverb. Education will not; the world is full of educated derelicts. Persistence and determination alone are omnipotent."* Everything we try and everything we grow within our life - successful or not - adds to our life experience and our soul development.

The Magickal Trees

Tree	Energy and Magic	Related Sephira
ASH	might, immortality, a universal source of life, Norse gods held council under it; Odin sacrificed on it	Tiphareth, Geburah
ASPEN	calms anxieties, resurrection, soul fearlessness, communication, releases energy to enter subtler planes of life	Hod, Tiphareth
APPLE	all healing energies, promotes happiness, Tree of Knowledge, Fruit of Avalon, magickal powers, home of Unicorn	Netzach, Tiphareth
BEECH	awakens soul quality of tolerance, aids contact to higher self, can be used for all patterns of growth	Binah
BIRCH	staffs of birch used by shamans to awaken energy to pass from one plane to another, healing	Yesod, Netzach
CEDAR	protective, healing to imbalances of emotional or astral level, healing	Yesod, Tiphareth
CHERRY	realizing insights, openness, unconsciousness, threshold of new awakening, Tree of phoenix	Netzach, Chesed
CYPRESS	healing, understanding of crises, awakens comfort of home and mother	Binah

The Magickal Trees (cont.)

Tree	Energy and Magic	Related Sephira
ELDER	mysteries of all burial rites, contact with the Mother Goddess, protection and healing	Netzach, Malkuth, Binah
ELM	lends strength, aids overcoming exhaustion, tree of intuition, inner call of Nature spirits and elf contact	Binah, Malkuth, Netzach
EUCALYPTUS	oil used in ancient Mystery schools to clean aura during growth, protective, healing, stimulates the third eye	Chokmah, Chesed, Yesod
FIG	releases past life blockages, links conscious with subconscious with correct perspective, sacred tree of Buddha	Chesed, Tiphareth, Hod
HAWTHORNE	fertility, creativity, growth on all levels, sacred to the fairies	Netzach
HAZEL	magickal tree, as in all fruit trees, the fruit is hidden wisdom, hazel twigs make powerful dowsing instruments	Hod
HOLLY	(technically a bush, but with all the power of trees), protection, awakens love and overcomes hate, birth of Christ within	Tiphareth
HONEY-SUCKLE	energy that helps learn from the past, stimulates energy of change, sharpens intuition, opens psychic abilities	Yesod, Chokmah

The Magickal Trees (cont.)

Tree	Energy and Magic	Related Sephira
LEMON	cleansing to the aura, draws protective spirits, good for purification at time of Full Moon	Yesod, Tiphareth
LILAC	spiritualizes the intellect, mental clarity, activates the kundalini, draws good spirits	Binah, Chokmah, Netzach
MAPLE	balances the yin and yang, draws money and love, grounding to psychic and spiritual energies, chakras in feet	Chesed, all of the Middle Pillar
MAGNOLIA	energy top locate lost ideas, thoughts, or items; activates heart chakra; aligns heart with higher intellect	Tiphareth (aligned with Daath)
MISTLETOE	sacred tree of Druids, female energy, all lunar aspects of universe, protects children or the child within	Yesod, Binah
OAK	sacred tree of Druids, male energy and all solar aspects of universe, strength, endurance, helpfulness	Tiphareth, Geburah
OLIVE	tree of peace and harmony, restores peace of mind, regeneration, enables the touching of inner guidance	Tiphareth
ORANGE	assists in rising on the planes and astral projection, brings clarity to emotions	Hod,

The Magickal Trees (cont.)

Tree	Energy and Magic	Related Sephira
PALM	tree of peace, protection of an area or group, leaves prevent evil from entering an area, Christ energy	Tiphareth Hod, Tiphareth
PEACH	awakens realization that immortality can be attained but only in legitimate ways, calms emotions, artistic	Netzach
PINE	calms emotions, awakens true occult Christian salvation, understanding sacred tree of Mithra, Dionysian energies	Geburah, Netzach, Binah
SYCAMORE	brings life and gifts, nourishment, beauty, female energies, sacred tree of the Egyptians, used to draw Hathor	Netzach, Yesod
WALNUT	hidden wisdom, power for transition, catalytic energy, freedom of spirit, following one's path, laws of change	Chokmah, Chesed
WILLOW	healing, removes aches, flexibility in thought, realization of links between our thoughts and external events	Yesod, Chesed

Chapter Two

The Power of Imagick

"Using the plan of the Tree of Life as his guide, the magician invokes the lower gods or archangels, as they are named in another system, desirous of mingling his own life with and surrendering his own being to the greater and more extensive life of God."

- Israel Regardie,
Foundations of Practical Magic
Aquarian Press Limited, 1979

Magic is one of the most misunderstood terms in metaphysical and spiritual studies. Magic is not some form of hocus pocus or prestidigitation. It is not burning candles and casting spells. Neither is it mere divination or pacts with spiritual beings of any sort. At its root, it means "wisdom", and to enter into its practice without the appropriate reverence, respect and understanding will lead to many problems down the road.

Magick is a divine process, based upon wisdom. It is the expression of wisdom. It is a means to an end. It is the development of mastery over life (or aspects of life) with the expression of that mastery within our everyday activities. Anyone who has mastered some aspect of life can be viewed as a magician. Being able to handle conflicts with patience, tolerance and insight can seem magickal to many people. To someone who knows nothing about plumbing, a plumber's ability to effect repairs is magickal.

Magick is the application of knowledge, understanding

and wisdom to life. It is discovering that the Divine already exists within us. It is discovering that life is supposed to go right. It is discovering how to make it right. It is amazing how often I hear people exclaim, "The most amazing thing just happened!", when they receive answers to their prayers of experience miraculous and magickal happenings within their lives.

The truth is that prayers are supposed to be answered. Miracles and magick are supposed to happen. It would be truly amazing if they did not occur. It is our own doubts, fears, recriminations, sense of unworthiness, and refusal to look beyond our limited perspectives that delay and hinder the manifestation of a magically wonderful existence.

Magick is one path in the quest for the spirit, the search for that innermost part, the point of our greatest reality. As with all spiritual paths, it is not a path that leads up to some Divine light into which all of our troubles are dissolved or from which there is no return. It is a path to finding the Divine Light within so that we can shine it forth.

The Qabala is rich is mystical symbols and images. These symbols and images are magickal tools that we can use to link our consciousness to other levels, planes and beings. By learning to use them in a controlled and directed manner, we can manifest their energies in such a dynamic manner that we become living, loving examples of the highest and best. We become living beings of light. This constitutes a true alchemical change. This awakens the higher self in a fully conscious manner.

Imagick

Imagick (coined from "imagination" and "magick") is this process of using symbols and images to tap and bridge deeper levels of our consciousness as described in chapter one. (Imagick is pronounced with a short i sound as in "it" - such as in the word from which it originated - imagine.) Imagick helps us to consciously align to corresponding powers of the universe and link them with our normal state of mind. Such a process involves dynamic visualization, meditation and/or physical activities in a prescribed manner according to natural principles.

It must be understood that a mere intellectual study of the correspondences will not generate any magickal changes. Neither will a mere arousal and awakening of the energies. it is not enough to merely touch different levels of consciousness and dimensions of energy. They must also be grounded and manifested into our daily lives if we are to achieve our hopes, wishes and dreams. The imagickal techniques, particularly when employed with the pathworking process, are powerfully effective. They build a bridge between the inner worlds and the outer world in which we operate. They link the spiritual and the physical, creating a flow between them that augments our energies, abilities and potentials in all areas of our life.

The images and correspondences within the Qabala are effective because they have been used in a manner similar to that described throughout this book for many hundreds of years. The effects of working with these symbols and images upon the day to day life are very definable because they have been used in such similar fashions with such similar results.

By focusing upon a particular image, color or symbol, we stimulate a specific level of the subconscious. It awakens it and its untapped potentials, opening us to our innate abilities and to spiritual forces outside of us to which we have access. We use the Qabalistic images to open and activate the subconscious mind's reservoirs and abilities. We expand the conscious boundaries within which they can operate in our daily lives. Their energies not only become more available to us, but we become more aware of their influence within our life circumstances as well.

Through the Qabalistic images and symbols we can set energy in motion on higher, more subtle planes of life. These in turn trigger a corresponding action or effect within our physical, daily lives. Learning these images and symbols and how to use them to create magickal effects within our life is what this book entails.

DRAWING UPON THE SUBCONSCIOUS

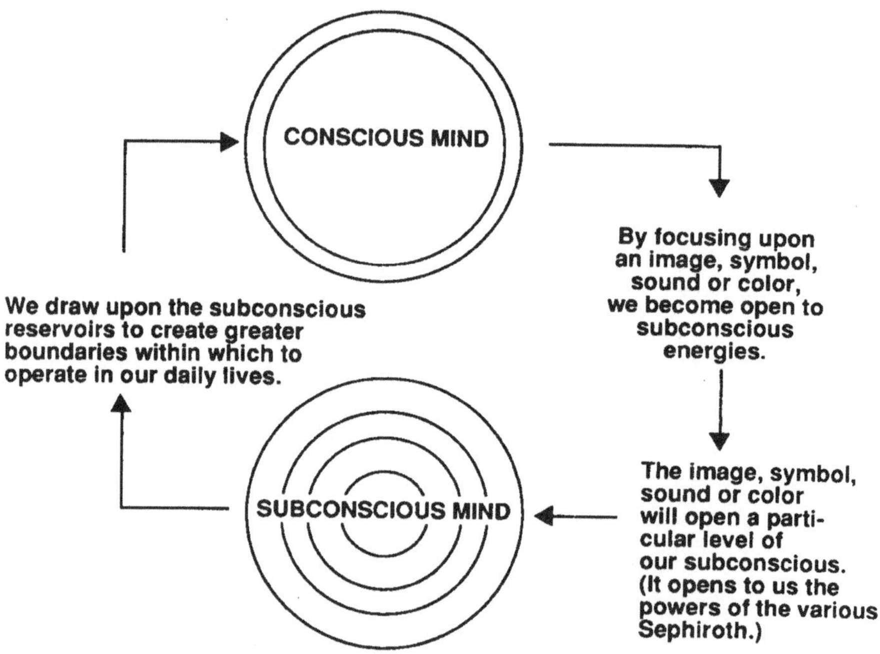

Awakening the Tree of Life

There have always been certain laws and principles that govern manifestation and existence on both the physical and non-physical planes of life. Called by different names in different societies, each civilization taught its own expression of these universal or natural laws. Regardless of their label(s) in other traditions, the process of applying them to create and manifest our highest potentials through the Qabala is called *"Awakening the Tree of Life"*.

Two principles in particular are important to understand how it all works. In the Hermetic tradition, these principles are known as *THE PRINCIPLE OF CORRESPONDENCE* and *THE PRINCIPLE OF CAUSE AND EFFECT.* Together they are employed dynamically in the Qabalistic process of Imagick.

The Principle of Correspondence states: *"As above, so below; as below, so above."* (Three Initiates, The Kybalion.)There is always a correspondence or link between the phenomena of the various planes of being within the universe. All planes and dimensions affect each other. What happens on one level has impact upon others. We cannot do something on one level without it affecting us on another. What we do on one level will play itself out on other dimensions - a corresponding energy.

This is why so many societies had their own versions of sympathetic magic. An action on one level can be focused to release a corresponding energy on another level. For example, pouring water out ritually upon the ground was used by many shamans to bring the rains. They recognized the corresponding impact of a properly focused rite.

The ancient Hermeticists used this principle as a means of prying aside the veils to other worlds and dimensions. By observing the physical and reflecting upon higher correspondences, they could understand some of the spiritual forces impacting upon physical life. Through this principle, we can pry aside some of the obstacles that hide the subtle dimensions and forces playing within our lives.

The Principle of Cause and Effect states: *"Every cause*

has its effect; every effect has its cause; everything happens according to law; chance is but a name for law not recognized; there are many planes of causation, but nothing escapes the law." (Three Initiates, *The Kybalion.*)

Simply put, every action has its effect - not just in the physical but upon other dimensions as well. In other words, if we take a focused and concentrated action - physical, mental and/or spiritual - it will have its impact upon our lives. It will create an effect. The type of action and how it is performed determines the strength and clarity of its impact.

With the Qabala, our focus and work with particular images and symbols in a carefully crafted manner will elicit results that we can define and determine. All images and symbols are tied to some archetypal force within the universe. Our focus upon it creates a release of that force that will play itself out within our daily lives.

When we work with the Qabala and these principles, we are learning:

1. To tap energies and forces previously unrecognized,

2. To understand how they are likely to manifest,

3. To control the amount of force in which they manifest, and

4. To direct where they manifest within our daily lives.

The Seven Hermetic Principles

Three Initiates, *The Kybalion.* Chicago: Yogi Publication Society, 1940.p.25.

1. THE PRINCIPLE OF MENTALISM:

"The All is Mind; the Universe is Mental."

2. THE PRINCIPLE OF CORRESPONDENCE:

"As above, so below; as below, so above."

3. THE PRINCIPLE OF VIBRATION:

"Nothing rests; everything moves, everything vibrates."

4. THE PRINCIPLE OF POLARITY:

"Everything is dual; everything has poles; everything has its pair of opposites; like and unlike are the same; opposites are identical in Nature but different in degree; extremes meet; all truths are but half-truths; all paradoxes may be reconciled."

5. THE PRINCIPLE OF RHYTHM:

Everything flows, in and out; everything has tides; all things rise and fall; the pendulum swing manifests in everything; the measure of the swing to the right is the measure of the swing to the left; rhythm compensates."

6. THE PRINCIPLE OF CAUSE AND EFFECT:

Every cause has its effect; every effect has its cause; everything happens according to law; chance is but a name for law unrecognized; there are many planes of causation, but nothing escapes the law."

7. THE PRINCIPLE OF GENDER:

Gender is in everything; everything has its masculine and feminine principles; gender manifests on all planes."

The Imagickal Process

Through symbols and images we set energy in motion on higher, more subtle planes of life, which will in turn trigger a corresponding action or effect upon the physical plane - specifically within our own lives. Learning the symbols and images, along with how to use them to create these seemingly "magickal" effects within our lives is what the Qabala teaches. It is what this text will help with.

Psychology has the task of interpreting symbols and images. Magick lives through them. The symbols and images that we use should energize our awareness on many levels, expanding our perceptions and thus changing our world. The first area of change is usually ourselves.

All images contain magickal seeds. When we use the image as a symbol of special significance, its magick is awakened. The greater the significance that we attach to the image, the greater the power it will have within our lives. Its magick grows.

Even though any image or symbol can be imbued with great energy, some images are better suited for magickal purposes. It may be that they have been used for centuries, and thus they contain a tremendously powerful thoughtform. It could be that they are very primal. If so, they are more purely connected to the energy they reflect. The symbol or image may also intimately reflect the archetypal energy at its source, imbuing it with greater magickal potential. An archetype is a matrix or key image which gives shape and direction to energies arising out of the primal source of all being. All images reflect an archetypal force in some manner and according to Carl Jung, all images andsymbols reflect one of seven specfic archetypes.

The *Imagickal Process* is one of imbuing images and symbols with greater energy and strength to impact upon our conscious lives powerfully and effectively. It requires accessing and stimulating the primal core of their essence and then releasing and directing their force in a controlled manner into

The Basic Archetypes of Carl Jung

Archetype	Characteristics	Common Symbols
Self	ego individual	temples, homes, books, star, egg, weeds, lit candle, births, gifts, weddings
Feminine	creates relationships, flow, beauty, birth, receptivity and acceptance	vessel, cave, womb, queen, doorway, priestess, wells, moon, veil, scabbard
Masculine	fathering, making, directing, organizing, building, active and assertive, penetrating, initiating	kings, unicorns, phallus, sun, sceptre, sword, tools
Heroic	facing difficulties and the insurmountable, conquers, heals	battles, struggles, teachers and new knowledge, youth, shields, healing balms
Adversary	agent of change, destroys or wounds what is, brings unexpected, tearing down of old, uses anger, moroseness	monsters, tyrants, beasts, demons, suffering, walls, the abyss
Death/Rebirth (transition)	end of one and beginning of another, crisis, change bringing sacrifice and new life	Solstice and Equinoxes, rite of initiation, altar, clock, dance, prayers
Journey	movement forward, development, aging, building on previous, new directions	Tree of Life, winding roads, ascent upward, mountains, staff, guides, rivers, streams, vacations, pilgrimages

our daily lives. There are four distinct steps to this imagickal process:

1. *Become conscious of the image reflecting a primal force or energy.*

We must first become aware that every symbol and image that we use is a connection to and a reflection of a more primal, archetypal force. Carl Jung taught that all symbols and images could be placed in one of seven categories of archetypal forces within the universe. (See the chart on the previous page.) The closer we connect to an image's archetypal source, the greater the power we unleash. To accomplish a more primal connection, we must go beyond our usual logic in working with them. We must draw increasingly deeper associations and conclusions about the energies activated by the symbol or image that we use.

In the beginning we reflect upon the outer surface or most obvious significance and associations of the image. Even the most superficial focus upon an image or symbol will release some energy into your life from its archetypal source. As we continue to work with it, such as through the techniques in this book, we delve deeper into the cosmic spiral of its archetypal origins, and with each use of the symbol or image, we release more of its primal archetypal force into our outer physical world and daily life.

2. *Immerse yourself more deeply into the energy of the symbol or image.*

The immersion into the image or symbol is sometimes called "the magickal action". It involves techniques that bring to the surface more of the archetypal energy hidden behind and operating through the image. This can be done through meditations, creative visualization and even through specific physical activities. It involves using techniques - such as pathworking - to adopt and absorb the energy of the image as our own. We learn to release it into our lives.

We then absorb and manifest the forces reflected by the images into our own individual essence. The various meditations and pathworking techniques will help you to link and merge your essence with the essence of the image's archetypal force. This is when we begin to create the magickal body; we begin to manifest our most ideal potentials and essence. Techniques for creating this magickal body will be explored in greater detail later in this book.

To facilitate our merging with the archetypal forces, it is important to use some of the same symbols and images with all aspects of the Tree of Life. Each time we use them, we strengthen our connection to them and their archetypes. It enables us to get beyond surface levels of energies. For this reason, every time you enter one of the ten temples or a pathworking scenario, do so in the manner of the exercise, *"Entering the Tree of Life"* at the end of this chapter.

Tapping Archetypal Forces through Symbols

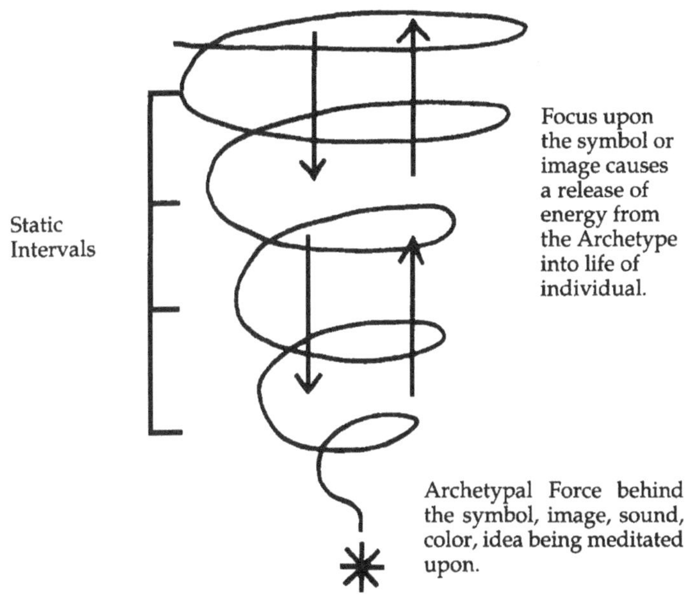

3. Ground or earth the energy into our physical, waking and conscious life.

The grounding of the energy accessed is most critical to creating the magickal life. This more than anything else is what distinguishes the effective techniques described in this book from fanciful imaginings, illusions, dreams and impotent creative visualizations and meditations that so many people complain about in the metaphysical field. All techniques may touch similar archetypal energies, but unless they are grounded, taken out of that ethereal mental realm, they will never work efficiently nor powerfully.

We are spiritual beings, but we live within a physical body and physical world. Those more ethereal, spiritual and archetypal forces we are accessing, must be earthed or grounded if they are to benefit us. If some tangible, physical activity is not used to ground the energies - to draw them out of the more subtle realms so they can express themselves more dynamically within our physical lives, they can create problems and imbalances.

Inappropriately grounded energies can often be identified by the following symptoms. They can stimulate nervousness, hypersensitivity, emotional outbursts, inability to sleep, a general sense of uneasiness, malaise, and other feelings of mental and emotional discomfort. Occasionally a sense of disruption and chaotic energies may also surface. If after a day or two of performing the exercises in this book you are experiencing several of these symptoms, you will need to reground yourself. *Energy that is not grounded properly will find its own outlet - usually a disruptive one.*

On the other hand proper immersion and grounding of the energies will generate new awareness, insights, inspirations and creativity. There are, of course, the specific benefits and gifts that we attain through each temple and pathworking which are described later in the book. There are though more general responses that we will experience from properly accessing and grounding those archetypal energies.

Dream activity will become more vibrant and lucid.

Physical energy will increase. Health will improve, and one of the more commonly experienced effects is that of increased sexual energy. Our sexual energy is a physical reflection of our creative life force. When we immerse ourselves more deeply into archetypal forces, our creative energies grow tremendously. The increased sexual energy is a tangible confirmation that the exercise worked, that the archetype was accessed - that the creative energy is flowing into your life.

The grounding begins with contemplation of the exercise, especially in the week following it. What have we experienced on all levels of our being since that time? What activities and events have unfolded since our performance of the exercise? Keeping a journal at least through one entire working of the Tree of Life is most essential to gaining the insight.

The performance of a physical action - even with something as simple as a journal - grounds the energy we have accessed into our physical lives. It allows it to express itself in a more unbalanced fashion. The contemplation and reflection upon the exercise and what has unfolded in our life since we performed the exercise is personal. It should be kept private and shared only with those who can truly help you to understand, i.e. a study group or a teacher. Sharing the experiences with others can dissipate the accessed energy, or through the responses of others may create blocks for the future. Comparing your responses to others will also create barriers.

The bridging and grounding of the archetypal energies to our physical life should at the very least involve the following. These physical activities are essential to experiencing the most powerful and beneficial effects of the exercises:

Begin and end all exercises with a physical activity.

Use a vocal prayer, a posture or series of movements to reflect the opening and closing. Performing the "Balancing Pillars" described in part three will help, or you can create your own. Physical movement creates electrical changes in the body that help make us more receptive to the energies. They will amplify and facilitate your ability to access the archetypal energies, and they will help you also to ground them so that they manifest and work for you in a more balanced manner.

Act out the lesson/experience of all pathworkings and temple visits.

Act out or pantomime the lesson or experience of the pathworking or temple visit. If you are trying to release energy that will bring more choice into your life, this might involve choosing to involve yourself in some new activity or endeavor within your life within 24 hours of the exercise. It is a physical way of sending a strong message to the universe that you will use all energy that you have activated. It also sends a message to the subconscious that you intend to utilize and act upon any energy that is released to you. The subconscious then feels free to access and release the archetypal energy into your life in great abundance.

Keep a Tree of Life Journal.

This doesn't have to be complicated or time consuming. Keep track of the date of the exercise, your feelings at the end of it and what occurs in your daily life over the next 48-72 hours or even a week. If you follow my suggestion of only performing one temple visit/ pathworking per week, it will be easier to discern how the energies are manifesting and playing out within your daily life. In part three are guidelines for creating and using a path working journal

Just the physical act of writing about the exercise, and then keeping track of the major events that unfold will serve several functions. First it helps you to understand what you set it motion and how it is likely to play out within your life each time you do the same exercise. More importantly, it is a physical activity which helps ground the energy, helping you to handle it in a more balanced fashion.

At the end of each exercise, eat something.

It doesn't have to be a full course meal - something light. A few crackers will often suffice to help you feel more grounded and less flighty and disconnected.

Stretch and perform some light physical work.

If you planted a tree as suggested in the exercise of the previous chapter, dig and work the soil. Again, it is a physical action that allows the energy to become earthed into your life, but in a more balanced fashion. If you feel disconnected and experience some of the symptoms mentioned earlier, perform some more vigorous physical activity. It will help to dissipate the disorienting effects.

4. *Assimilate and evaluate the experience.*

When we immerse ourselves in the images and symbols (step two) through the various exercises within this book), they will elicit responses within ourselves and within our lives - usually in a noticeable manner within 24-48 hours. Events that unfold in that time frame have often been triggered or brought to the forefront by your work with the symbols. Your work enables them to manifest more intensely.

After the immersion and grounding of the energy, there must be time to contemplate and assimilate the experience and its teaching. We must discern, examine and understand the intensity to our internal responses (physically, emotionally, mentally and spiritually). We must also monitor external effects as well by observing and noting what ensues in our daily life following the various exercises. This is the importance of the journal.

We must assess both our inner reactions and the outer effects. It is this monitoring and assessment that ultimately enables us to develop control and to open newer and greater forces. This may take a day, a week, a month or even longer - depending upon the individual, the method used, the symbol or images employed, and the circumstance in your life at the time.

When we use the imagickal process, we are learning to control and direct what we set in motion within our lives. We want to release energy to play itself out as intensely or as gently as we desire. When we can do this, we are living a magickal life. Problems are resolved more easily. Tasks are accomplished more smoothly. Opportunities arise more frequently. People may see us as living a "charmed existence", when in reality we are just working with the natural laws of the universe. It is this monitoring and seeing what actually unfolds within our lives following our exercises that provide the key to what seems to others as a "magickal" control of life.

Developing the control is in part a trial and error process. If events that follow in our life are too intense or chaotic, then we know that next time we should change the manner in which we worked with the images. We can soften our focus and thus soften the impact within our life. In this way we learn to temper what we set in motion. This is what we will teach later in the book.

Yes, we know that certain images and symbols will generate certain kinds of effects within our life, but through the Qabala - through the imagickal process - we learn to generate the effects with great force or great gentleness. It is the assimilation, the post grounding process that enables us to understand the archetypal force and to delve only as deeply into it as we need each time.

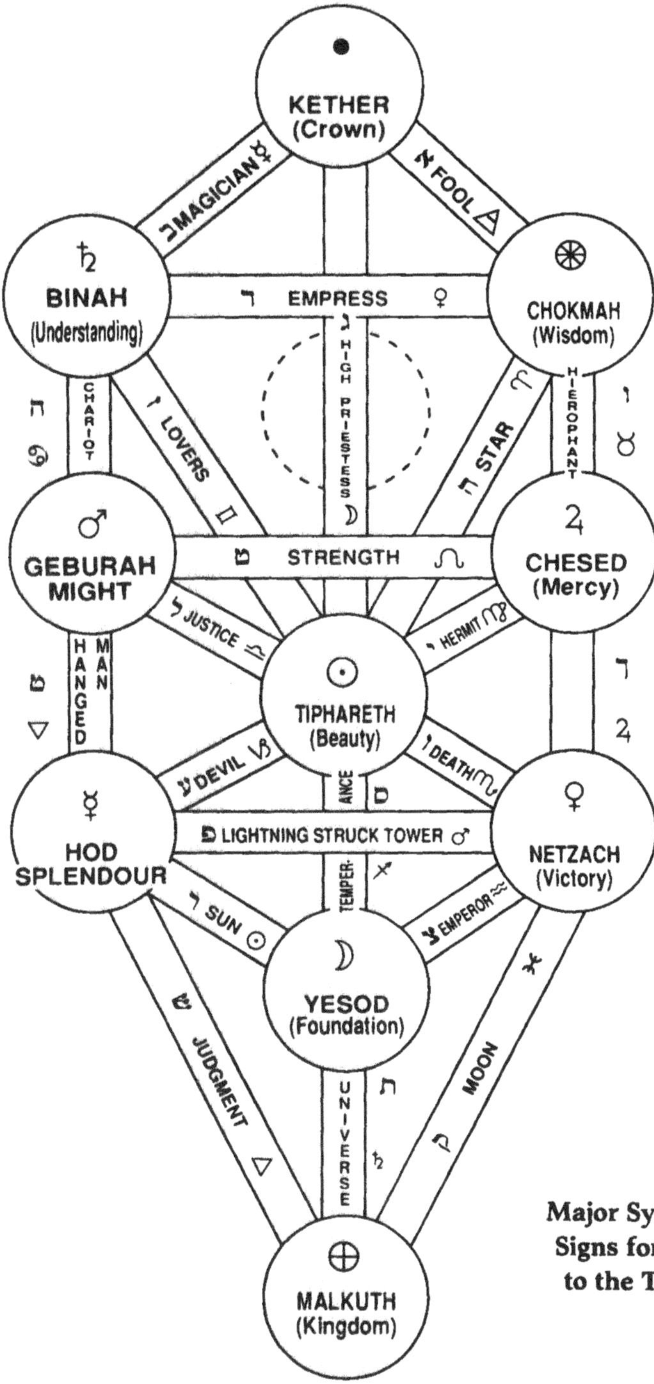

Major Symbols and Signs for the Paths to the Tree of Life

Meditation Stones for the Tree of Life

Sephira	Stone and Associated Activity
KETHER	DOUBLE-TERMINATED QUARTZ: Kether leads to the Malkuth of the next level of consciousness or the next Tree.
CHOKMAH	OPAQUE FLUORITE: Fluorite activates high energies and wisdom. The opaqueness corresponds with the clouds to be cleared away to reveal the light within
BINAH	OBSIDIAN: Awakens the darker self within so we can transmute it into the higher. A powerful stone to use for giving birth to the new, bringing the light from the womb. Most people have difficulty with its energies.
	BLACK TOURMALINE: The highest of the black stones, protects and nurtures. Like obsidian, teaches us how to bring more light into the darkened world. A devoted servant to the light, helps us to radiate spiritual consciousness in all situations.
CHESED	LAPIS LAZULI: The gold within the blue of this stone is power and royalty. With it one can learn to become a representative of the gods and empower one's life.
GEBURAH	GARNET: Once known for their powerfully protective energies, garnets provide strength and courage. They balance and uplift. The Hebrews called the garnet barak, which means lightning. Garnet is often associated with Kamael and his assistance in our lives.

Meditation Stones for the Tree of Life

Sephira	Stone and Associated Activity
TIPHARETH	ROSE QUARTZ: For the heart chakra and the heart of the Tree of Life, awakens self-fulfillment, healing, and inner peace. Gentle like a child, loving like the Christ, and strong like a king.
NETZACH	MALACHITE: Helps those dedicated to the grounding of higher healing energies into the planet and all growing life. A good friend, bringing us into line with nature and all its forces.
HOD	CITRINE: Awakens the brain to higher knowledge. Its yellow-orange ray can shine like a sun into our lives. Excellent for applying spiritual energies to accomplish earthly matters.
YESOD	AMETHYST: An excellent meditation stone, facilitating the change of consciousness from our normal waking state into the more ethereal levels. Yesod is the gateway to the deeper levels of the Tree.
MALKUTH	SMOKY QUARTZ: Grounds our energies and helps to lift our energies and consciousness away from the physical. It helps the mixing of the energies of the earth with those of the spirit so we have our feet upon the ground and our heads within the heavens.

EXERCISE:

Entering the Tree of Life

Benefits:

- **opens temples of the mind**
- **awakens perceptions**
- **increases gifts from spirit**
- **altered states of consciousness**

The techniques described and outlined throughout this book need not be held to the letter. We each have a responsibility to adapt them to our own unique energy system. To confine the Qabalistic Tree of Life and all of its energies, attributes and potentials to specific manifestations and uses only serve to limit its effectiveness. As we become used to these techniques and to linking the various levels of our consciousness through them, we will want and need to adapt them more specifically to our individual lives. We will have to separate being from reading about being.

Most of the imagickal techniques throughout this book incorporate very dynamic symbols and images to awaken the energies and potentials of consciousness. When performing the exercises, it is always beneficial to reflect upon the symbology and imagery prior to the actual working. It is not necessary to memorize all of the symbolic significance or to keep them constantly in mind. Reflecting upon some of the more predominant ones prior to the exercise though will sow the seeds that will enable you to experience the effects more tangibly.

Use as many aids as possible to facilitate tapping the specific level of consciousness. Use candles of the appropriate color, and use a fragrance that will also serve to trigger the appropriate level. The more aids we use, the stronger the effects. One of the more effective aids is a meditation stone. Crystals and gems have an electrical frequency that can assist in tapping levels of the subconscious more easily when used in meditation. The chart on the following page will help in determining the appropriate stone and its effects for the individual temples on the Tree of Life.

This exercise is one that opens the doors to the inner temples of the tree. In essence we are awakening the inner Tree of Life. This exercise can be used to enter any of the ten levels and to perform any of the pathworkings. The process will be the same for all of them:

1. *You are in a meadow, in which a great tree extends into the clouds.*

2. *You enter into the tree and its cloak of darkness.*

3. *You use the divine names to awaken the temple in the darkness.*

4. *You encounter angels, magickal gifts, and/or a variety of other aspects.*

5. *You close the temple down, using the divine names.*

6. *You exit the tree.*

When used regularly and consistently, this process of going into the tree creates a subtle shift in your consciousness automatically. When used regularly and consistently as a prelude to every meditation and exercise, it will help you to achieve an altered state of consciousness at will and in full awareness. It will enhance other meditative tools you use and deepen your work with them.

It also provides a safety feature to all of the exercises within the book. If something feels uncomfortable or thoughts and images arise that are unwanted and not easily brushed aside, using the divine names and stepping from the tree is a way of dispelling them and preventing them from being activated accidentally. The tree and its inner temples (all of which already exist within you) are places of safety, security and warmth. We use this process to create a spiritual haven within ourselves. This process allows for a more comfortable awakening of our inner perceptions and innate potentials.

Preparing for the Imagickal Working

Certain preparations should always be made prior to any magickal exercise or working. At the very least, the following steps should be followed:

- **Eliminate any possibility for distraction or interruption.**
Take phones off of the hook and inform others that you must not be disturbed. When we use altered states, such as in meditations, we become hyper aesthetic or hyper sensitive. Lights are brighter; sounds are louder. Touches are more intense.

- **Set the correct atmosphere.**
Everything that you do should be done deliberately. For every pathworking and for every exercise there are fragrances (incenses and oils), candles of an appropriate color, stones and crystals and other tools that can be used to facilitate your

accessing the level of consciousness you wish. The charts in chapter one will help you in choosing the appropriate colors and fragrances to assist your efforts in accessing the ten inner temples. You may even wish to use some non-intrusive music. Later you will be provided with similar tools to help in the pathworking exercises.

- Make yourself comfortable.

With the atmosphere set, make yourself as comfortable as possible. For most, the upright seated position is best. I often discourage reclining positions because this is what we use to fall asleep. Using it in meditations may result in too much of an altered state of consciousness - sleep itself. More importantly though use the position you find most comfortable.

- Perform a preliminary relaxation.

This helps you to focus and to eliminate the mental and emotional distractions that can have a tendency to surface. There are a variety of breathing techniques to help us relax. We can also perform what is commonly known as a progressive relaxation. Focus on each body part, starting at the feet. Visualize warm thoughts and energy, soothing and relaxing each part of the body in turn. This will help distract you from thoughts of the day. Take your time with this. The more relaxed we are, the exercises become easier and more effective. In time, you will find that just preparing for the relaxation will trigger it. We are simply retraining the conscious mind.

When these steps are accomplished, then we need to just visualize the scenario described or the variation that we create. The exercise that follows is the technique for entering into the Tree of Life, specifically for the Temple of Malkuth. The process will be the same though for every level - for every Sephira. This specific exercise is available on my audiocassette and CD – *Entering the Tree of Life*. It has the exercise and music on one side, and just the music on the opposite so that the listener can use the music to facilitate awakening the other temples as well.

One of the more frequent concerns of those working with the Qabala has to do with proper pronunciation of the various levels and names. I have provided a pronunciation guide with phonetic spellings and other basic guidelines in the appendix. It is important though not to get hung up on this in the beginning. Yes, the names do carry great power, and yes, that is enhanced through proper intonation. Any effort initially though will work - as long as it's somewhat similar. Intention has great impact in all magickal processes.

Entering the Tree of Life

A meadow forms around you. There is the fragrance of spring flowers and new mown hay. The sun is warm upon the face and body, and in the distance is the sound of birds. As the scene begins to take form around you, you see that this meadow has a path that leads from one end of it up to a distant mountain. The path is lines with stones and flowers of every color and kind. At the opposite end of the meadow, the path continues leading down to as distant valley.

As you look down that path toward the valley, you see your present home within it. And you begin to understand. This meadow is a plateau, an intersection of time and space. It is a place where the finite meets the infinite, where heaven unites with earth. It is a haven.

In the middle of the meadow is a giant, ancient tree. Its massive branches and trunk dwarf you, and its bark is twisted and gnarled like the skin of some giant, ancient entity. The upper portion of it roots are exposed, like the twisted limbs of some giant mythological serpent. There is no doubt that they extend deep into the heart of the earth itself.

As you stand underneath it, staring up its length, the tree seems to extend forever. Its upper branches are lost in the clouds. If ever there were a single Tree of Life, this would surely be it, as it stands bridging the earth with the heavens. You feel a little small and insignificant standing next to it. A part of you feels as if the tree has chosen to ignore you in your slightness, an appropriate metaphor for anyone who begins to explore the universe and all of its possibilities.

As you lower your eyes to its base, you see a small opening - just large enough for you to squeeze through if you bend slightly. You stare in awe and amazement. How had you not noticed that opening sooner? Was the tree acknowledging you after all?

You step forward, trying to peer into the opening, but it is so dark, that nothing can be seen. You take a deep breath, relaxing even more deeply, and you step cautiously out of the sunlight and into the darkness of the opening.

The darkness envelops you like a warm cloak. The air is thick, and you breathe deeply, forcing yourself to relax. No light penetrates through the opening, and you cannot see a thing in the inner blackness. You reach out tentatively with your hands, unsure what to expect. You touch the underside of the tree, and you are amazed at how warm and soft it really is. You press your hand flat against its inner side, and you can feel the life blood flowing through the tree itself.

You step forward carefully, waiting, trying to see something. Nothing but darkness envelops you. And then there is a soft voice inside your head.

"This is your temple, and only you can bring it to life."

Realization begins to melt over you. If it truly is your tree, then the ancient words will awaken and restore life to the inner temples. To test it, you softly speak into the blackness, the divine name for the Temple of Malkuth.

"Adonai ha Aretz."

The blackness seems to shift around. The inner tree lightens and takes on the shade of olive green. The second of the four colors associated with Malkuth. You smile, beginning to understand, and you speak the name again.

"Adonai ha Aretz."

The olive shimmers, and begins to take on a russet tone. Within this light you begin to discern shapes. You see that the area is circular, and in the center before you is a large stone altar and other objects that are still no clear.

You speak the name a third time.

"Adonai ha Aretz."

The russet shimmers, and the room is filled with a citrine, sunshine yellow light, a reflection of the sun. It fills the room and everything within it stands out clearly.

Yes, there is an altar. Upon it is a small lamp, burning softly. But it begins to glow brighter as if it had been waiting on you. The floor is pitch black and the ceiling is stark white. The walls are engraved with sigils, glyphs and ancient writings from every civilization and religion around the world. Most make no sense to you, but there are a few glyphs and writings that you do recognize.

You step forward and begin to examine everything more closely. To your right is a life size stone statue of a young maiden, seated upon a throne. You recognize her as the magickal image for this temple.

On the altar is a bowl of water, a piece of flint and steel, a plate with salt and a fan - all representing the four elements. At the foot of the altar are three baskets, shaped like cornucopias. In the first are wheat, corn and other grains from around the world. The second is filled with stones and gems of every color and kind. Next to these is a third that is filled with exotic powders and oils and whose fragrance fills the room.

You stand before the altar and look upon the lamp. Its flame has steadied and turned a crystalline blue. Its light warms and heals every aspect of your being. It fills you with a sense of "coming home". This lamp burns eternally within the temple. Though its flame may diminish from neglect...it is never extinguished, and it burns in all of the temples.

Carved into the altar beneath the lamp is a large circular talisman. Around its outside are the insignias of all the names of the Divine throughout history. Inside the talisman at the top is inscribed your name. At the bottom is your name in a foreign and ancient script. This was you name when you first entered the mysteries of the inner temples. It is your soul name.

You begin to understand. This is your temple! The tree is your Tree of Life! The scriptures upon the wall are the teachings of wisdom to which you can open by working from this temple and others within your consciousness.

As this realization fills you, a soft spark of light begins to shimmer and dance behind the altar. You watch as it grows, filling the room with even greater light. As you watch intently, you begin to see a vague form within that light. Then you realize, this is the Archangel of Malkuth, and you whisper the name.

"Sandalphon."

There is a brilliant flash of light, and then standing before you - behind the altar is that great being the ancients called Sandalphon. This being is dressed in shades of autumn and the earth. Though young in appearance, there is something ancient to the eyes. They hold you fixed, looking through you, seeing all within you and loving you all the more. Never have you felt such complete acceptance, and you are filled with love for this being.

Sandalphon extends his arms outward to the side, and the floor begins to vibrate. A roaring sound fills the temple! Two stone columns burst through the floor on either side of the altar to the back of the temple. One is of blackest ebony. The second is silver white crystal. They lodge themselves permanently, and the peace returns to the temple.

Now it is complete. The pillars of balance are in the temple and now within your own Tree of Life. The may now manifest more strongly within the outer life. The magic of the tree and the inner temples is now alive and active! The lamp shines more brightly, reflecting off the pillars, chasing all shadows from the temple. The entire room brightens, taking on a crystalline clarity.

Without saying a word, Sandalphon reaches forward and touches the front of the altar. A spark ignites and a fire begins to burn across the front edge of the altar. It is so hot and intense that it burns into the altar. You watch in awe as the spiritual fire inscribes the altar and your heart with ancient words that you had forgotten:

"BEHOLD THY SOUL IS A LIVING STAR!"

As the flame fades, leaving its message permanently within the temple, you feel rejuvenated, alive for the first time in a very long time. You know that the universe is truly available to you now. Nothing can be denied to one who will work for it. You are heir to all the wonders, magick and light within the universe. By re-entering this

Tree of Life, you have once again declared your right to this Divine inheritance.

It is then you notice a movement to your right. Your eyes widen, as you see the young maiden of stone has come to life. She is young and beautiful. She wears a small crown upon her head. She stands before you and gazes into your eyes with recognition and love. She smiles softly.

Slowly she reaches into the first basket and draws out a handful of grains. She takes you hand and fills it.

"So you will never hunger." Her voice is like soft music.

She turns and takes a small crystal upon a leather necklace from the basket of jewels. She places it over your head.

"So you will know wealth is your Divine right."

She then turns to the third basket. She takes from it a small vial of oil and anoints your brow and your heart.

"So that you will always see and know the Divine in all things."

You feel the warmth of the oil, and everything around you becomes clearer.

She then cups your face gently within her hands, and places a soft kiss upon your cheek. Before you can respond, she shimmers and melts into you. You breathe deeply feeling her come alive within you, and you see yourself truly as a son or daughter of the Divine.

You look toward the altar and Sandalphon bows to you. Your heart is ready to burst. You are filled with such love and wonder. You had forgotten how much promise there is to life. You feel the doors to blessings opening wide for you.

The light begins to swirl around Sandalphon. His essence begins to draw into it. Before this magnificent being fades from your view, you see a streak of light pass over the three baskets. They begin to shudder and overflow, spilling out their contents. And you know it is a reminder that there is never a lack within the universe for those who truly work to manifest a higher destiny.

You hold the grain in your hands, and you touch the crystal about your neck. You feel the warmth of the oil upon your brow and in your heart - gifts to take with you into the outer world. You know that the time here is finished for now, but there is no doubt you will return.

There are too many wonders, too many blessings to discover.

You step back from the altar, and you speak the name that awakened it.

"Adonai ha Aretz."

The bright light shimmers and changes back to a russet orange, beginning to cloak the inner temple.

A second time you speak the name.

"Adonai ha Aretz."

The russet, shimmers, turning to an olive green.

A third time you speak the divine name.

"Adonai ha Aretz."

You are encloaked in blackness. You turn and step from the Tree of Life, bring out from it the gifts. You breathe deep the sweet air, and the entire world seems so much brighter. Your life seems filled with so many possibilities. You close your eyes briefly, and you see the maiden alive within you. You open them, looking around to see the meadow and tree fading from the vision until next you call it into life. And you realize that the images fade from the inner vision only so that they may be born into your outer life.You breathe deep the essence of hopes fulfilled, for you are the heir to the Divine.

Pathworking is
the process of
using archetypal
symbols and images in an
imaginative
and sometimes
mythologized journey
to elicit specific effects
within our daily lives -
opening the psychic and
spiritual planes more
consciously.

Chapter Three

The Temple of Knowledge

"We live in a time in which supersensible knowledge can no longer remain the secret possession of a few but must become common property of all those in whom the sense for life in this age stirs as a need of their soul existence"

- Rudolph Steiner

In more ancient times mystical knowledge was hidden from the general public. Today, mystical and metaphysical knowledge is more available to the general public than ever before. There exist tremendous amounts of knowledge about all aspects of mysticism. This abundance of knowledge influences all levels of awareness and consciousness - even as it is reflected within the Tree of Life.

We have more knowledge today of the workings of life on Earth than at any other time in history. The mysteries of nature are being unveiled at an unprecedented rate. The once theoretical and invisible atom is today a scientific and physical reality. This is an example of knowledge influencing us through Malkuth or Earth.

We understand the psycho-structure of the human mind in ways never before comprehended. This is knowledge influencing us through the level of Yesod. Scientific realms are aligning with the alchemical teachings of the past. Science and magick are not as distant as once believed. This is knowledge - influencing us and manifesting through the level of Hod.

Meditation on the knowledge inherent within each Sephira will yield great benefits to the spiritual student.

Knowledge of every aspect of the Tree of Life is more available to the general public than ever before. Knowledge and its ability to stimulate and affect different levels of consciousness is more predominant than ever with an increased ability to accelerate the awakening of our sleeping potentials. This increased mystical knowledge is a reality, and it is only hidden in that it lies behind and influences all aspects of the Tree of Life.

If we wish to climb the Tree of Life and ascend to greater heights of awareness, we must have a disciplined inner schooling. Such schooling can enable us to attain knowledge of the divinely creative worlds and the beings that belong to them. Through careful preparation our inner potentials can be realized.

In the modern Qabala - in modern work with the Tree of Life - this is accomplished through the hidden Sephira referred to as *DAATH.* Daath is not an original concept of the Qabala. In fact, early Qabalistic teachings speak of ten and only ten sephiroth or levels on the Tree of Life. Daath or Knowledge is only mentioned in conjunction with either Binah or Chokmah. Today we must view it as a separate level of consciousness in its own right.

Daath has been called the invisible level, hidden within the Great Abyss that separates the bottom seven levels from the three upper. As seen in the following diagram, it bridges the seven lower levels of consciousness to the three higher, more abstract levels.

It bridges the levels of consciousness that are easier for us to access to those which are more difficult to work with and control, and it is only hidden today in that it lies behind and influences all other levels of consciousness.

When we can bring the upper levels to play more dynamically within our lives, along with the lower seven, then we are truly living the Tree of Life. Through Daath this becomes more easily accomplished. Daath, or higher knowledge, becomes the bridge to heightened consciousness and higher initiation for the modern spiritual student. But that greater knowledge also entails *much greater responsibility.*

Daath Becoming Visible on the Tree of Life

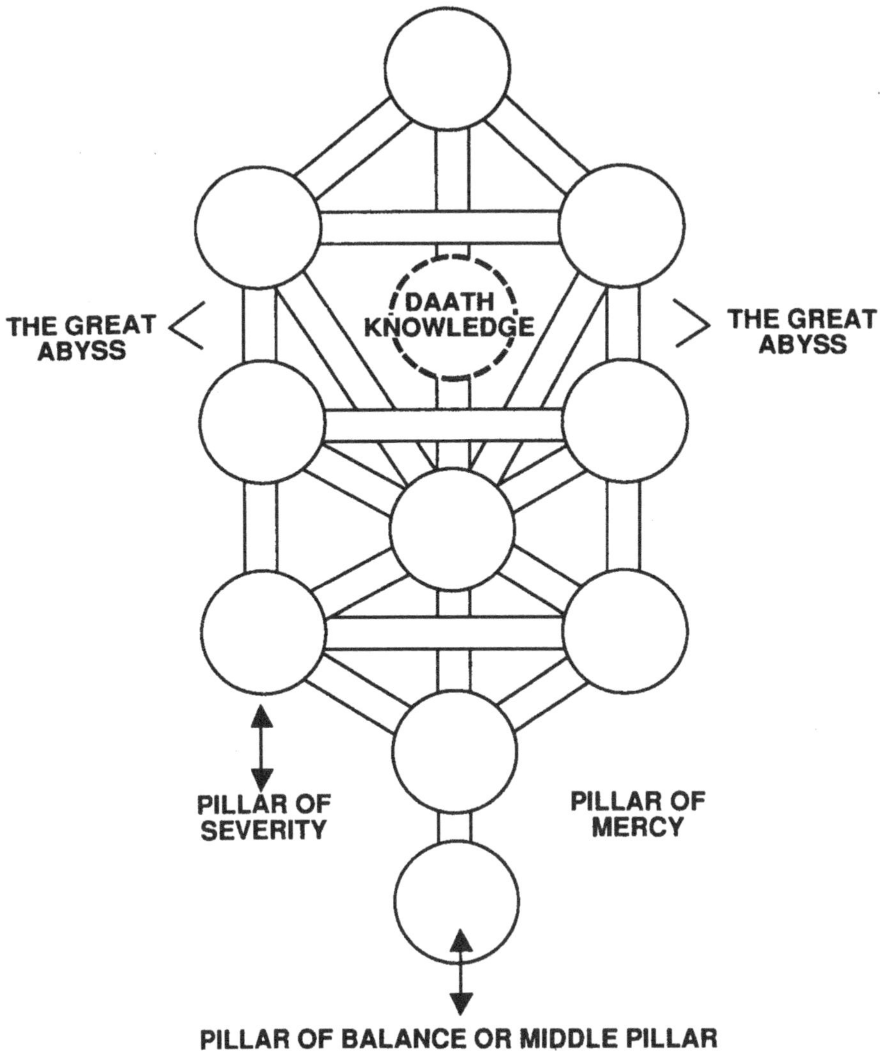

The Power of Daath

Daath is the eleventh Sephira on the Tree of Life. It is the hidden temple of knowledge. Although absent from the earliest teaching of the Qabala, it has found itself increasingly part of Qabalistic lore over the more recent centuries. As mentioned, it is called the invisible Sephira, hidden within the Great Abyss that separates the seven lower levels from the three upper.

It is significant that Daath falls within the area of the Tree of Life known as the Great Abyss. Knowledge brings to light many of the fears and superstitions that we hold. Knowledge serves to move us through the abyss of our darkest doubts and superstitions in every area of life. Knowledge sheds light upon the natural and supernatural worlds.

Many times in unfolding our spiritual energies, the heightened initiation we seek does not occur until we are able to tap more fully those levels of consciousness that serve to integrate the more pure, abstract energies of the universe. The levels of our consciousness that work with these abstract forces are what we call Binah, Chokmah and Kether in the Tree of Life.

We can manifest tremendous potentials from the other seven - often times more tangibly than the upper three, but until we link the upper three with the lower seven, even the lower levels will have limits of manifestation within our lives. This is what makes Daath so critical to our path of spiritual evolution.

Daath becomes the bridge between the lower seven and the upper three. It is what creates the true alchemical transmutation within us on a soul level. It is this crossing of the abyss through higher knowledge that is reflected in the Biblical story of Elijah who "saw God and was no more". He accessed the energies on the other side of the abyss, and it created a permanent change in consciousness and perception. The old no longer existed, for something new was created.

Daath or knowledge helps us to work from all levels of consciousness associated with the Tree of Life. As our knowledge of the energies available to us at each level grows, we are propelled more strongly along our own unique path in life. Universally, Daath operates and affects the awakening of all energies at all levels of our consciousness. The more we know about a particular level of consciousness, the more we can use it to benefit our lives.

It is because of Daath that we are able to work on each individual level and awaken their corresponding energies, thereby increasing our understanding (Binah) of our own purposes in life and increasing our wisdom (Chokmah) so that we may act upon that understanding. By doing so, we may touch the highest aspects of our own consciousness (Kether), linking us more solidly with the Divine.

Prior to fully tapping the level of Daath, the spiritual student is still in the process of "becoming" - still awakening to the various levels of consciousness and their energies. When we learn to unite Daath with the others, when knowledge operates fully and consciously with each of the other levels of consciousness, then we are capable of integrating present physical life with universal life. Then we enter true discipleship, and we are thereafter involved in the process of "being" rather than "becoming". At this point the soul has access to all that was, is and will be. This does NOT mean though that the soul can employ it all, but it would have access to it.

There is great significance to Daath being placed upon the middle pillar of the Tree of Life. Knowledge can balance us, but knowledge misused will result in misplaced force and imbalance within our lives. The idea of "a little knowledge being a dangerous thing" is apropos here. Our fears and doubts, and even our inbred, societal superstitions - represented by the Great Abyss - can cause us to use our knowledge inappropriately. Daath on the middle pillar reminds us to balance information and knowledge with appropriate discrimination (Malkuth), independent testing and work (Yesod) and appropriate devotion (Tiphareth) if we are to touch the crown of our own divinity (Kether).

Daath in the Human Microcosm

On a more personal level, within the human body Daath is associated with the throat chakra. This is our center of will and creative expression. The throat chakra is very important to the modern spiritual aspirant, for it contains a key to the secret of regeneration. Through it can be found the teachings for the magical power of sound and voice.

The Divine aspect associated with the heart of the Tree of Life (Tiphareth) and thus our own heart center is called *Jehovah Aloah va Daath* or "God made manifest in the sphere of the mind". In other words our thoughts are at the heart of what manifests within our lives. They create most of our life circumstances. When we give voice to those thoughts - appropriately or not - we draw their energies out of the ethereal mental realm and ground them, releasing them more dynamically into our physical lives. Yes, our thoughts affect us, but when we give them voice, their effects manifest more quickly and more clearly.

The creation and manifestation of our thoughts into our physical world is part of the power of Daath acting through the throat chakra. We are activating our own innate Daath consciousness, giving greater power to our thoughts. Remember that Daath is the link between the energies of the higher mind with the lower levels of consciousness. It is why the ancient masters strongly encouraged and practiced reticence of speech.

Daath, like all of the sephiroth, has specific energies associated with it and with its function within our lives. It too has a Divine aspect that is most predominant, as well as archangelic and angelic beings that can be touched by learning to tap this level more fully. It is linked to specific energies within the physical universe as well, with its corresponding virtues and vices (unbalanced expressions of the energies tapped).

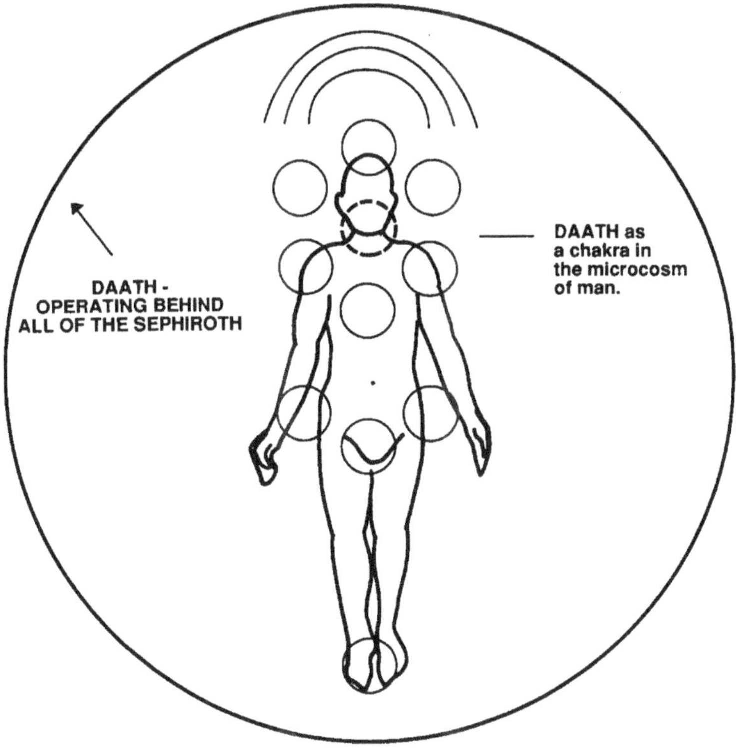

Daath not only works to release knowledge of each level of consciousness, but also serves as a separate consciousness as well, wherein universal knowledge of all the spiritual and esoteric sciences can be attained. On a lesser level, it also corresponds to the throat chakra, the center of will and creative expression within humans. It is a center of cornucopia because through proper use and understanding of it, we can learn to manifest all we need from any of the other levels of consciousness.

The Power of Daath

That aspect of the Divine which can be experienced at this level of our consciousness is actually a combination of the Divine aspects associated with and experienced through Binah and Chokmah. The Divine name *Jehovah Elohim* is the name most appropriate for the Divine force accessible through Daath. This name can be interpreted as *the Divine which manifests the perfection of creation and the life of the world to come.* This fits Daath and Daath's function within our daily lives, for through knowledge, we can create a new life or a world to come.

Because of Daath's association with the throat chakra and thus the power of voice, we can use this Divine name with proper visualization to add tremendous power to all of our affirmations, mantras and other words of power. It literally empowers the throat chakra for greater manifestation. Toning the name prior to and just after our prayers and affirmations will make them ever more effective and powerful.

No single archangel was ever associated with the level of Daath. Usually, the archangels of the four cardinal points are assigned and more accessible through this level of our consciousness. Raphael is for the East, Michael is the South, Gabriel is the West and Auriel is for the North. This is appropriate because learning comes to us from all directions if we learn to recognize it. These magnificent beings can help us learn from all things within our world. Invoking their aid and guidance before any work on the level of Daath surrounds us with protection and helps us to use knowledge with fewer imbalances.

On the other hand, since all of the archangels serve as teachers for the different sephiroth, any archangel can work through Daath. Teachers disseminate knowledge, and Daath is the sphere of knowledge. Any teacher we work with - human or angelic - helps us to activate the Daath level of our own consciousness.

Working with the archangels is a group of spirits or angelic beings similar to the seraphim. Qabalist Gareth Knight describes them as having the appearance of silvery gray serpents with golden darting tongues. My own personal experience has been very similar. I have found them very serpent-like, casting a silver flame or light about them. Their eyes always appeared mist like, shifting like the mist upon a lake in the early morning. I find this appropriate in that our knowledge is always shifting our perceptions into new waves and forms. With everyone though there will be some differences because these beings will interact with each person's energies in a unique manner.

On a more mundane level the energy available to us through Daath is astrologically comparable to Sirius, the Dog Star. In Egyptian mythology the name Sirius is traced to the god Osiris, and it was considered the resting place of the soul of Isis. In fact the Isis mythology can be used most easily in awakening the energies of Daath within ourselves.

Osiris and Isis are both attributed to Sirius and thus also to Daath. Isis is the supreme feminine (Binah) and Osiris is the supreme masculine (Chokmah). Their union occurs on the mundane level in Daath. The technique of using myths and tales to tap the various levels of our consciousness is explained in later chapters.

In astrology if Sirius is well placed, it denotes or can contribute to wealth, fame, honor, etc. within one's life. All of these are things which greater knowledge can lead to within our individual lives. The world is a world of abundance, an abundance that everyone can share in if we KNOW how. Through Daath we come to know. Not only does it reflect the union of Binah and Chokmah (the union of the female and the male from which comes new birth), but it also unites Geburah and Chesed, energy and abundance.

There are other aspects associated with Daath that can help us tap this level of consciousness. Candles of the appropriate colors and a corresponding fragrance can make our task more easily accomplished. The colors that reflect and which can be used are grays and lavenders - particularly the grays. Gray is like a cloud which hides knowledge behind it.

Some fragrances are also effective in creating an atmosphere that facilitates touching this level of consciousness. Lilac, bay oil and wisteria are three of the more effective for Daath. More generic fragrances, such as sandalwood or frankincense, can also be used.

Temple of Daath

WHAT CAN BE ATTAINED THROUGH ACCESSING THIS TEMPLE OF THE MIND:
Hidden knowledge; past life information; creative expression; higher visionand greater perception;knowledge and information that can increase wealth and prosperity; opportunity to balance the male and female aspects of our life; greater clarity of mind; revelation of past life karma.
Symbolized by the Magical Images & Gifts of:
Books of Knowledge; Janus, Crescent, Pentacle

DIVINE FORCE AVAILABLE: Jehovah Elohim
(Creation through Knowledge)
- Combination of Jah and Jehovah Elohim -

ARCHANGEL MOST ACCESSIBLE: Raphael, Michael, Gabriel, Auriel
(Archangels of the four directions)

SPIRITS MOST ACCESSIBLE: Serpents of Knowledge
(help us to shift our perceptions)

TOOLS & IMAGES TO HELP ACCESS THIS LEVEL OF THE MIND:

Colors:	grays and lavenders
Fragrances:	lilac, bay oil, wisteria
Meditation Stone:	herkimer diamond, flourite
Astrology:	Sirius, the dog star
Magickal Image:	Janus type figure (man with 2 faces, looking in opposite directions); Isis figure

MAGICKAL GIFTS: Book of Knowledge, crescent, pentacle

WEAKNESSES THAT HINDER DAATH'S POTENTIALS:
doubts; fears, fanaticism; apathy and blame

STRENGTHS THAT ASSIST DAATH'S POTENTIALS:
openmindedness; willingness to face karma; courage to express

Magickal Images and Symbols of Daath

Learning to change our world creatively is what we attempt through the Qabala and the imagickal techniques of working with it. The symbols and images of Daath are vague at best because the energies they awaken are fluid and changeable. Each new bit of knowledge changes all that was previously learned. When we change our imaginings, we change our world. Through working specifically with Daath the images and symbols we use at all levels are empowered to become reality. Our dreams become more capable of manifesting. Daath gives the images and symbols life, stimulating the cosmic spiral on the middle pillar.

The magickal image of Daath operates in many ways like the archangels - as a teacher. It is usually the image of a man with two faces, each looking in opposite directions. This is the mythical image of Janus. In Roman mythology Janus was the planter of seeds and the god of good beginnings, ruling the past and the future. He protected the health, happiness and material wealth of the family. Janus was the guardian of doors, gateways, bridges, entrances and exits. Janus was believed to open and close the gates of heaven. All of this reflects the power of Daath and the importance of knowledge in life.

The image of a face looking in opposite directions reminds us that unless knowledge is used correctly, it will result in either looking or using it only where we have already been. We must use it to move us beyond where we are, across the abyss to higher evolution. It is also a reminder that knowledge must always be balanced.

JANUS

CRESCENT

PENTAGRAM

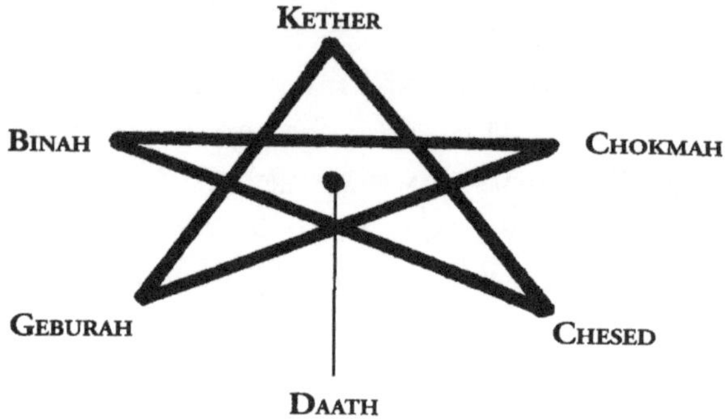

As you will discover, this image will help open your own vision across the abyss. Just as Janus opened the doors to heaven, Daath opens to us knowledge of the heavens and how to achieve it. This image helps to awaken a vision of the new life to come - a life which can bring hope, fulfillment and a heightened sense of will and destiny.

One of the other symbols associated with Daath is the pentagram. Daath is the heart of the pentagram, with the five points touching Kether, Binah, Chokmah, Geburah and Chesed. (See the diagram.) It links the lower sephiroth with the three supernals in the Tree of Life. It is a geometric shape which activates the higher energies of the individual so there is dominion of the spirit over the elements - reason over matter.

The pentagram, the five-pointed star, is an ancient sign of the microcosm. It is a symbol of humanity with arms and legs extended and the head touching the creator. At the heart of the microcosm is Daath - knowledge which helps us realize that all of the energies of the universe already exist within us.

The crescent is also a symbol for Daath. This moon symbol is more strongly related to Yesod, but Daath is a deeper level of Yesod. They both reflect energies of the subconscious, with Daath supplying the knowledge of how to use those energies more appropriately. Daath can be taken as the higher, more spiritual energies of Yesod.

The crescent is an ancient symbol. This geometric shape can be a link to the archetypal forces that enhance healing of emotional imbalances. It can be used to help with problems of expression. Both of these aspects relate it to Daath. Through greater self-knowledge we can face and transmute our lower emotions, freeing our own creative expressions.

The crescent also awakens the feminine energies of our soul - our intuitive, receptive aspects. We are all a combination of masculine and feminine expressions of energy. This is part of what the Qabala teaches. The feminine are the intuitive, illuminated and enlightened aspects of the soul, our birth giving energies. Knowledge, innate within us all, has the potential to illumine and enlighten. When it does, we begin to give birth to our higher self.

The crescent is a shape that is also connected to nada yoga, the dynamic and creative use of sounds and mantras. Again, this reflects the association of Daath with the throat chakra in the human body. It reinforces the influence of Daath as tied to our center of expression for creativity and manifestation.

Daath is located in the Abyss, the center of our deepest levels of subconscious fears and inner demons. Tapping Daath places us right in the midst of them, where we have little choice but to deal with them. It is for this reason that Daath is also known as *THE SPHERE OF JUSTICE.* True justice involves confronting and dealing with what must ultimately be faced.

Through Daath, we open to knowledge of all deeds - past, present and future. Through Daath, knowledge of things hidden is revealed and brought to full consciousness. This can be severely disruptive to the soul and mind. Because of this: **Do not enter Daath unless you truly are willing to face all**

that you are and all that you have done!

Learning to work at the Daath level of consciousness will awaken the virtue of detachment. Knowledge helps us to control in a detached manner the desires we all have. The person who learns to tap this level will be able to go about their business with a detachment that will prevent distraction. It awakens a strong sense of destiny.

The Daath powers in balanced function, of course, give the type of person with a mission or a sense of destiny who will have sufficient detachment to cut his way through any abstruction to his aims, at no matter what cost and who has absolutely no concern for what danger the future may have in store, such is hi faith in his powers and acceptance of destiny.

- Gareth Knight,
Practical Guide to Qabalalistic Symbolism
York Beach: Samuel Weiser, Inc.,
1978, p.105.

This aspect of Daath can work against us though. It can serve to cut us off from the mainstream of society and people. It can create a kind of misguided fanaticism. It becomes misguided when the other virtues from the tree of Life are not integrated. Those virtues most important to integrate into our life to prevent the unbalanced fanaticism are devotion to the divine, humility, love for fellow humans, and a sense of charity. Detachment should always be from the lower aspects of our personality and not from humanity itself.

On the other hand, Daath will open us to higher knowledge. Through it we can awaken a true confidence in the future. It enables us to see across the abyss of our daily lives. We come to *KNOW* that there truly is a better life for us, one that we are capable of creating!

Do not enter
or work with Daath
unless you truly
are willing to face
all that you are
and all that
you have done!

Cardinal Rules for Working with Daath

There are two primary rules to keep in mind when working with Daath:

1. Do not perform Daath exercises too frequently.

With most exercises with the Qabala, I often recommend they be performed three days in a row. Three is a creative number and its rhythm amplifies the effects of the exercise we are performing. With Daath, perform the exercise **ONCE, and then leave at least a month after working it so you can truly discern the effects on your life!**

Work with Daath in small doses. Our bodily systems and our individual lives must be able to assimilate the experience of Daath with all of its archetypal force. To explore Daath without creating imbalances requires time and patience. Knowledge without true understanding or the wisdom of how to apply it for the benefit of all is very dangerous. It takes time to re-assimilate and integrate the increased knowledge and awareness in the most beneficial manner.

Too much, too soon will overwhelm and create a collapse or fall within our own lives. If knowledge is to be used correctly, we must be able to discern how it affects us individually and how it can affect everyone and everything else in the universe. Treating this cardinal rule too lightly is what causes the sharp, serpent bite of knowledge.

2. Only explore Daath if you are truly able and willing to handle the responsibility and repercussions (good and bad).

Knowledge is often given as the cause for the fall of humanity, as depicted in the story of Adam and Eve eating the fruit from the Tree of Knowledge. Knowledge has its consequences. If we are to use knowledge, we must be willing to take upon its responsibility.

Touching Daath creates opportunities to learn about ourselves. It can show our darker aspects. Those aspects that we would rather ignore and which can be disruptive to the personality may surface so we can face them and transmute them. Daath is direct. It does not sugarcoat.

Daath can disrupt the conditions of our life with an intensity that can be difficult to rebalance. Here we learn and face true cosmic law. We see what we have done, and we know it must be balanced. For those who have lived many, many lives, karma can be frightening. It is for this reason that many of the ancient, esoteric schools cautioned students against past life exploration. It has the potential of releasing energies that have already been balanced. it can open wounds that have already healed. It can also release the balancing of karma with an intensity that can be agonizing for the soul.

Daath can open a Pandora's box of past-life karma. The exercise at the end of the chapter can be easily adapted for exploring past lives through Daath, but even with this exercise, caution is recommended. The old saying holds true: **"Be careful of what you ask, for you may get it!"** When we tap Daath, we will get what we ask.

EXERCISE:

The Temple of Knowledge

Benefits:

- **knowledge of hidden things**
- **past life information**
- **self-examination**
- **secrets of the universe**
- **future knowledge**
- **revelation of personal destiny**
- **greater knowledge of the Tree of Life**

The symbols and images within this exercise have been chosen carefully to elicit the strongest and safest effects from Daath. It is best to familiarize yourself with the meditation and its symbols prior to the working. Contemplating and reflecting upon their significance will help to trigger an even stronger response.

The effects of this exercise are very powerful but very subtle. They will manifest into your daily life in a manner that must be dealt with and transmuted. The exercise works gradually, but it WILL work.

The first time I used this exercise, the effects were felt for months. Old emotions and thoughts arose that had to be dealt with. Numerous individuals commented or inquired about my change in energy. It was not recognized as positive or negative, just different. I discovered information about others that I didn't want to know. I discovered things about myself that I did not want to admit.

Knowledge of the self is one of the benefits of this exercise, but knowledge can be painful. It can reveal the thorns in our life that need to be removed. The removal hurts, but in the long run, it is not as painful as allowing a thorn to remain, becoming infected and festering within us.

Remember: **Once you set the energies in motion, they will play themselves out!** If they seem to overwhelm you - and it can happen - the best course of action is to deal with what has been set in motion as best as you are able at the time. Using the protection and balancing exercises given later can also help. Take a break form working with the Tree of Life. Focus on the daily, mundane activities for a few weeks or longer. Spend a lot of time in nature; it will help ground the energies released and help keep you balanced as well.

The wonderful thing about Daath though is that anything cleaned out through knowledge of the self will be replaced by something much more beneficial to us. We find ourselves propelled along a higher destiny. Through it we enhance our learning in every other area of life. Through Daath we learn to read from the Holy Writ - the Book of Knowledge of the universe.

Knowledge can be painful, especially since it can be used to interfere with the free will of others. A misuse of knowledge draws to us strong repercussions. Through this exercise, you will have the opportunity to open to Daath - to open to knowledge, to read from the book of your life - past , present and future.

Before performing this exercise, make some preparations:

1. Familiarize yourself with Daath and all of its symbols and energies. This includes the sigils on the following page.

2. Make sure you will be undisturbed.

3. Review the benefits and precautions.

4. Set the tone with the appropriate fragrance, candle, etc. Although with many meditations music can be a wonderful aid, for working with Daath, no music is usually most beneficial.

5. Perform a progressive relaxation.

Sigils of the Archangels

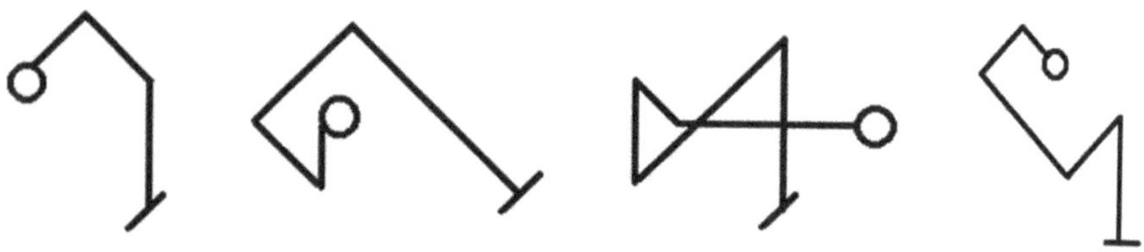

Raphael **Michael** **Gabriel** **Auriel**

The sigils are symbolic signatures of the four great archangels. They are based upon Golden Dawn techniques of applying Hebrew letters to the ancient symbol of the Rose and Rose Cross. There are many ways of forming the signatures of these beings; this is only one. For a complete elaboration, you can refer to *THE GOLDEN DAWN* by Israel Regardie (Llewellyn Publications, 1986; p.9-47).

These sigils in Daath (and in the Daath exercise) serve to balance the expression of knowledge within our lives. Any meditation or work with Daath should utilize the sigils or other symbols/images of the four great archangels. They provide strong protection and grounding of the energies awakened in Daath.

This exercise is a guide. Do not worry about remembering all of the details. We must use our own insight and allow the basic imagery to adapt them to us. At first hold as closely as possible to the scenario. Once familiar with it, it can be adapted more freely. Each may find their own variations occurring.

There will be different responses to this exercise, but once the temple is opened - as it is through this exercise - then we can go back and read from the Book of Knowledge. This book can open us to knowledge on almost anything we wish to learn - especially if we are ready for it. Keep in mind that someone who does not know basic mathematics will not be able to perform calculus. The knowledge that opens to us will be relative to that for which we are prepared.

Every reading of the book does have its accompanying bite, usually at the end. (It will vary from individual to individual.) The pain of the bite varies according to what knowledge is being revealed and its potential for misuse. The bite is our reminder that misused knowledge has its price!

The time frame in which to work this exercise and experience results varies. It could take as long as a month to recognize the effects, but usually it takes no more than a day or so for the first confirmations to make themselves known. It usually comes through new revelations, new opportunities for knowledge, discovery of hidden things going on around us, or a variety of other possibilities. Pay attention to what reveals itself to you in the days following the exercise.

The ancient mystery schools taught their students to "KNOW THYSELF". This is the kind of energy released through this exercise. It releases the energy that stimulates and awakens insight into ourselves and our lives. It releases energy to help us see aspects of ourselves and our lives that we have not seen or not seen as clearly as we should. It helps manifest conditions that enable us to have knowledge of ourselves and of things affecting ourselves - good and bad.

It is usually best to wait a month before repeating this exercise, but it is only a guideline, especially upon its initial working. The month period enables us to determine the effect that this exercise will likely have on our life. This requires some self-examination.

In the days that follow this exercise, ask yourself some questions:

- *Have your emotions been more charged or volatile since performing the exercise?*
- *Have new situations arisen - good and/or bad?*
- *How are you relating to people in your life or they to you since the exercise?*
- *Are there certain things upsetting you more?*
- *Have new learning opportunities (formal & informal) presented themselves?*
- *Have new people come into your life? What are they like?*
- *Are you having things revealed - good and/or bad?*

Examine every aspect of your life. Remember that knowledge throws light upon shadows. It forces us to look at things from a different perspective. Suspicions may be clarified. Secrets may be revealed. Hidden insights may occur.

Self-knowledge is most important. Unless we can become aware of those aspects of us that limit us, we can never clean them out and replace them with energies that are more beneficial. This exercise sets energy in motion to bring out new perspectives on ourselves. This will happen in both obvious and subtle ways. Thus we need some time to assimilate what has been released into our life or we may bring on too many learning circumstances too quickly. When that occurs, the learning is disruptive rather than healing. This is why some time be given before repeating this exercise.

Use your own judgment. Remember that the Qabala will show us our greatest strengths and our greatest weaknesses. If not controlled, especially when working with Daath, this can be troublesome. If you find yourself going to Daath to find out things for which you have no direct use, to intrude into the privacy of others or to satisfy some unbalanced urge for gossip, there will be a price!

There is with most people a craving for more knowledge. It must always be balanced. Those who have much, often want more. Those who have access to much, often want it opened and augmented, even at the risk of imbalance. There are times to seek and use knowledge, and there are times when it is best to leave it alone. Through Daath, the old axiom of a little knowledge being dangerous can reveal its truth. Part of this will be explored in the last chapters.

The autonomy of the individual must be recognized unqualifyingly. No one has the right to use knowledge to impinge the free will of another or to over ride it. Free will is one of the greatest gifts humanity has received, and it does have its responsibilities and consequences. To use knowledge inappropriately to impinge upon anyone's free will has dire consequences.

Through Daath and through what unfolds within your life after accessing it, we learn that knowledge is most powerful when it is used to serve!

Entering the Temple of Daath

You are standing outside the ancient tree of life. As always, its immense size astounds you. It grows even larger and more impressive with each visit. Today though there is a heightened sense of anticipation and anxiousness. It is the first day of school as far as you are concerned.

The Temple of Daath - the Temple of Knowledge - is something you have looked forward to for a long time. To be able to finally know! To have the knowledge of all the ages at your hands - what joy! Knowledge has done so much good and yet caused so much pain, and a temple that encompasses all knowledge fills you with a sense of wonder.

Humans know so much about the physical world, and so little about other worlds and dimensions. Humans can be arrogant. Humans like to believe that no one knows more or better. Fanatics have always believed they knew better than the ordinary person. History books are filled with such individuals and the chaos they create.

Knowledge entails responsibility and it requires continual discernment.

You see the opening at the base of the tree. You take a deep breath and then bend slightly, stepping into the now familiar darkness. You are not sure that you know how to open this temple, so you breathe deeply, relaxing.

As the darkness of the inner tree encloaks you, you here a soft whispered voice.

"What is it you seek?"

Startled at such a voice within your tree, you are unsure how to respond. The voice speaks softly again.

"What is it you seek?"

You are a little confused. Have you done something wrong? And you cannot answer because you do not know the answer.

A third time the voice speaks the question.

"What is it you seek?"

Your mind races, knowing there must be a correct response. Then as if from some primordial remembrance, the words come forth. Though you speak them softly, hesitantly, they echo in the hollows of the tree with great power.

"I seek to know that I may serve."

A dim light begins grow inside the tree. You wait, your breath becoming a bit more rapid in anticipation. You remind yourself to be patient - that a long awaited dream is about to be fulfilled.

As the light grows, a stone gray, nearly empty room is revealed. Your eyes widen and your shoulders sink in disappointment. This can not be the Temple of Knowledge!

You had come expecting the magnificence of the libraries of Alexandria, and you find only an empty room. No books. no scrolls. No writings or markings of any kind, except for insignias carved into the upper part of each of the four walls. Each is different and somewhat familiar, but they tell you nothing. It makes no sense. And you are filled with disappointment.

There is not even an altar in this temple - if in deed it is a temple. Near the back of the room sits a wooden pedestal. Its base is in the shape of a pentagram and three rods upward out of it to a crescent-shaped surface. Upon this crescent surface sits a large leather-bound volume. On either side of the middle rod of the pedestal are two stone carved snakes, resting in a circular coil on the pentagram base.

As you step forward to the pedestal, the surface with the book is chest level - heart level to you.

"We enter the mysteries through the sphere of the mind, but only so we can worship at the shrine in the heart."

It is the same voice as before, but its sound softly echoes in your mind and in the air around you. You are not sure if they are your own words from some deep level of your own consciousness or the words of some being that you have not yet discovered. It is very puzzling indeed.

"It is good that you are puzzled, for the asking of the question is the beginning of the answer."

The voice rings again. You look about to search the shadows, but there are no shadows! There is dim lighting at best within this room, but there are no shadows! It is as if they have been chased away. There are no blacks or whites. Only grays.

You turn slowly back to the pedestal, a little disoriented. But a part of you knows that new knowledge can change the world. Above the book burns a pine cone shaped lamp that provides the only light within the temple. You know that it must have significance, but it eludes you at the moment.

You focus your attention on the large volume. It is closed, wrapped in a leather binding that is strapped and locked. You reach out gingerly to touch it. Your fingers brush it softly, lightly. You feel its texture, and your hand traces the image of a man with two faces looking into opposite directions. As you touch the image the lamp grows brighter.

You fumble with the latch, and it pops open. You lean forward, preparing to open the volume. You lay it wide, like wings across the pedestal top. And there on the top of the very first page is your name.

You stare with utter surprises and disbelief. you fail to notice in your surprise that the coiled snakes have shimmered into life. They slide upward, crisscrossing and intertwining around the middle rod of the pedestal. Slowly they begin to climb toward the book.

As you lean forward to read what is written about you in this book, the heads of the snakes appear around the sides. Before you can respond to their appearance, the twin serpents strike - each biting you on the temple behind the eyes. You jump back, drawing your hands to your face, feeling a quick sharp pain piercing your entire head. The book snaps closed with your movement. You watch, eyes wide, as the serpents draw back, receding down that middle rod to settle once more at the base. There they shimmer once more into stone. The pain in the temple disappears, and all that is left is a soft, soothing tingling to remind you what has occurred.

"The first bite of true knowledge is always the hardest to bear and catches one off guard."

You look around the room in amazement. Everything is brighter, more distinct. The bites from the serpents of knowledge have somehow cleared your eyesight. The insignias on the walls begin to glow, casting the grays back and filling the temple with crystalline white light. For a brief moment you see the images of four great beings overlaying the insignias. The four great archangels!

As the images fade upon your recognition, the temple begins to shake and vibrate as if to collapse upon itself. You fall to the ground, curling up and covering your head in fear. The temple roars!

Then nothing! Everything stills. There is silence.

You are lying upon the floor. You have no idea how long you have been there. You shiver and realize that you are completely naked. You draw yourself up slowly, confused and bewildered.

"All knowledge has its price, but its blessing is greater than any discomfort. By opening to it, you can strip away the old. You can tear down the old foundations so that the new may be laid. Only then does new light and life enter in forever. Knowledge brings light only when it is balanced with love. Knowledge is only painful if we don't use it to serve. Knowledge with love will create a new world."

The voice fades again. All is quiet, but something is different. Why does the room feel so strange? Why is it so much more crystalline? You pause to listen for the voice.

Nothing. Silence is your only answer.

You turn to leave. You glance back once more to the pedestal. The pine cone lamp brightens in response. The book lays itself open for you. A soft breeze moves through the temple, passing through you and filling you. You feel energized, healed, strong and balanced.

The breeze flips the pages of the book. You smile, beginning to understand. A part of you knows that the Book of Knowledge is now open to you once more. In it you will be able to read from your past, the present and the future.

You feel alive and more in control of your life and what is to unfold than ever before. It's as if a part of you knows that all is needed for you will reveal itself. The future is something to look forward to, not run from. You know that it is there for you to create in any manner that you choose.

You step from the Tree of Life, and as the inner visions fade, they do so only to be born into the outer life. You breathe deeply, your heart and mind at rest, secure in the knowledge that awaits you!

What is
psychic
is not always
spiritual.
What is occult
is not always
beneficial.
And what is desired
is not always
uplifting or
useful.

Chapter Four

Symbols, Images and the Magickal Body

"Within the body all of the energies of the universe, heaven and earth, play themselves out. As we learn to use the body in a more consciously directed manner, we open ourselves to the universe, and we awaken and manifest its powers within ourselves and our lives. We become the living universe!"

- Ted Andrews
Magickal Dance

A multitude of methods, tools and techniques exist for awakening our innermost energies and potentials. Most of these though do little more than just that. They simply awaken. For many people, this is comparable to stirring up a hornet's nest. Energy awakened inappropriately (especially when ill prepared) results in chaos. Energy unused or misused once awakened becomes disruptive.

Although there are lessons we can learn from chaos and disruption, there are much easier ways of learning. The key is knowing how to absorb and integrate the energy awakened. As we will discover later in this chapter, this is accomplished through creative imagination and the magickal body.

Most methods for awakening our potentials and for accessing the universal and spiritual energies of life fall into one of two categories: **meditative** and **ceremonial.** One is neither better nor worse than the other. Both include the use of symbology, visualization, creative imagination, pathworking, mantras, yantras, and many other tools to awaken the universal energies. The primary difference is that ceremonial methods often involve more intricately ritualized physical activities.

The Qabala employs both kinds, but this book will focus more upon the meditative techniques and tools. These can be adapted to more powerful ceremonial methods. The imagickal, meditative techniques throughout this work are created to elicit very specific results. They will allow you to experience the power of the Qabala and to use it more effectively. They will enable you to increasingly manifest the universal forces more tangibly into your daily life, without being overwhelmed by them.

With every meditation, with every imagickal working, we are planting a seed thought. Planting a seed thought means placing a clear magickal or mystical idea or image into our visualizations with strong intention. This consigns the seed thought or image to the subconscious mind, where it will begin to grow and increase in energy on its own. If we repeat this process every day, if only for a few moments, the magickal idea, image and/or working will become a bridge to the Divine world. At the very least, it energizes our entire life, increases our creativity and enhances our expression of life while in the physical.

The symbols and images associated with the Tree of Life are the tools for opening doors beyond the realm of our physical environment. The Qabala provides a system of using these symbols and images to explore the more subtle realms without getting lost. It provides a powerful "how-to" for almost any image and symbol.

Symbols and images are guideposts. In the Qabala, certain ones have been used in a similar fashion by many people for many centuries, thus the paths are already laid out for us, with built in markers to prevent our getting lost. All we need to do is learn to read the markers and walk the paths in order to link our energy with the universal energy activated by this work with the images and symbols.

Tapping Hidden Levels

Empowering our life through the Qabalistic symbols, images and seed thoughts requires understanding the language of symbols, and then it requires setting up the conditions that cause a mental shift to a new way of processing information - an altered state of consciousness. Through the meditations and related techniques in this book, we learn to use the language of symbols to delve into parts of our mind that are too often obscured by the endless details of daily life. Through proper use of Qabalistic symbols, images and seed thoughts, we can create a mind-set that perceives life in a new manner. We begin to see underlying patterns, and we access our greater potentials and release them into our normal consciousness. We discover solutions to problems and we add energy and animation to our lives.

In working with the Tree of Life, we are consciously learning how to use specific symbols and images. We are learning to tap energies represented and reflected through them. Each sephiroth - each level of consciousness - is a temple in which specific energies are more available to us. These energies are translated to and awakened within us through symbols and images.

The colors, names, letters, tarot associations, astrological glyphs and all of the other images and symbols associated with each level of the Tree of Life help us to understand the energy within us. They also help us to access and express those energies more directly and consciously. In essence, we are taking an "intangible" expression of energy and potential within us and giving it a tangible representation through the symbol or image. In this way we activate their influence upon us more dynamically and in turn we can manifest and express those energies more effectively within our lives.

To achieve results, to tap deeper levels of consciousness and to manifest our innermost powers, we need only to learn how to shift our awareness in the appropriate manner and then maintain it for the time and purpose necessary. This is a learned skill! The Qabala provides all of the tools (often in the form of images and symbols) necessary to accomplish this, and the more we use them, the more energy, power and magic manifests within our lives.

Qabala symbols and images help us access forces and energies latent within us and the universe. They open doors to ever-deepening levels of consciousness and perception. The images, symbols and correspondences of the Tree of Life are ways of controlling specific aspects and manifestations of archetypal force that are playing within our lives.

Most effective occult techniques are very simple. They depend upon capacities that can be developed by any intelligent man or woman. Yes, depth of control requires much more time and energy, but *everyone* can achieve some results almost immediately. When we use symbols, images and seed thoughts to develop controlled creative imagination and then use that creative imagination to give birth to the magickal body, our life takes a quantum leap. We become the living Tree of Life!

Tapping Hidden Levels Through Symbols and Images

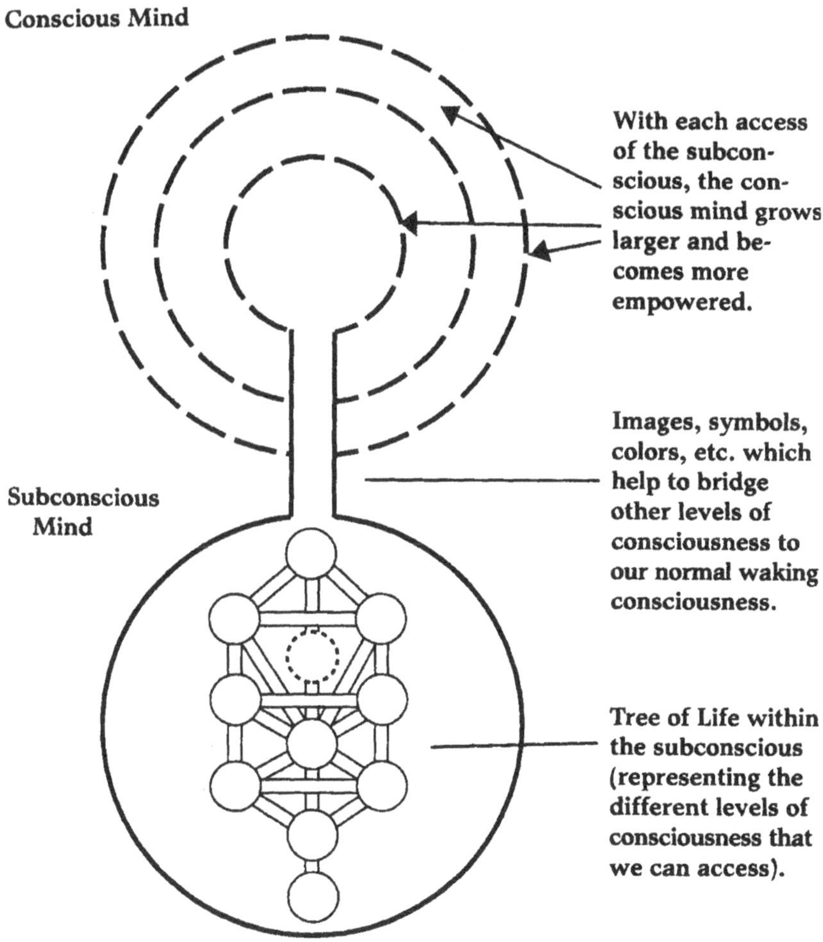

By focusing upong specific images, symbols, colors and sounds, we can open up specific levels of our subconscious mind. Symbols and images, when used through such techniques as imagick and pathworking, enable us to draw upon our subconscious reservoirs to create even greater boundaries within which to operate in ourwaking lives. The symbols refdlect other realities. By working with them more consciously, we bridge all aspects of ourselves, which in turn opens higher understanding, greater mysticism and access to all realms and times.

Imagickal Symbology

Symbology is the language of the unconscious, and each of us at some point will need to learn more about it and how to use it to our fullest capability. If we intend to step out on the path of controlled evolution, we must become aware of the power and significance of symbols within our lives.

To understand symbols is to understand ourselves. They help us to understand what our beliefs, superstitions, fears are based upon. They can also open us to levels of our being that we have either ignored or been unaware of. Symbols span the world of thought and the world of being. They provide a means of understanding and interacting with the true world of hidden realities within us and our life. They express what we have no words for.

Symbols bridge the rational and intuitive levels of our being. They lead us from the limited regions of the conscious mind to the unlimited regions of the subconscious mind. They touch both objective and subjective realities. They are a means for the subconscious to send forth information to the conscious mind that might not have discerned it otherwise. They bridge the finite aspects of us with our more infinite potentials.

Good guided imagery and symbols are derived from archetypes and thus at some point in our use of them, they lead us back to those archetypes. The archetypes are the manifesting energies of the universe. The archetypes are the points where the abstract divine forces begin to take upon themselves more substantial forms of expression. If we do not attempt to work with the archetypes and clear the debris from our life, we will not progress beyond a certain point. The symbols and images assist us in merging our finite mind with the infinite mind of the universe.

Symbology and imagery are a part of our essence and have tremendous spiritual import to us. They are accumulators of energy which, if used properly, release archetypal forces to play out within our lives. The techniques of this book are designed to teach how to use symbols and images of the Qabala for the greater activation and control of archetypal energies in all areas of our life. In this way we discover that we can truly change our world.

Understanding the relation between the archetypal forces of the universe and the symbols and images that bridge them into our daily lives is critical to leading a magickal existence. At the core of every symbol and image lies some archetypal force. Energy translated from the archetypal to the sensible ones of physical life take the form of images and symbols in order for us to recognize them and work with them. Likewise, it requires proper use of symbols and images to connect back to the archetypal forces. This is why the Tree of Life places such an invaluable role in unfolding our potentials. It provides the tools for working with them properly.

Through the Tree of Life we learn to use images as a carpenter uses wood, hammer and saw. Qabalistic images and symbols are the tools we use to build perception of the spiritually creative worlds and their energies playing within our lives. This means we must be able to construct a passive, reflected thought or image and then transform that thought through our ***creative imagination*** into a living, empowered energy. When we can accomplish this, we can consciously open the doors, communicate and interact with all of the spiritual realms.

A physically and spiritually creative person is one who can process information in new ways. A creative individual intuitively sees possibilities for transforming ordinary data and everyday experiences into new creations. It is an individual who can see the creative possibilities that exist in limitations. To accomplish this, we must be able to learn in new ways.

Inside each of our skulls we have a double brain with two ways of knowing and learning. The different characteristics of the two hemispheres of the brain have a dynamic role in releasing higher potentials into our daily life expression - especially when working together.

Each of the hemispheres gathers in the same sensory information, but they handle that information in different ways. One hemisphere (often the dominant left in Western society) will inhibit the other half. The left hemisphere analyzes, counts, marks time, plans and views logically and in a step-by-step procedure. It verbalizes, makes statements and draws conclusions based on logic. It is sequential and linear in its approach to life.

On the other hand, we do have a second way of knowing and learning. This is known as right-brain activity. We "see" things that may be imaginary - existing only in the mind's eye - or recall things that may be real. We see how things exist in space and how parts go together to make a whole. Through it we understand metaphors, we dream and we create new combinations of ideas. Through the right hemisphere we tap and use intuition and have leaps of insight - moments when everything seems to fall into place but not in a logical manner. The intuitive, subjective, relational, wholistic and the time-free mode is right hemisphere activity.

One of the marvelous capacities of the right hemisphere is imaging, *seeing an image or picture with the mind's eye*. The brain is able to conjure an image and then hold it and work with it. These images reflect our sensory information and data - past, present and future. Something imagined is not something unreal. It is simply a product of the imaging faculty of the brain that has a source, even if unidentified.

Because of this faculty, symbols, visualization and creative imagination are often a part of developing higher potentials. The symbols and images assist us in accessing that part of our brain and mind which bridges into deeper levels of perception and consciousness. Learning to use the right brain to tap and access specific level of consciousness in a balanced and fully conscious manner - to bring it out and then apply it to some aspect of our daily lives - involves hemispheric synchronization - working with both sides of the brain.

The Qabala teaches us how to do this. It provides an organized system of images to access and connect deeper levels of our subconscious mind to our normal waking consciousness. It is a system (left brain) of image and symbol usage (right brain). Our unfoldment becomes a safer and easier process when we control and work through a balanced system. By working with such a system in an appropriate manner, we use both sides of our brain and more fully tap our subconscious - which opens all the doorways to our intuitive, higher self.

When we control, direct and focus the inner energies consciously, we are doing what the teacher and mystic Rudolph Steiner referred to as "grabbing the serpent of wisdom by the neck". We are choosing and directing the movement of energy within ourselves and our lives. We do it consciously and with full responsibility. We learn to make the energies work for us when we wish and how we wish.

The key to empowering our life is setting up conditions that create a mental shift to a new way of processing information. Through the techniques in this book, we will learn to delve into parts of the mind and its perceptions that are often obscured by the endless details of daily life. Through the proper use of images and symbols, we create a mind-set that begins the process of unveiling the hidden to us. We begin to see underlying patterns, and we access greater potentials and manifest them within our daily lives.

The Four Main Worlds of the Tree of Life

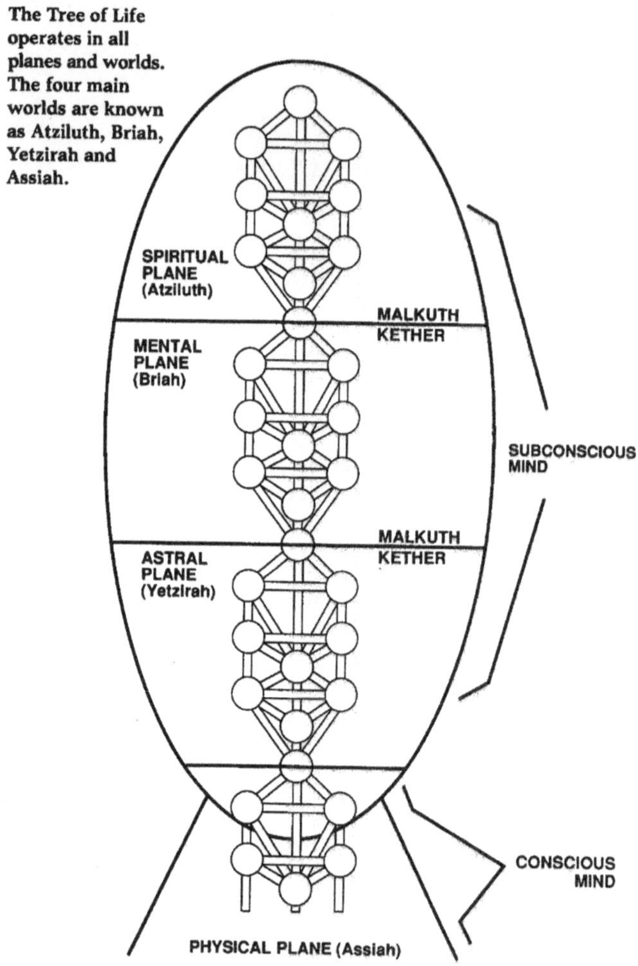

The Tree of Life operates in all planes and dimensions. As we learn to work with the symbols and images appropriately, we not only manifest the energies of a level but we also open the doors to the next. All dimensions and realms are available to us and can be accessed by us through the proper use of symbols and images, such as is described throughout this book.

The Power of Creative Imagination

The capacities that must be developed for true success with the Qabalistic symbols and images are **visualization, concentration** and **creative imagination.** These - when truly developed - will lead to higher forms of inspiration and a fully conscious perception of the spiritual realm and all of its manifestations of life.

VISUALIZATION is the ability to create a mental picture and to hold it steady within the mind for a reasonable time. The image should be as clear as anything seen within the physical life. It should be made as lifelike as possible - in color, texture, fragrance, etc. A simple exercise is to visualize an orange. Clearly visualize its shape, size and color. Feel the skin on it. Experience how it feels as you press your finger into it and begin to peel it. Notice the fragrance as the juice squirts out. Then create the image of its taste.

Some individuals are not visual and thus may feel that their work with the Qabala will be hindered. Nothing could be further from the truth. Even if we can't picture in our minds, by simply bringing the thought or idea of an image or symbol to mind, we open the doors that will elicit the same result.

CONCENTRATION is the art of holding the thought or image that you have created within your mind without the mind wavering or wandering to other things. We should develop a concentrated focus that is strong enough to hold one image or thought to the exclusion of others. This takes practice. If we find our mind wandering, bring it back to the image or thought - no matter how often it wanders. By doing so, we train the mind. In time it will respond with increasingly concentrated focus when and how we wish.

The third fundamental ability to develop is controlled **CREATIVE IMAGINATION.** This is enabling the mind to create images and scenes associated with our meditative thought or seed image. These created images should be in a three-dimensional form. They can be like highly concentrated daydreams or even very lucid night dreams. The ensuing scenario relates entirely to our key image or seed thought. In such occurrences, we become absorbed within the framework of the unfolding scenario, losing track and awareness of time and the ordinary world around us.

Creative imagination or imaginative cognition is a key to opening the doors to the spirit realm. Its proper development will reveal the spiritual background of life. Through it we begin to see the spiritual essences and energies surrounding and interplaying with the physical world at all times.

What we consider imagination is a reality on some level beyond the normal sensory world. Through creative imagination, we create new awareness in relation to our daily life, a new kind of experience in form and color. Through creative imagination, we build up significances of the images and symbols that we employ, imbuing them with greater relevance to our life. Then we learn to assume a union with them. Through repeated use, we activate more of the image's archetypal origins, releasing it more dynamically and tangibly into our life.

This in turn triggers higher forms of inspiration and intuition. It begins to unveil the spiritual universe working within our day-to-day lives. We begin to gain a better understanding of the conditions of the true conditions of our lives and the spiritual laws governing them, along with the spiritual hierarchies that inhabit them. After the doors are opened through creative imagination, we begin to explore through inspiration, experiencing more direct spiritual perceptions rather than through images that must be translated.

To establish this more direct contact, we must first develop the use of creative imagination. We must work toward greater knowledge of the entire school of inner esoteric schooling, so as to distinguish the true from that which only appears to be true. We must learn to exclude all thoughts and images of the physical world for definite periods of time. We must also be able to extinguish by our own resolve those same images and thoughts that we created and used to open the doors. When we can do this, we can consciously connect with our own spirit/soul being or higher self.

The Magickal Body

One of the greatest benefits in working with the Tree of Life is the creation of the "magickal body". The magickal body is the new, more conscious you that is created through the work. When we work with the Tree of Life, we bring to life the unexpressed, inherent energies and abilities within us. We use the Tree to awaken our higher, more powerful selves.

Each Sephira reflects specific energies that are a part of our essence and can manifest within our reality - physical or otherwise. Work with the Tree is work with ourselves. Through it we awaken our innate potentials and begin to manifest them within our lives.

For some people the awakening of these internal abilities and capacities is very subtle, but for others, the awakening is quite apparent. If we are to truly empower our essence, we need to be aware of this process. Anything we do with the Tree will affect that part of us which corresponds to it.

What we are working to accomplish is to consciously bring to life those aspects of ourselves that we wish, dream and hope to manifest. The magickal body is the ideal you, with the ability to be the most powerful and effective that you can be in your life. Through work with all of the levels of the Tree, we develop the ability to assume the powers and potentials for whatever a task may require within our life.

In order to accomplish this though, we must first awaken the energies, abilities and powers necessary. We are creating a new *me*. We are not just changing the old. We must keep this in mind at all times. We need to focus and apply creative imagination to the ideal within us - physically, mentally and spiritually. In this way, the images and symbols remain strong and vital for us.

The creation of the magickal body begins with the creation of the imagickal body. Imagine the ideal you. What would the ideal you truly be like? Remember that if you can imagine it, then it can be. *When you change your imaginings, you change the world.*

All energy follows thought. Where we put our thoughts that is where energy goes. Form follows idea, thus thought and image create an energy matrix or blueprint by which the form will manifest within our life.

The process is rather simple. Visualize exactly what it is you wish to be, with all of its variations and in as much detail as possible. Visualize it as if you are already it - as if it is already accomplished.

Then do whatever is necessary in the physical to help it along. Act according to the way you have imagined. The key to magick is being who you truly are. Our magickal essence is merely a reflection of our higher, truer essence.

Begin by asking yourself some basic questions:

1. **What is the highest, brightest, most creative image of yourself that you can imagine?**
2. **What characteristics would you have?**
3. **What would you most ideally like to be able to do?**
4. **What abilities would you be able to express?**
5. **How would you ideally like others to see you?**
6. **How would being this way change your life at home and work?**
7. **If you could manifest those abilities now, what are some ways you could use them to your benefit and that of others?**
8. **How would you be able to help others without them knowing?**
9. **What would you be able to accomplish and how would you do it most effectively?**
10. **What new possibilities would unfold for you?**

When we use symbols and images in the proper manner, we are opening to the creative powers of the universe. The amount of energy available to each of us is limited by our capacity for realization. If we increase our awareness, at the same time removing our inhibitions and limitations, we increase our intake of universal or cosmic energy. Whatever we are or are becoming is intensified. Every aspect of our nature is intensified!

We are physical beings. This means our primary focus should be within the physical world, but we can use other dimensions and levels of consciousness to create more productivity within our physical lives. If we are to use other, deeper levels of consciousness for our betterment, then we need to transform the energy potentials of the inner to the outer life. It is the magickal body tat assists us with this. With each touching of the sephiroth, we release energy that assists in molding, creating and empowering the ideal self - the true magickal person that lives within us. The magickal body is a reflection of the divinity that is inherent within us.

Associated with each Sephira is a magickal image and magickal gifts. This magickal image is a tremendously powerful thought form that has been created through constant work on the Tree of Life through the ages. Tapping these thought forms assists us in creating our own variations and expressions of the energy represented and reflected by the image.

These magickal images reflect a tangible expression of the more abstract energies available to us through that level of consciousness. In touching each level, we assimilate the energies of the magickal image into ourselves. This in turn enables us to more fully tap and use the energies of the Tree of Life more fully within our daily lives. The magickal images help us move from merely developing a magickal body to becoming a very real magickal being.

Magickal Images and Gifts Associated with each Sephira

Sephira	Magickal Image	Magickal Gift
Kether	Ancient bearded king, seen only in profile	spinning top
Chokmah	bearded male figure	sceptre of power
Binah	mature woman, matron	Black cloak with rainbow interior, cloak of concealment
Chesed	mighty crowned and throned king	king's cup
Geburah	mighty warrior in his chariot	sword
Tiphareth	majestic king; sacrificed god; child	crown that's too big
Netzach	beautiful naked woman	rose
Hod	hermaphrodite	caduceus pendant
Yesod	beautiful naked man; very strong	silver slippers and a mirror
Malkuth	young woman, crowned and throned	grains, oils & gems

EXERCISE:

Creating the Magickal Body

Benefits:

- **personal empowerment**
- **awakens perceptions**
- **healing**
- **greater control of life**
- **problem solving**
- **shapeshifting**

The magickal images are reflections of archetypal forces that are always active within the universe. We work with the images to help us in working more consciously and in a more controlled manner with those same forces that exist within us. They reflect divine aspects of our selves that we are relearning to incorporate and express more fully within our lives.

The qualities symbolized by the images are awakened within us through the magickal image and gifts. As our own personal experience and knowledge of them grows, so does the archetypal force that they represent. Ultimately, the energies associated with the magickal images and gifts become integrated and expressed more dynamically within our own life. It is then that we are creating the magickal body and a true magickal existence.

The idea of taking on the attitudes and energies of the sephirotic images is very ancient. In the Western world we are frequently told to live according to the examples of others - especially in the image of saints and masters. With the magickal images we link the archetypal forces associated with the images to our own lives more dynamically. We set them in motion to manifest in specific areas of our life.

Remember that the images of the Divine take many faces and forms. Through the magickal images of the Tree of Life, we are learning to distinguish and incorporate the energy more tangibly within our lives. One of the most common techniques of using the magickal images to create a magickal body is through the individual sephiroth. The process is simple, and a more expanded version exists in the exercise at the end of this chapter.

1. Using the methods previously discussed, we enter into the Tree and bring the particular temple to life.

2. As the inner temple comes to life, allow the magickal image to step before you.

Let it speaks of what it reflects or symbolizes. Let it explain how you can manifest the same energies in your own life. The image can teach you how it has operated and been used by you in the past - positively and negatively.

3. Let this wonderful, powerful form show you how to use its energies to amplify your own - thereby creating your own magickal body.

4. After the teaching has occurred, allow the image to step forward. Feel it melt over you and into you.

Feel yourself becoming one with the image, inseparable. The image breathes with you and in you - you are the image. It becomes strengthened in you and by you. It infuses you, adding to your repertoire of magickal energy.

5. Then leave the temple of the Tree, knowing that as you carry the image and its essence into the outer world, with all of its energies and powerful awakened within you.

Know that by relaxing and visualizing the image within you, its powers are brought to the forefront to be expressed within your life.

Through this process we learn to become the alchemist - the master shapeshifter. If the need arises to use the energies associated with the image and the level of consciousness that it affects, all we need to do is relax and visualize the image coming to life within us.

We all adapt ourselves, according to situations and people, everyday of our lives. Through the magickal image we learn to shapeshift more consciously, more powerfully and so much more effectively than we ever could do otherwise. Since all life situations can fall under the rule of one or more of the sephiroth, through use of the magickal image and its gifts, we can learn to transmute all situations. We need only practice assuming and shifting our shapes - calling forth our magickal essence (or an expression of it). That is when our magickal body begins to truly live.

EXERCISE:

Empowering Your Magickal Essence

Benefits:

- **dynamically healing and empowering**
- **opens the doors to new opportunities**
- **stimulates abundance and increase**
- **strengthens self-esteem**
- **opportunities to explore inner potentials surface**

One of the simplest methods for creating our own magickal body is through the magickal images associated with each level on the Tree of Life. This exercise helps us to become a living Tree of Life, inherent with all of its energies and possibilities. Although a little longer than most exercises, it is powerful at awakening and building the Tree of Life within ourselves.

A simpler version than what follows is described in the previous exercise with the individual going into each Sephira and working only with the magickal image, temple and gift for that temple. Either method will work, but regardless of how this exercise is employed, it will empower you and energize all levels of your life.

Empowering the Magickal Essence

You are standing in that same meadow - with a great mountain in the distance and the valley below. In the heart of this meadow is that magnificent tree that is becoming so familiar to you. Your hand reaches out and gently touches the bark - in almost a caressing fashion. You feel the warmth beneath the ancient bark, and it is comforting.

Faintly, the bark before you shimmers slightly and the diagram of the Tree of Life, as tall as you, stands out against the tree. You know instinctively that it is a doorway being presented for you. A part of you also seems to know that not always will it be such. At some time, you must learn to create your own doorways - when your own magickal body has become empowered.

You breathe deeply and step through the Tree of Life outline and into the inner darkness of the tree itself. This is becoming so familiar to you now, and you smile a bit. No longer is there any fear that you first experienced. Humans haven't come as far as what they often try to profess. They still fear most what they cannot see.

Softly you whisper the name for the Temple of Malkuth.

"Adonai ha Aretz."

The blackness around you shimmers and becomes a soft olive green. Again you speak the name.

"Adonai ha Aretz."

The olive green shimmers and the inner area is filled with the colors of autumn. Now you can see the outlines of the temple furnishings. You breathe deeply and a third time you speak the name forth:

"Adonai ha Aretz."

The room fills with a citrine, sunshine light, and you see the temple as you last left it- the altar, pillars, baskets before you. Today the scent of sandalwood is strong within the temple. You breathe deep its fragrance, and the lamp upon the altar shines strong and true.

But all is not exactly as you remember. There is now a doorway behind the altar. This puzzles you. You can see stars through that doorway, as if it leads into the heavens themselves, but how was it opened - and why.

A movement from your right draws your attention away from that open doorway. Then the young crown woman - the magickal image of Malkuth - steps before you. She smiles warmly, and it fills your heart. She takes your hands gently within her own and places a piece of bread within them.

"Eat of this bread. As with all foods, it will nourish you in your journeys. As you eat, know that all you will ever need to nourish your life is upon the Earth - and is your birth right. Just as any prince or princess knows that he or she will inherit a kingdom, so too must you realize. On Earth we all must work, but there is always a harvest. It is not the finishing though that leads to the harvest. It is the participating in the work that holds the key to acquiring the treasures of your birth."

As you place the bread within your mouth, her image shimmers and as you swallow, she is drawn into you. You are filled with simple confidence, and her sense of innate royalty comes alive within you. A part of you knows that you will never be without again.

You whisper a prayer of thanks and as you raise your eyes, there steps through the doorway and around the altar, a beautiful, naked man - strong and vibrant. He smiles with confidence at you and then kneels at your feet. Lifting each of your feet in turn, he places a silver sandal upon them. They fit you perfectly. As he stands, he places over your head a necklace with a silver mirror, framed with intricate carvings of the moon.

"These sandals allow you to move freely in all worlds and in all dimensions. They will keep your steps firm, steady, light and quick. They will give you agility in all areas of your life. You will move with greater ease and less restrictions. You will step around obstacles more easily.

"The mirror will help you see how all things reflect within your life. Like the phases of the moon, it will show you the phases and patterns moving through your life. It will help you to see yourself and others more clearly."

You test the sandals, rising up on your toes. You feel light and unbound. It is as if there is no gravity and yet you feel very connected to the earth. As you look upon the young man and thank him, he shimmers, melting into you...becoming a part of you. You glance into the mirror, and you see the image of this young man strong within you. You feel independent and assured. And then you see the young woman as well.

As you raise your eyes from the mirror, there steps through the doorway behind the altar a third figure. At first it appears masculine, but as the figure draws your eyes, you are not so sure. Its cloak disguises its sex. Upon the forearms though are copper bracelets of two intertwining snakes. The orange cloak is embroidered with wings. The eyes are soft and speak of intelligence far beyond anything humanity has ever experienced. Then you realize that before you stands one of the many forms of the hermaphrodite.

The figure smiles at your confusion. It takes your right hand within its own and in a quick - snakelike movement - removes a bracelet and fits it securely upon your forearm. Your forearm tingles. The metal feels alive - as if the snakes are alive.

"I am knowledge. Knowledge is universal - neither male nor female. Neither is it for one or the other for knowledge and truth is for all. Especially is it for you. But knowledge and knowing how to use it are two different things. Do not confuse them. We each must understand how to use it, when to use it, where to use it and to what degree. To ask the question is the first step to receiving the answer - the first step to awakening your true magickal essence."

And with a quick movement, the figure melts into you before you can even respond or assimilate what was said. But the thing you do know now is why the door is open...so that the archetypes throughout the tree can help to awaken your own magickal essence!

From the doorway steps a beautiful naked woman - bright, warm and fertile. Her eyes melt your heart and stir you. She seems to be bathed in the fertile greens of the Earth. It is obvious that she is in love. She radiates it and it warms your heart and amuses as love truly should - whether it is our own or others'. As she looks upon you, you feel newly born and beautiful. Her eyes see all beauty in all things. She extends a rose, and you take it with your left hand.

"The rose lives forever within the heart of every man and woman. It is the rose of beauty. It is the rose of the child, the mystic, the poet. Beauty lives within all life. We must learn to look upon the rose within those we encounter rather than at the covering that hides the rose.

"We are all meant to love and be loved. As you discover your

own rose, it will be a magnet. As we learn to see the rose in others, they will see it within themselves. When we deny the beauty of ourselves, we also deny the beauty and wonders of the universe."

Then with a soft embrace that melts all doubts, she melts into you. For the first time in ages, you feel alive and beautiful and as striking as the rose. You realize that you can never be alone or lonely for there is life and love on all dimensions.

Stepping through the doorway is a child. He has a playful look upon the face - innocent and puckish. He is dressed in the colors of a golden sun, and he motions for you to lean down, and as you do, he places a crown upon your head. It is too large and sits lopsided upon your head. you are afraid of moving too suddenly in case it should fall. The child grins.

"All the masters taught that it is necessary to become again as little children if we are to touch the heavens. To be a child is to be open enough to still hear the elves whispering in your ear, and it is to know that nothing is impossible. "

"We are all children of the Divine, growing and learning and earning the inheritance that is ours."

Your eyes widen as the image of the child changes before you. Now there is a god hanging upon the tree of sacrifice. Only the eyes of the child remain within the image.

"We can sacrifice the child so that we can learn to live the life of the divine, but only by obeying the spiritual over the physical can we accomplish this. This alone will retain or recapture the purity of the heart necessary to manifest the force of the universe in our lives and the lives of those we touch."

Again, the image shifts. Before you now is a majestic king, standing upon the globe of the Earth. The eyes of the child still remain.

"The crown is to remind you of what you will inherit upon your path. Now it is too large for the child within you. As you grow, as you learn...as you sacrifice the lesser for the greater, the lower for the higher, the physical for the spiritual, you will grow into it. As you do, the world becomes your own."

The image shimmers and melts over and into you. You feel like a child...so much to learn, so much to do, so much to explore. You understand that it is time to put certain aspects of your life away, for you are destined to inherit and to rule. The world truly is yours!

"Sometimes the world must be won!"

The words snap you from your reverie. Through the doorway steps a mighty warrior with sword drawn and blood red armor..

"A sword is an instrument that can kill or defend. It can protect or attack. There is no right or wrong; the sword is double edged - as are all choices and decisions.

"Before the new can be built, the old must be torn down. That demands strength and courage. If one is to grow and evolve, one must become a spiritual warrior. That means you must carry the Flaming Sword of Truth. You must wear it in the scabbard, but be able to draw it and use it when necessary. Remember that what you tear down, you must build up. What you protect, you must strengthen. What you wound, you must heal. And what you kill, you must restore to life."

With that, the warrior salutes and places the sword in the scabbard and fastens both around your waist. He nods, shimmering and melting into you. In that instance, you know what it is to be a true warrior. You know what it is to fight unnecessarily. You know that you will have whatever strength any task will require. Never again will you face what you can not handle.

From the doorway steps a mighty crowned king, dressed in royal blue robes trimmed in gold. He holds within his hand a chalice of gold. His eyes are warm and merciful. There is no doubt that this man is kindly, generous and gracious to all within his kingdom.

"A king has many things. He has great wealth - a never ending supply. He has people who love to do his bidding. He can get anything made, anything done, and anything he wishes - when he wishes. He rules the entire kingdom. He may divide the work, but he reaps the rewards. It is his right as king.

"All of the Earth is yours to claim, but care for it as well. Allow your kingdom to provide for you. Be willing to accept what it gives, but be willing to give back for what it provides. Abuse is not only taking too much without giving back, but it is also NOT taking when it is offered.

"Royalty has great responsibility. By requesting treasures

from your kingdom, you provide opportunities for others to fulfill and add to their lives. Each is a king or queen, but we all must claim our kingdoms. We must not give up our rights out of fear or self-righteous sacrifice. A king provides for his subjects, and they in turn reward is favors. A king helps others find their own kingdoms.

"Express appreciation for what you have, and give up what you do not need or use...pass it on to others. Drink from the cup and know that it is forever full. It is the Grail of Life and all of the treasures within it. To drink from it is to claim your divine inheritance."

You take the cup from his hands. The nectar is sweet upon the tongue. You stand taller, and there is no doubt that the world is yours to claim! You close your eyes and revel in the abundance and prosperity that you know is coming your way.

"If you wish to truly claim the kingdom, do so in silence."

You stare as a matronly woman in a black robe steps through the doorway to greet you. Her eyes are warm, nurturing, motherly, and there is a strength about her that is only developed through time. She is capable of tremendous nurturing, but she can also be stern when necessary - especially for the protection of her children.

"On the journey of life we each must learn to express our energy in the most creative manner. Plans and goals should be held close to one's heart until truly safe to be brought out. There are times to speak and times to be silent.

"Giving birth can be both pleasure and pain, and that which is created must always be watched over. To give birth to the higher requires great care. There are many unenlightened who will always seek to hinder you in your plans."

She removes a black robe from her shoulders and places it over you. As she does you see the inside lined with colors that shimmer with life with each movement.

"This is the Robe of Concealment. Within it is hidden the lights of creativity - to be revealed when you decide. From the darkness of the womb comes new life. This robe is for your protection and your care. This robe will protect your creations until they are ready to be brought out into the light. Do not use it to hide yourself, rather use it to care for and protect your creativity - to give birth to your own inner radiance!"

She steps forward and places your head against her chest. She kisses you lovingly upon the top of the head. It is so safe and comforting, and then she melts quickly into you.

As you look up, there now stands before you a tall bearded figure. He resembles the ancient master Abraham or even Melchisedek. The power surrounding this figure is intense, and you feel the urge to back away. A hint of amusement at your response passes across his face.

"All that you need to do for yourself is to act. Make your plans and act upon them. All that you need to fulfill your dreams already exists within you and within your life. Initiating the action is often the most difficult part. Once set in motion, it will move of its own accord. If you wish to change your life, take an action. Give the change a push.

"To you I give this sceptre of power. It will strengthen you in your faith to initiate actions. It will help prime the pump, arousing and directing your creative forces and those surrounding your life. It will help impregnate your dreams with the power of reality. Your thoughts, feelings, beliefs and actions are all expressions of your creative forces. We all give birth through all of our expressions.

"Like all mature men, the ability to impregnate is inherent in all. Use this sceptre to awaken the wisdom to know how and when to act upon your creative forces so that you initiate only that which will benefit you and those in your life."

He hands to you the sceptre and melts into you. A strong sense of maturity and responsibility for your own creative power flows through you. You have done so much, but there is still so much more to do.

There now stands before you an ancient bearded king, seen only in profile. One side of the face is hidden. You understand that as long as you are in the physical, there will always be an aspect of the divine that will be hidden.

The image shimmers and then swirls, spinning in vibrant, crystalline light. It forms a spinning whirlwind that shoots out toward you. You raise your hands in defense, but then it rests lightly within the palm of your hands as a small pulsating ball of energy. The swirling takes the appearance of an atom and spins like a top in the palm of your hand. It pulses and hums, and then a voice issues forth from it.

"Nothing is ever the same. Everything moves; everything changes. We each must learn to focus our energy so that it spins and flows with us and for us. This is the cycle of life. We live that we may grow and we die so that we may be born again to learn some more. It is the cycle of all things."

The spinning ball of light rises from the palm of the hand and then enters into you through the crown of your head. for an instant you see yourself as a baby, born again.

You look about you, the room is empty, except for a mirror off to your left. You feel so strong and energized. Never had you realized that you had so much within you. You move to stand before the mirror. As you stand before it, a light grows bright around you. You can see your own aura, and you see a Tree of Life within you. You see each of the magickal images in turn within you as well. You are filled with a sense of the sacredness that is you.

Never have you known there was so much to you. Within the Tree of Life - within yourself- are the keys to empowering your life. You offer a silent prayer of thanks, and you bow to the inner temples.

The truth is
prayers are
supposed
to be answered.
Magick and miracles
are supposed to happen.
The amazing thing
would be
if they did not.

Part Two:

The Sacred Paths

"This is an age in which psychic phenomena will increase to such a degree that past techniques of dealing with them will become obsolete. Only those who develop the ability to penetrate into the deeper mysteries will be able to help people who are exposed to such psychic experiences."

- H.P. Blavatsky
"Theosophical Forum"

Chapter Five

The Paths of Wisdom

"Do not let it be forgotten that there is a Mystery tradition of the race which has its mature aspect in the sun worship of the Druids and the beautiful fairy-lore of the Celts, its philosophical aspect in the traditions of alchemy and its spiritual aspect in the Hidden Church of the Holy Grail...All these have their holy places, mounts and pools of initiation, which are part of our spiritual inheritance."

- Dion Fortune,
Avalon of the Heart

One of the designations for the Qabalistic system of development is *"THE THIRTY-TWO PATHS OF WISDOM"*. It is the wisdom that unfolds for us in all the paths of life. In reality, there are only 22 major paths that link the ten levels of our consciousness in the Qabalistic tradition. These are considered *true paths*. The individual sephiroth (the ten temples) are also counted though as paths and thus the ten sephiroth plus the linking 22 paths comprise the 32 paths of wisdom. Although this can be a bit confusing, don't get hung up on it. Just remember that the numbering of the actual paths begins at 11 and goes to 32. And when we are beginning we start at the bottom of the tree (Path 32) and work our way upward (Path 11).

As with the ten sephiroth or temples, there are many associations with the various paths. Each path has symbols, magickal images and gifts, colors, astrological and tarot correspondences and a variety of other symbolic associations. All of these can affect us in the same manner that the symbols and images for each temple can affect us. They are links to archetypal forces. When they are used in a specific meditative or ceremonial manner - such as in pathworking - they elicit specific effects that will play themselves out within our physical lives.

The path descriptions that follow provide guidelines for the major symbols, images and keynotes to the paths of wisdom. For each there is a spiritual experience, and a life path keynote. In chapter six we will examine how to determine which of the paths of wisdom is our life path - a path whose lessons and potentials are most important to us.

Three of the other correspondences given are most important, in that they reflect the primary energies of the path and hold the key to creating astral doorways that we can use. The remaining correspondences provide tools for fine tuning what is activated within our lives through the exercises provided in part three.

1. The Hebrew Letter

The first symbol is the Hebrew letter. The esoteric aspects of language and alphabets hold the key to many mysteries of life. In their simplest aspects, the shape of the letter, its meaning and other associations with it have significance. In the Tree of Life, the Hebrew letters are a potent reflection of the essence of the path. This text will not explore all of the significances of the paths, but it will provide a starting point for deepening studies. Some of the works listed in the bibliography will provide even deeper insight into the power of the letters. As we will discover in the part three, they can be used to open astral doorways.

The ancient Hebrew alphabet, one of the fore runners of our own, has great mystical significance. There is not space within this text to cover all of the subtleties of it, but in essence each letter has a numerical significance, color attribution and other symbolism. Those who wish to immerse themselves in

Path Numbers and Hebrew Letters

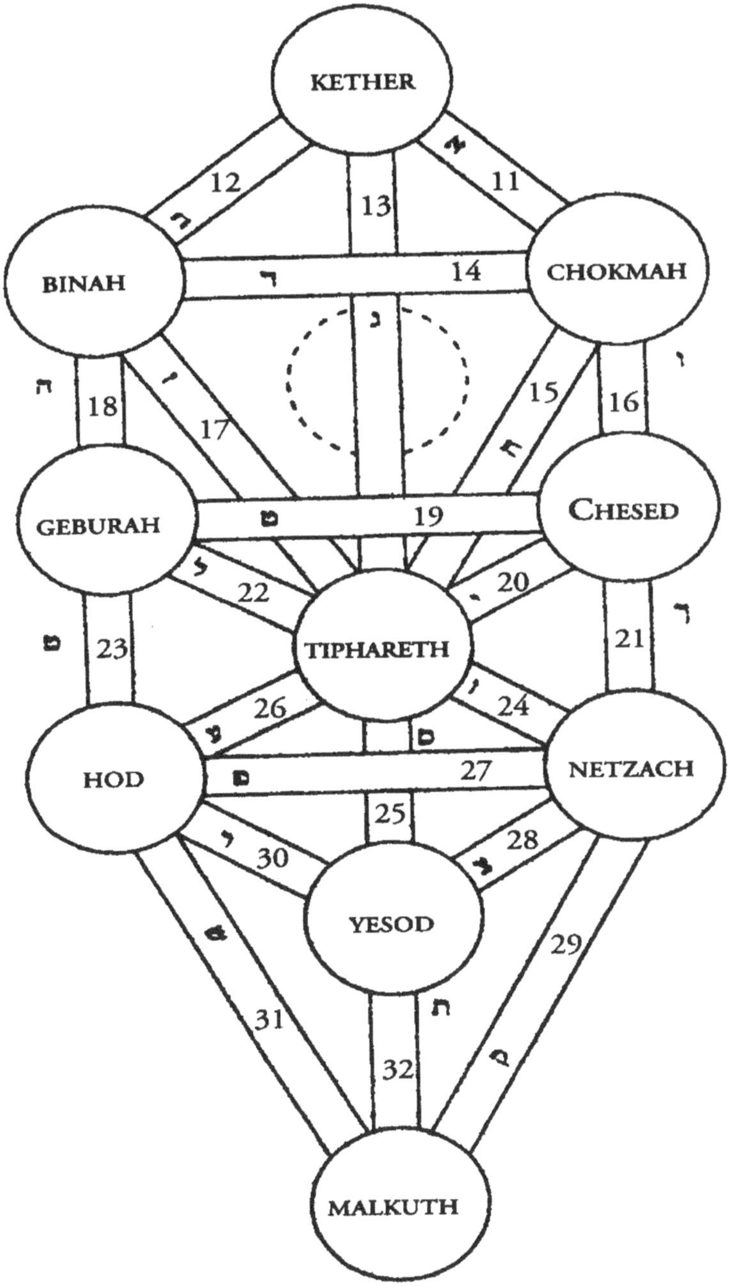

esoteric linguistics will find much inspiration. An earlier work of mine, *The Magickal Name*, examined some of the esoteric aspects of alphabets and how they translated into our modern alphabet to influence us. Although no long available, it will be released in 2010 in a revised edition. The reader can also consult some of the sources listed in the bibliography.

2. Astrological Influence

The second most important correspondence with the path is its astrological sign. The astrological aspects of the path reflect some of the cosmic energy that will be released into our lives (or stimulated more strongly) through our work with the particular path. The stars and planets can have an influence upon us, although it is subtle. A study of astrology can provide some insight into some of the subtle influences of the path.

The glyph (symbol) for each of the signs of the zodiac, planets and elements can be a powerful tool for opening psychic doorways. As we will examine in part three, an examination of the path associated with your personal astrological sign can provide some wonderful insight into your own potentials, strengths and weaknesses.

3. Tarot Designation

The third most important correspondence is the tarot card that corresponds to the path. Tarot cards are pictorial reflections of spiritual and physical patterns and energies at play within our lives. And like the other two primary symbols, they can be powerful doorways into the more subtle realms of life. Yes, there can be differences as to which card applies to which path. Those given are the more commonly accepted and are guidelines only.

The images on the tarot cards reflect certain archetypal forces. That and the thoughtform energy that has developed around them through the centuries of use make them powerful bridges. The 22 cards of the major arcana reflect the energies that are inherent within the paths of the Tree of Life. They also reflect the combined energies of the Sephiroth they link.

Astrological Associations on the Tree of Life

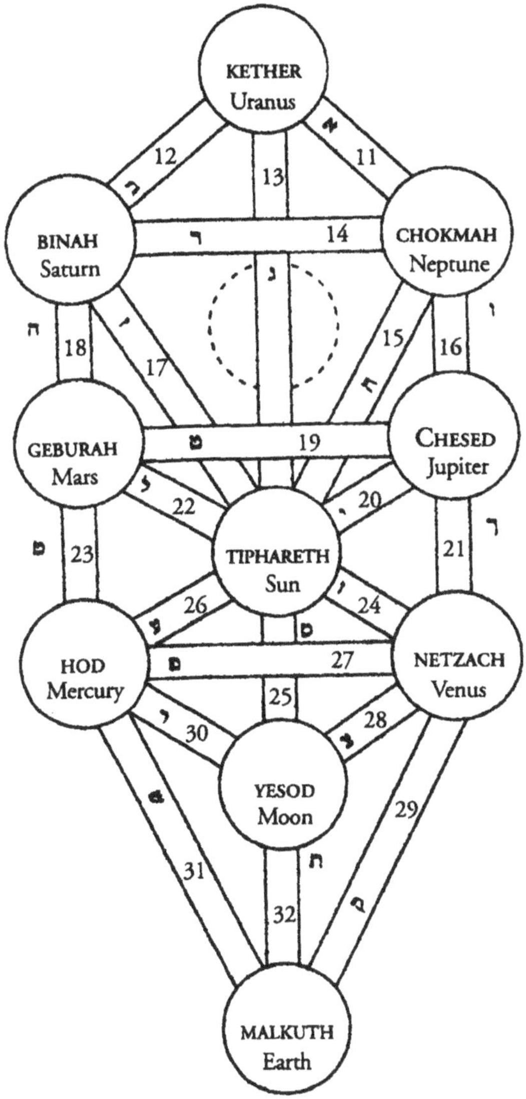

32 Saturn
31 Primal Fire
30 Sun
29 Pisces
28 Aquarius
27 Mars
26 Capricorn
25 Sagittarius
24 Scorpio
23 Primal Water
22 Libra
21 Jupiter
20 Virgo
19 Leo
18 Cancer
17 Gemini
16 Taurus
15 Aries
14 Venus
13 Moon
12 Mercury
11 Air

4. Benefits, Strengths and Weaknesses

For each path there are also listed the primary benefits that can unfold from pathworking, along with the strengths and weaknesses that can be achieved and revealed. Often these are strengths and weaknesses within us, but they can also reflect strengths and weaknesses of others in our life or qualities likely to show up in various endeavors within our life. As to whom or what they apply specifically is usually determined by the actual pathworking.

Also, each path has a list of specific myths and tales which reflect and symbolize some of the major energies and aspects of the particular path. These mythical tales and stories can be a powerful way of activating the paths energies more dynamically within our lives. Specific techniques for using these myths and tales will be provided in chapter seven.

5. Other Correspondences

For each path there are other correspondences and associations. The color serves to trigger and ring the doorbell of the level of our mind appropriate for our task. Color has a great potential to affect us physically and spiritually. There are also magickal gifts with each path as there are with each temple. We bring these gifts out of the Tree of Life with us after the pathworking. These gifts represent the positive benefits that will unfold in your life as a result of the pathworking.

For each path there is listed a set of tales and myths whose symbols and imagery reflect the basic energies of the path. Stories, tales and myths can be powerful transformational tools. They can heal and enlighten. They can empower and balance. The use of stories and tales in the ancient bardic tradition was explored in an earlier work of mine, *Sacred Sounds.* In the Part III is a method of using these tales to further amplify the energies of the path in our lives.

As you continue your work with the Qabala, you will find a multitude of correspondences associated with each temple and each path - more than what I have provided. In time you will want to incorporate them into your work as well. The more images and symbols that we include in our pathworking, the stronger the impact upon our physical and spiritual lives.

The following pages contain the basic descriptions of the paths and the major energies that are activated through them. How to use these descriptions comes later in the next part. These aspects can be used to create astral doorways, for specific pathworking purposes and illumination, for determining our personal life path, for divination and for a variety of other purposes. Once you are familiar with the various paths, their lessons and gifts, you will be guided through a variety of ways to use them.

32nd Path – Malkuth to Yesod

Prayer Psalm:

"Let my cry come before you, O Lord;
in keeping with your word, give me discernment.
Let my supplication reach you;
rescue me according to your promise.
My lips pour forth your praise,
because you teach me your statutes.
May my tongue sing of your promise,
for all your commands are just.
Let your hand be ready to help me,
for I have chosen your precepts.
I long for your salvation, O Lord,
and your law is my delight.
Let my soul live to praise you,
and may your judgments help me.
I have gone astray like a lost sheep; seek your servant because your commands I do not forget."

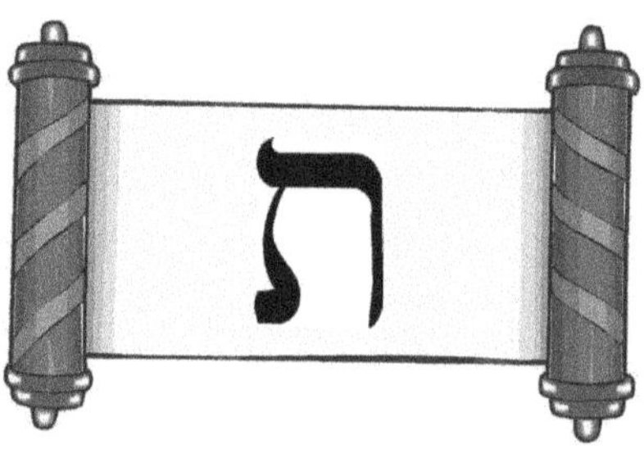

Malkuth to Yesod

The 32nd path takes the seeker from the material to the astral, helping to open the astral more consciously. The keynote for those who have this path as a life path is opening to the spirit. Here begins the evolution toward spirit. It is a path that reveals the light within illumination. This is the path of descent into the subconscious with all of its hidden fears. It is also the path of ascent to the higher self where we learn that when we face our fears, our higher self emerges. This path awakens the promise of new life.

On this path, the symbols and images awaken fears that burden the imagination and block our flow of energies. The working of this path clears and liberates us from the weight (in its many forms) of physical existence. In pathworking, it will release the energy to overcome depression, to develop greater intuition and to strengthen the light bodies.

This is a path of wisdom whose effects are not always felt immediately but whose wisdom (to the degree of understanding why events within your life occurred) is gained with the passage of time. Clarification is stimulated but comes slowly. This path's symbols release energies into our life that initiate experiences of self-discipline (or the need for it) which can lead to liberation on many levels.

This path can show us, through our life experiences, the limitations of life so that we can lay the proper foundation for growth. It forces confrontations with subconscious fears which will play themselves out or reveal themselves within our daily, physical lives. This is a Saturn type of influence. Saturn is the teacher. By facing the fears, we find that they dissolve in the facing or in combating them that they are not as powerful as we imagined.

The images and symbols of this path also can release energy that brings upon us helpful limitations, greater self-discipline, common sense and a greater understanding of the need for structure within our lives. It may also manifest conditions that show us where we have needless restraints within our lives, or too much calculation and a lack of human feelings. It is through the energies of this path that we begin the process of dying to the physical focus of life, expanding our awareness of what lies hidden behind our physical life and its events. This path reveals to us that there is life beyond the physical even if we don't understand it.

Pathworking used with The World card of the tarot will release energy of the spiral dance of creation into our lives. The world is ever growing and gives way to the newer and the better, even if we don't always recognize it immediately. This path with this card can open up new worlds, perspectives and awareness. It activates energies that let us know that we are free to go in any direction. It lets us know that each day contains opportunities to grow and learn.

The World Card with this path stimulates the release of pressures, sometimes by bringing them to a head. It can manifest situations that help us recognize how insignificant many of our self-created troubles are in relation to other things within the world. This path and its symbols help us to hear the voice of the higher in times of darkness. It helps us prepare the consciousness to reach out even higher.

The gifts that ultimately come from this path is a balance between flow and restriction, reflected by the cauldron and the girdle. The cauldron is a symbol of the womb, the cup, the cornucopia. It is a source of birth - of stirring new life. The girdle is used to bind - abundance, love, etc. - to ourselves or to a higher purpose. Both gifts have ancient significance, closely connected to the divine feminine, often represented by the Earth (Malkuth) and the Moon (Yesod).

The gifts of this path teach us that we can create and manifest. They teach us that creation and manifestation can easily be accomplished when we align ourselves with more universal rhythms, but we must learn to work with those rhythms and their ebb and flow. These gifts teach us that what we have and don't have is within our own hands.

Malkuth to Yesod

Pathworking Benefits:	**Overcomes depression, awakens intuition, dreamwork, strength ens light body, astral projection**
Spiritual Experience:	**Vision of the Holy Guardian Angel and Vision of the Machinery of the Universe**
Life Path Keynote:	**Awakening to the Spirit**
Hebrew Letter:	**Tau (the cross)** ת
Astrological Influence:	**Saturn** ♄
Tarot Designation:	**The World Card**
Colors:	**Indigo and Black**
Magickal gifts:	**Cauldron and the girdle**
Tales and Myths:	**All descent myths; Orpheus and Eurydice; Alice and the Looking Glass; Persephone and Pluto; Madagascar tale of Sand Chil dren**
Strengths Achieved:	**Discrimination, independence, motivation, facing fears, common sense, self-discipline, grounded-ness**
Weaknesses Revealed:	**Greed, idleness, depression, lack of discipline, hidden fears, lack of feeling, depression**

31st Path – Malkuth to Hod

Prayer Psalm:

"Princes persecute me without cause but my heart
stands in awe of your word.
I rejoice at your promises, as one who has found
rich soil.
Falsehood I hate and abhor; Your law I love.
Seven times a day do I praise you
for your righteous judgment.
Those who love your law have great peace,
and for them there is no stumbling block.
I wait for your salvation, O Lord,
and your commands I fulfill.
I keep your decrees and
love them deeply.
I keep your precepts and your decrees,
for all my ways are before you."

Malkuth to Hod

The 31st path is a path of relationships. For those whose life path is the 31st, lessons and blessings from relationships is the keynote. It is a path whose symbols release and stimulate energies within our life so that we can truly discover our relationships to others - and what they say about ourselves. It provides the energy that stimulates vision of what needs to be transformed and/or renewed. It will also increase the will to endure.

This path can activate a trial by fire that we must all go through in our quest for the higher. Fire destroys and creates, for from its ashes we can always rise like the phoenix. This is the path of fire and all that fire symbolizes and entails, activating its forces within our lives - physically and spiritually.

This path can be used to strengthen the kundalini, and to free ourselves from emotional problems. Remember that we use pathworking scenarios associated with the symbols to release energies into our life. We can use the images and symbols so that the effects will play themselves out in the manner we desire. Such ability takes time and practice, and with this path, it is even more necessary.

It is through the fire of our relationships that we grow. Cloistering is escapism. This path releases energy so that we begin to see our relationships for what they truly are - not for how we wish they were.

This path and its symbols stir up situations where greater strength, courage and self-assertiveness arise or needs to arise. It releases a sense of idealism into our life, activating our life more strongly.

The energy of this path may manifest in a variety of ways. We can experience within our life ruthlessness and self-imposition - and how they disrupt our lives and the lives of others. We may have revealed where we are self-indulgent and loud, but as a result of confronting and facing these qualities, we find ourselves more ardent in our beliefs and with a greater sense of inspiration, initiative, courage and creativity.

Through this path we discover that behind the fires of difficulty and negative expression are opportunities to uncover hidden treasures and blessings. This path brings the light of fire to our lives - thus, the magickal gifts of flint and steel. When struck, they create the sparks of fire. The ability to create fire on any level is a great power. Learning to create fire and control it for our needs has much hidden significance for those who are willing to truly examine it.

The Judgment card when used in pathworking, releases the archetypal energies that show us our links to the past and to all of humanity. This is the path of karma - of cause and effects. Through this pathworking we can unveil the causes of events within our life and the effects that can unfold.

Through the Judgment card we stimulate situations in which we must face responsibility and take on more of our individual divine purposes. This card in pathworking calls forth, through our daily life circumstances a realization of what our life purpose is. It also clarifies how all situations within this life have added to that purpose. It reveals how to deal with situations and people from the perspective of our life purpose.

This card can also add to the trial by fire. It can manifest situations that force and activate greater choice in our mission in life. It will reveal unwanted ties and it will uncover the blessings of the divine operating within our lives.

Malkuth to Hod

Pathworking Benefits:	Energy for transformation, relationships clarified, idealism, opportunity for renewal, truths revealed, balance of give and take
Spiritual Experience:	Vision of the Holy Guardian Angel and Splendor
Life Path Keynote:	Power of Relationships
Hebrew Letter:	Shin (the tooth) ש
Astrological Influence:	Fire △
Tarot Designation:	Judgment
Colors:	Orange and Scarlet
Magical Gifts:	Flint and Steel
Tales and Myths:	Prometheus and the Stealing of Fire, The Necklace of Brising, The Tinder box, The West African Tale of the Fire Children, Tales of the Phoenix
Strengths Achieved:	Discrimination, truth, strength of will, fortitude, self-discovery; helpfulness & kindness, inspiration
Weaknesses Revealed:	Avarice, dishonesty, weak willed, fear of change, ruthlessness, irresponsibility, inertia

30th Path – Yesod to Hod

Prayer Psalm:

"Behold my afflictions and rescue me,
for I have not forgotten your law.
Plead my cause and redeem me;
deliver me according to thy word.
Far from sinners is salvation;
for they seek not your statutes.
Your compassion is great, O Lord;
according to your word, give me life.
Though my persecutors and foes are many,
I turn not away from your decrees.
I beheld my transgressors and I knew
they had not kept your word.
See how I love your precepts, O Lord;
in your loving kindness give me life.
The foundation of thy word is truth,
and each of your judgments is everlasting."

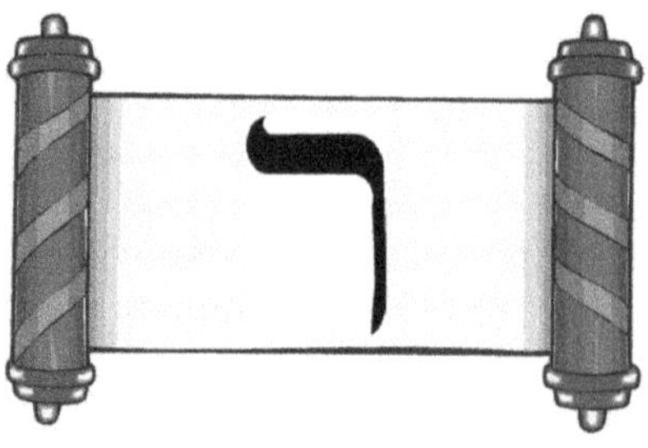

Yesod to Hod

This is the life path of finding light within the dark, of opening to vision in all environments of our potentials. The symbols and images of the 30th path release energy to shed light into the dark corners of our consciousness. It is the path of enlightenment, comparable to opening the windows and shutters to admit the sun. It releases energies that uncover hidden parts of us that need to see the sun, including our half-formed ideas. It stimulates artistic inspiration.

This is the path of science and occult astrology with ties to ancient alchemy. It can stimulate and awaken greater power in healing (of ourselves and/or others). Through this path our visualizations become more fruitful, and we open ourselves to prophetic insight and intuition.

Within our physical life, pathworking with these symbols and images may result in circumstances that require and release greater courage, energy and pride. Situations may arise to test our stamina or to show us where we lack it. We will encounter situations that reveal our lack of self-confidence, and we may see where and to what degree we may be overly egocentric.

This path releases energy into our physical life that animates all aspects, so that we develop greater individuality and so we learn to use our vitality more productively. The symbols and images of the 30th path bring on circumstances that help us develop self-mastery.

The Sun card of the tarot, when used in pathworking, can open up doors to the ancient lodges and mystery schools with all of their magickal and ritual tools and techniques. This path with the Sun card literally stimulates new sunshine in all things. Its energies can also give rise to circumstances that reveal our own selfishness and fears, so that we can bring new sunlight to shine upon them.

Pathworking with this tarot card will also manifest conditions in our life that help us realize we have been granted a place in the universe. It creates circumstances and situations that assist us in recognizing our purpose in this incarnation and why we should be thankful for it.

The magickal gifts of this path are the lion and the sparrowhawk, two ancient solar symbols. All birds of prey at some time have been associated with the sun, as has the lion. As totems, the sparrowhawk, as with all birds of prey, teach control and speed by which opportunities can be seized.

The lion is the second largest member of the cat family and is one of the most ancient symbols for the sun, whose keynote is assertion of the feminine and the power of the female sun. In essence this symbol when used with pathworking on this particular path will awaken a more dynamic aspect of our intuition. It becomes clearer, more accessible and more prophetic. This symbol awakens us to a new sun - creativity, intuition and imagination - all of which will shine more brightly within our lives.

Yesod to Hod

Pathworking Benefits:	Healing, enlightenment, artistic inspiration, prophecy, insight into alchemy
Spiritual Experience:	Vision of the Splendor of the Universe and its Machinery
Life Path Keynote:	Vision and Enlightenment
Hebrew Letter:	Resh (head) ר
Astrological Influence:	Sun ☉
Tarot Designation:	The Sun Card
Colors:	Orange
Magickal Gifts:	Lion and Sparrowhawk
Tales and Myths:	Tales of Phoebus Apollo, Grimm's Rumpelstiltskin, Snow White and Rose Red
Strengths Achieved:	Recognition of purpose, optimism, self-mastery, power in healing, balance of reason & intuition
Weaknesses Revealed:	Selfishness, fears, lack of diligence, egocentricism, overly rational, idleness, dishonesty

29th Path – Malkuth to Netzach

Prayer Psalm:

"I call out with all of my heart; answer me, O Lord;
I will observe your statutes.
I call upon you, save me,
and I will keep your decrees.
Before dawn I come and cry out;
I hope in your words.
My eyes greet the night watches
in meditation on your promise.
Hear my voice according to your kindness, O Lord;
according to your laws give me life.
They draw near who follow after mischief
who are far from your laws.
You, O Lord, are near, and
and all your commands are permanent.
Of old, I know from your decrees,
that you have established them forever."

Malkuth to Netzach

This is the life path of sexuality in all of its many expressions. Its symbols and images activate such energies and their play within our lives on many levels. Because sexuality is a reflection of our most creative life source, this is also the path of creativity and physical evolution. Its energies symbolize and reflect spiritual progress shared in fellowship with other students of the mysteries. It releases energy that is often experienced and expressed as heightened sensuality in everything.

This energy is tied to the transformative aspects of healing and sexuality, and because of this the two magickal gifts are most closely significant to this path. The scarab and the dolphin are the two magickal gifts of this path. They are both ancient symbols of birth, sensuality and protection. The scarab or beetle in Egypt was a powerful symbol of protection and resurrection, because its young were born from ox dung in which the beetle laid its eggs and at the appropriate time, immersed the ball of dung in water. They reflect the metamorphosis of life and of nature, especially when we learn to control our creative forces (sexuality). Wearing a scarab while performing the pathworking enhances activation of energies that attune us to new insights and to nature.

The dolphin is a social animal known for its subtle and yet powerful ability to heal. They live harmoniously within their family or pod and thus they help the energies that can restore harmony to relationships, especially family. They augment healing and new life. Dolphins can show you how to enter the waters of life and then with breath and sound call forth from the waters what you most need or desire. Both animals are associated with water in some form, as is the astrological influence for this path. A study of the sign of Pisces and the symbolic significance of water will help us activate the power of this path and its symbols.

Pathworking between Malkuth and Netzach releases energy that teaches us about life that exists in all things - not just humans. It increases understanding of nature and animals, opening us to the spirit and language of the natural world. It aligns our individual energy with those of nature and all of its life forms and expressions.Pathworking here creates situations that teach us to see only what is, without the additions of ungoverned imagination. These situations help us to see that we are part of all living things and only require a simple life.

Many benefits come from working this path. Its symbols can instigate the resolving of family disputes and the spreading of harmony. They can open us to scrying, particularly with techniques of mirrors and crystals. Working this path prior to scrying with crystal balls can be very effective. For more information on scrying with crystal balls you may wish to consult my book *Crystal Balls and Crystal Bowls.* It also increases the imagination, and thus it can assist in developing greater and more effective creative visualization ability.

This path can also be used to stimulate opportunities to increase prosperity or for stirring up those aspects of ourselves that prevent us from having what we need or desire. This is also a path between levels of our consciousness that governs our attitudes toward others (including the physical aspects of sex). Its symbols and images will stimulate old and manifest new personal relationships.This path can manifest situations where we must be more unselfish and innovative. We may also find ourselves in situations where we or where others seek to control through giving. Sometimes our potentials can become so blocked within that there is a tendency to withdraw. Working this path, helps counteract this tendency, and at the same time, a unique individuality and separateness within our life begins to emerge.

Pathworking with the tarot card of The Moon awakens greater faith and intuition. Its energies draw us into contact with those who make us feel happy and beloved. As a life path, its energies often bring a testing of individual faith. Without faith we become vulnerable and can succumb to failure much more easily.This path's energies, when stimulated by The Moon card, help us to see future possibilities so that we will not lose sight of our lofty goals that we have come to attain. They help us to realize that the blessings we receive daily are often very real. They are also very subtle and frequently unnoticed.

Malkuth to Netzach

Pathworking Benefits:	Creativity, scrying abilities, attunement to animals and nature, increased sexuality, discrimination
Spiritual Experience:	Vision of the Holy Guardian Angel and Beauty Triumphant
Life Path Keynote:	Creative Power of Sexuality
Hebrew Letter:	Qoph (back of the head) ק
Astrological Influence:	Pisces ♓
Tarot Designation:	The Moon
Colors:	Crimson
Magickal Gifts:	Scarab, Dolphin
Tales and Myths:	Eros and Psyche, Romeo and Juliet, Navajo tales of Coyote Trickster, Tale of Tontlewald, Artemis and Endymion, Rescue of Aphrodite from Typhon
Strengths Achieved:	Unselfishness, simplicity, faith, family harmony, innovation, understanding animals and nature
Weaknesses Revealed:	Greed, ungoverned imagination, sexual obsession, separatism, excessive empathy, withdrawal,

28th Path - Yesod to Netzach

Prayer Psalm:

"You are just, O Lord,
and your ordinance is right.
You have pronounced your decrees
in justice and in perfect faithfulness.
My zeal consumes me
because my foes forget your words.
Your promise is very pure
and your servant loves it.
I am small and despised,
yet I do not forget your commandments.
Your justice is everlasting justice
and your law is permanent.
Though distress and anguish have come upon me,
your commands are my delight.
Your decrees are forever just; give me understanding
and discernment and I shall live."

Yesod to Netzach

This is a life path of learning to use our energies to manifest our dreams. This path will release the energies that force us to examine and deal with the higher aspects of sexuality. Its symbology releases tremendous creative power into our life. This is often experienced in an initial sexual physiological response. This energy ultimately imbues our hopes, wishes and dreams with greater life force. This energy stimulates tremendous inspiration.

This path will manifest opportunities to explore and test our resolve to manifest our personal dreams, as opposed to humanity's greatest dreams throughout the ages - youth, beauty and wealth. We will find ourselves placed in a position of having to assess and choose according to our highest aspirations.

We are also brought face to face with the dangers and difficulties of following our dreams. Are we giving up security for a pipe dream? Is the dream truly achievable? Have we prepared properly for the pursuit of this dream? This path awakens our doubts, but it also awakens our inspiration and hope.

This is why the magickal gifts of this path are so apropos. All of them have represented in the past the traditional dreams of humanity but also the more spiritual and personal dreams of the individual. The grail is a cup of life and health, but it is also a symbol for our personal life quest. The apple has represented the dreams of knowledge and eternal youth and the eagle and star are ancient symbols of spiritual inspiration.

Pathworking here will manifest situations that will construct new attitudes in our affairs. It can be used to gain new insight into astrology, particularly in relation to planning careers. It releases the energies that promote peace at any level, and it helps manifest situations to find suitable work and educational opportunities.

The 28th path will stimulate a willingness and increased opportunities to experiment. New ideas, inventions and social activities increase. We often find ourselves becoming more loyal to some cause. It can also manifest overtalkativeness and a flightiness of behavior. Some find themselves and those around them demonstrating more fanatical ideas. There may arise a tendency toward imposing ideas on others or others imposing ideas on us.

The Star card of the tarot is most often associated with the 28th path. Sometimes The Emperor card is also used, although it is most often associated with the 15th path. The two can be interchangeable. Remember that the correspondences are guidelines. Study both and choose the one that is more in line with your purposes of working the path.

The Star awakens energies that tie us to our inner strength and to that of the universe. It helps manifest greater understanding of all situations in our life. The 28th path is the path of all temples and their peaceful grounds. Because of this, when the Star is used in pathworking, it inspires us to realize that there is always light to be drawn upon. It helps us to pierce the darkness by submitting ourselves to the divine.

This card when working with the Qabala manifests situations that make us aware of our individuality. We will have to face our petty desires so that we can get rid of them. It also reveals the earthly concerns that must be eliminated before we can reach fully into the universe.

This is a path of creativity, and it can manifest great inspiration and zany schemes. It can even stimulate impracticality. Whatever it manifests helps us learn to handle the creative energies more productively.

Yesod to Netzach

Pathworking Benefits:	Creative and sexual power, higher aspirations, peacefulness, loyalty, dream opportunities, unselfishness and independence
Spiritual Experience:	Vision of the Machinery of the Universe and Beauty Triumphant
Life Path Keynote:	Dreams and Inspiration
Hebrew Letter:	Tzaddi (fishhook) צ
Astrological Influence:	Aquarius ♒
Tarot Designation:	The Star (sometimes The Emperor)
Colors:	Violet
Magickal Gifts:	Grail, Star, Apple, Eagle
Myths and Tales:	Zeus and Ganymede, The Elves and the Shoemaker, Rip Van Winkle, East of the Sun & West of the Moon
Strengths Achieved:	Hope and inspiration individuality, strength to follow dreams, greater will and understanding
Weaknesses Revealed:	Fear of following dreams, pettiness, self-doubt, impracticality, imposition of will, lust, idleness

27th Path – Hod to Netzach

Prayer Psalm:

"Wonderful are your decrees;
therefore I observe them.
The revelations of your words sheds light,
giving understanding to the simple.
I gasp with open mouth
in my yearning for your commands.
Look upon me and be merciful to me
because I love your name.
Steady my footsteps according to your promise
and let no iniquity rule over me.
Let thy countenance shine upon your servant
and teach me your statutes.
My eyes shed streams of tears
because they keep not thy laws."

Hod to Netzach

The 27th path is the first of three paths that cross the Tree of Life. Because of this, its energies are stronger and play more tangibly within the physical life. Its effects will be more discernible. The keynote of this path as a life path is development and rewarding of endurance, courage and faith.

This path will manifest energies for the tearing down of the old and the building of the new. Its symbology relates to conflicts and their resolution. Its symbols can bring on trials of endurance and of courage and faith. It unites us with emotional forces so that we have no choice but to deal with them.

This path brings to life circumstances that offer the chance to survey our entire personality. it creates situations that force us to see what can be salvaged and what can not. It stirs up situations so that we see what needs to be thrown away or torn down and what is still in good condition. It provides the opportunity to recreate ourselves.

This path can be used for any kind of balancing, banishing and cleansing within ourselves and our environment (physically, psychically, and spiritually). It will show us the doors that need to be closed for our benefit, and it provides the energy and opportunity to close them in the most beneficial manner possible.

Lightning strikes suddenly and powerfully. It has the power to swiftly destroy what is no longer useful, so that rebuilding can occur. Rubies are the stones of fire, and this path is like fire in that it destroys while it creates. Out of the ashes of what we tear down are the rubies, the new blood and new wealth within our life. Traditionally, the wolf and the bear have been two of the greatest teachers in the animal kingdom. They serve as teachers on this path to help us understand the why's of the changes and how best to clean out the old.

In the area of personality, this pathworking will manifest situations within our life that force us to see where we are fooling ourselves and others. It presents opportunities at the same time to correct it or continue it. We are forced to face our weaker aspects and to build upon the stronger. It reveals the ego at play within our life. It plays in our life dually - as a destructive force and as a creative force.

This path will also stimulate a stronger desire to succeed. It stimulates a fighting spirit. It will manifest situations that will reveal the animal nature we have yet to change, and it provides opportunities for such changes.

The Tower card when used with pathworking will stimulate karmic reassessment. It reveals outworn patterns and releases energy to build new ones. It is a beneficial tool to use in pathworking here for those who are striving and struggling in life and wanting to step or break out into a new life path.

The Tower card helps release the energies for changing our fortunes. It reveals the false securities of our hopes and dreams, and it manifests the energies of change, especially when we are clinging to old goals that can prevent us from accepting new and wonderful opportunities in the future. If we are feeling lost on the path of life, this card when used in pathworking will release energies to tear down the old walls and let new light into our life.

Hod to Netzach

Pathworking Benefits:	Cleansing; tearing down of old; courage and faith; balancing of psychic energies; endurance; change of fortunes
Spiritual Experience:	Vision of Splendor and Vision of Beauty
Life path Keynote:	Endurance, Courage and Faith
Hebrew Letter:	Peh (mouth) פ
Astrological Influence:	Mars ♂
Tarot Designation:	The Tower
Colors:	Scarlet
Magickal Gifts:	Lightning, rubies, wolf and bear
Myths and Tales:	David and Goliath; Greek tales of Ares; Jack the Giant Killer; Chinese Tale of Tseng and the Holy Man; Tale of Snowdrop
Strengths Achieved:	Endurance; courage; faith, self-awareness; fighting spirit; clarifying changes; truth
Weaknesses Revealed:	Emotional & mental conflicts; insecurities; self-delusion; feelings of being lost; imbalances

26th Path - Hod to Tiphareth

Prayer Psalm:

"I have fulfilled just ordinances;
leave me not to my oppressors.
Be surety for the welfare of your servant;
Let not the proud oppress me.
My eyes strain for your salvation
and your just promise.
Deal with your servant according to your kindness,
and teach me your statutes.
I am your servant, give me discernment
that I may know your decrees.
It is time to serve the Lord,
for they have nullified your law.
For I love your command more than gold,
however fine.
For in all your precepts I go forward;
every false way I hate."

Hod to Tiphareth

This path releases energy for the spiritual experience known as "The Dark Night of the Soul". This experience helps us to link our personality with our individuality. It throws us back upon ourselves to the well of truth that lies within each one of us. This is the life path for uncovering our faith in a higher power that expresses itself within us.

All of our wrong ideas are exposed to the sun. Our illusions and beliefs are challenged. Our ideals are challenged as well. We often find ourselves in situations of having to face what must be faced, so that we can be rid of it. It is a path of darkness, where situations arise that teach us to live on our faith and ideals. It is a path that can change our ideas of spiritual levels and consciousness.

The symbols and imagery on this path can serve as a form or exorcism. They can be used to provide protective energies for the home. They also can help us in overcoming domineering aspects, along with selfishness and conceit. They can awaken a need for tolerance.

The magickal gifts assist us in handling the energies that tempt us. The ass is an ancient symbol of labor but also humble wisdom. In Chaldea the goddess of death was pictured on an ass. Thus it was a symbol of death, and, of course, the life after.

The yoni and lingam are the symbols of the male and female genitalia. They frequently reflect (especially in the Western world) the temptations of sexuality and learning to use our energies of sex creatively and spiritually (as well as physically). A difficult task, but their transmutation is part of the alchemical process that can reveal the lead in our life that can become the gold.

Pathworking here releases the energies that manifest situations which in turn force pragmatism. We often find ourselves needing to be more prudent and self-sacrificing. Our personal trust and loyalty is tested, as is the trust and loyalty we place in others (especially of spouses and loved ones).

Organizational abilities will increase, if only out of necessity, and there will be an increased awareness of others needs. Some find themselves exhibiting miserly and demanding tendencies, and some become secretive, dictatorial, overly ambitious and opportunistic. Sometimes these qualities manifest in those around us so that we can learn to handle and respond more appropriately.

On the up side though this path, as a result of what manifests, always leaves us stronger and more spiritually balanced and pragmatic. We develop greater confidence in our life and where we are going, even though the exact location may not be clear. We learn to heed out inner voice and trust it, even over those outside authorities in our life.

The Devil card when used with this path releases energies that test our innate abilities and our trust in them. It helps manifest situations that teach us to use our innate power properly. This is the path of overcoming temptations, and pathworking with this card always tests those on the quest for higher consciousness.

This card and its symbology with this path, tests the seeker of light. Its energies can submerge us into the material, so that we will want to change. It creates situations that teach us to heed our inner voice. Through this path we learn that we must seek out spiritual help, just as we must seek medical help when ill or in pain.

The Devil card and the 26th path help us to contact and realize our true needs, especially when our life is in turmoil. It requires that we come as little children to ask for help. It is the path whose symbols help put our life journey back on course.

Hod to Tiphareth

Pathworking Benefits:	Truth; devotion; practicality; loyalty; trust; awareness of the needs of others; stronger inner voice
Spiritual Experience:	Vision of Splendor and Harmony
Life Path Keynote:	Faith in a Higher Power
Hebrew Letter:	Ayin (eye) ע
Astrological Influence:	Capricorn ♑
Tarot Designation:	The Devil
Colors:	Indigo
Magickal Gifts:	Yoni and lingam; the ass
Myths and Tales:	Pan and the War between the Titans and Olympus; Aladdin and His Lamp; Amalthea and Zeus (The Horn of Plenty); Krishna and Serpent; Ahriman
Strengths Achieved:	Strength of will; tolerance; pragmatism; stronger belief system; openness & innocence
Weaknesses Revealed:	Weak-willed; false pride; selfishness; dishonesty; conceit; domineering & demanding

25th Path - Yesod to Tiphareth

Prayer Psalm:

"I hate men of divided heart,
but I love your law.
You are my refuge and my shield,
in your word I hope.
Depart from me you wrongdoers
that I may keep the commands of my God.
Uphold me according to thy word and I shall live,
and let me not be ashamed of my hope.
Help me that I may be safe
and ever delight in your statutes.
Thou has rejected all of them that stray from thee,
for their deceitfulness is in vain.
Sustain me and I shall be safe, and I will always
meditate upon thy commandments.
My flesh shudders for fear of thee,
and I am afraid of thy judgments."

Yesod to Tiphareth

The keynote for the 25th path as a life path is the power of choice and vision. The 25th path will reveal the temptations of the physical world, bringing upon us choices. It is through this path that choosing can become painful. This path also reveals the benefits and detriments of past choices, so that we do not make the same mistakes again.

The 25th path is the path that will help us experience a rebirth and a major change in consciousness. The energies activated by its working manifest situations that develop greater self-sufficiency with all of its rewards, while demonstrating to us the need for faith in the deepest sense in order to experience those rewards.

The symbols and magickal gifts of this path can aid in the development of astral projection, higher forms of psychic ability and protection in all of our travels. The rainbow, bridge and even the bow and arrow are wonderful images to meditate upon before going to sleep. They help us to cross over into new thresholds of awareness, resulting in lucid dreaming, astral projection and clarity of perception.

The symbols, images and colors of the 25th path can present us with our deepest desires and manifest choices that will improve perfect understanding. If we feel bound and restricted, with little choice in our life, this path can loosen and open those restrictions.

Temperance is the tarot card for the path from Yesod to Tiphareth. This is the path that joins the moon and the sun, and their energies always work best when tempered. This card helps us align with the energies of beauty and harmony, giving them greater expression within our life.

Rising to a higher level can bring rapid development, and the Temperance card with this path strongly activates our psychic sensibilities. Because of this greater balance is required. Temperance is the card of balance, and on the spiritual path balancing the physical with the spiritual and the ways we express them in our daily lives is essential.

This card when used in pathworking stimulates experiences that reveal the need to balance what has been left unbalanced. Through the equilibrium that manifests we discover our true purpose in life. We create opportunities to try new things, while keeping our feet on the ground. We can explore without losing touch. This card and this path manifest opportunities to link with the Divine.

This path can also bring us face to face with the beast within. The power of Divine or spiritual energies can upset and unbalance our personal energies. This unbalancing may occur personally, revealing sides of ourselves that we may have ignored or shoved to the back of the closet. It may also occur in those around us who become mirrors for us.

This path will also stimulate greater vital energy - freeing more to do the things we have thought of doing - positive or negative. One way of looking at it is in association with electrical currents. Prior to this path we may have been operating at 110 volts. This path may release 220 volts into our life, which we must find a way of controlling and grounding without it unbalancing us or over stimulating our more negative characteristics.

This energy also awakens greater boldness and straightforwardness. It manifests opportunities to expand and inspire the mind. Through the 25th path we are able to see the larger issues at hand.

The images and symbols of the 25th path also can awaken or bring to light tendencies toward false exaggeration, gluttony and coarseness. However its energies manifest though, it always leads to self-discovery. It provides us with training so we can more fully participate in the more universal scope of life.

Yesod to Tiphareth

Pathworking benefits:	**Rebirth; self-sufficiency; astral projection; higher forms of psychism; understanding; devotion**
Spiritual Experience:	**Vision of the Universe in Harmony**
Life Path Keynote:	**Power of Choice and Vision**
Hebrew Letter:	**Samech (prop) ס**
Astrological Influence:	**Sagittarius ♐**
Tarot Designation:	**Temperance**
Colors:	**Blue**
Magickal Gifts:	**Rainbow; bow and arrow; bridge**
Myths and Tales:	**Biblical story of Joseph; Chiron & the Centaurs; Chinese tale of Tseng and the Holy Men; The Little Mermaid; Rapunzel**
Strengths Achieved:	**Self-sufficiency; responsibility; harmony; self-discovery; boldness; moderation**
Weaknesses Revealed:	**Temptations; irresponsibility; fear of choosing; gluttony; exaggeration; narrow sightedness**

24th Path – Netzach to Tiphareth

Prayer Psalm:

"A lamp to my feet is your word,
a light to my path.
I resolve and swear to keep your ordinance.
I am very much afflicted; O Lord,
give me life according to your word.
With the words of my mouth be pleased, O Lord;
and teach me thy judgments,
My soul is continually in thy hands;
I do not forget thy law.
The wicked have laid a snare for me,
but from your precepts I have not strayed.
Your decrees are my inheritance forever;
the joy of my heart they are.
I intend in my heart to fulfill your statutes truly,
even to the end."

Netzach to Tiphareth

This is the life path of death and rebirth. Through this path we learn to transmute our fears of change into acceptance of what is and what will be. This path and its symbols activate the archetypal energies for the transmutation of our personality. It initiates facing of our fears of change in all its respects. It is a path that shows us death (in whatever form) as being nothing more than part of the evolutionary process.

The 24th path and its symbols will stimulate circumstances that help us to assimilate and deal with grief. It enables us to see death as the beginning of rebirth. It can awaken energies that help us understand any change within life - physiological or spiritual. Because of this, it is a beneficial path for understanding such phases of life as adolescence and menopause. It also increases understanding of anyone with emotional problems.

The boat is one of the magickal gifts of this path. Many mythologies speak of traveling across the rivers of life in boats. Death boats enabled individuals to cross from death to life and back again.

The phoenix is also one of the most ancient of symbols for the process of life, death and rebirth. It dies in fire and rises from its own ashes. It is one of the symbols associated also with the sign of Scorpio, the astrological influence for this path. The eagle is reflective of the heights we can achieve if we make the right choices and work through death to the power of rebirth.

This path will manifest energy into our life that helps us recognize the subtle shifting and merging of new energies and patterns within our life. It presents us with choices and new opportunities, but when choices arise after pathworking with this particular path, we must be careful to make the most spiritual choice - even if it is the most difficult.

The Death card in the tarot reflects the energies of this path. It helps release and teach transition' sacrifice and change. Transition is a part of life. It is not a cessation of life. The 24th path is filled with images of death, transition and love, and it is reflected and amplified through this card.

The Death card when used in pathworking helps to awaken energies to renew the soul. It manifests situations that teach us that death is not real but an illusion. This path always involves lessons in resisting change, and teaches us that we have all the energy we need to handle change.

The Biblical words, "Thy rod and thy staff shall comfort me all the days of my life..." hold true for the energies of this path. The Death card and the 24th path will teach us how to leave the past behind. It helps us to realize that the past cannot be recaptured and that attempting to do so will only leave us foundering in limbo.

The energies of this path can manifest negatively unless controlled and watchful. Strong egotism may surface. The situations that arise can be seductive in that friends may be used inappropriately for personal gain and self-satisfaction. Psychic vampirism may manifest from us or from others around us.

Rebirth - and thus this path - activates our life force more strongly. This gives us greater energy to deal with situations on-going within our life or to initiate new and more positive situations. It stimulates creativity, with new opportunities to build or add to our life.

Healing can also be greatly stimulated by these energies. Friendships will have opportunities to deepen and strengthen. It also inspires faith and creates situations in our life that instill greater desire to merge the physical and spiritual. The 24th path releases energies that give us a choice of rising high into the light or falling into darkness. The choice is ours.

Netzach to Tiphareth

Pathworking Benefits:	Transformation and rebirth; devotion; unselfishness; facing of fears; healing; new & deeper friendships, opening to new possibilities
Spiritual Experience:	Vision of Beauty and Harmony
Life Path Keynote:	Death and Rebirth
Hebrew Letter:	Nun (fish) נ
Astrological Influence:	Scorpio ♏
Tarot Designation:	Death
Colors:	Green Blue
Magickal Gifts:	Boat; phoenix; eagle
Myths and Tales:	Adam and Eve; Apollo and Phaeton; Dickens' Christmas Carol; Chinese Tale of Tseng and the Holy Man; Sumerian tale of Gilgamesh; Utnapishtim and the Flood; Death of Siegfried
Strengths Achieved:	Acceptance; assimilation of grief; understanding of other's problems; ability to leave past behind
Weaknesses Revealed:	Fear of change; inability to understand others; seductiveness; misuse of friendships; egotism

23rd Path – Hod to Geburah

Prayer Psalm:

"How I love your law, O Lord!
It is my meditation all the day.
Your command has made me wiser than my enemies,
for it is ever with me.
I have more understanding than all my teachers
when your decrees are my meditations.
I have more discernment than the elders
because I observe your precepts.
From every evil way I withhold my feet,
that I may keep your words.
From your ordinances I turn not away,
for you have instructed me.
How sweet to my palate are your promises,
sweeter than honey to my mouth!
Through your precepts I gain discernment;
therefore I hate every false way."

Hod to Geburah

The 23rd path is the beginning of the more abstract paths and their energies. Because of this, it becomes more difficult to specifically define how the energies manifest within our life. As a life path, its keynote is the revelation and blossoming of power.

This is the path of breaking down outworn forms so that new vision and perspectives can flow. It creates situations that reveal aspects of us that are no longer viable or usable. It creates situations that reveal the attitudes and activities of our life that are no longer necessary. It enables us to take a new perspective on the world - our world - and everyone and everything within it.

This path and its imagery create circumstances that show us what needs to be dissolved within our life. We may see a breaking down of various aspects. Water (the astrological influence and the meaning of the Hebrew letter) washes away the old and keeps life moving. Water has a depth that is not always apparent. Although some situations may seem calm on the surface, we may need to dive a little deeper and trust our instincts. They tell us there are strong currents in motion. Initially, the effects may not be tangibly visible, but they will manifest.

The magickal gifts are the cup and sacramental wine and clay pots. The cup and wine was used in many traditions as part of initiatory rituals and celebrations to reflect the drinking in of new life. Initiations open us to new possibilities, revealing what is no longer beneficial for us in life and show us the doors available.

Clay pots hold and pour water. They are made by hand and can be shaped into many forms, and if broken, new ones are easily made with the proper effort and training. This path teaches us that our life can be formed and shaped with the skill and patience of a potter. This is the life path of ancient initiation and the forming and testing of character to learn our true purpose in life.

The Hanged Man card when used with this path stimulates new perspectives in all areas of our life. This card is aligned with the energies that involve learning to submit to the higher. In pathworking it teaches tolerance and upliftment. This card and its imagery teach us that we have chosen this earthly experience.

The Hanged Man awakens energies that help us change our vision so that we are less strongly focused upon the material. It opens the energies that enable us to merge the material with the spiritual world. When we are totally willing to hear, the words of the Divine will be spoken. Thus opportunities to exchange our views for new ones in which spirituality plays a more important role begin to arise.

This path and its symbols manifest conditions in the physical that can place us in a position to be put upon by others or others into a position in which we may be tempted to put upon them. We may become prone to unproductive daydreaming. We may even find ourselves becoming self-indulgent, with feelings being exaggerated out of proportion.

The path between Hod and Geburah will stimulate more psychic energy, making us more sensitive to everything. It can also make us more impressionable. It will awaken greater desire to be of service, thus helping us to develop greater compassion and understanding. Through this path - whether in pathworking or as a life path - we begin to learn our emotional limitations and our spiritual potentials.

Hod to Geburah

Pathworking Benefits:	Truth and courage; new perspectives; clarifyingemotions; upliftment; opportunities for new visions;heightened sensitivities and instincts; discovery of life purpose
Spiritual Experience:	Vision of Splendor and Power
Life Path Keynote:	Revelation and Blossoming of Power
Hebrew Letter:	Mem (water) מ
Astrological Influence:	Element of Water ▽
Tarot Designation:	The Hanged Man
Colors:	Deep Blue
Magickal Gifts:	Cup & sacramental wine; clay pots
Myths and Tales:	Noah's Ark; Hansel and Gretel; Story of Siegfried; Australian Tale of the Rainbow Serpent;
Strengths Achieved:	Tolerance; upliftment; compassion; sensitivity; greater service; trust of instincts; discernment
Weaknesses Revealed:	Intolerance; depression; focus on material; self-indulgence; dominance; overly impressionable

22nd Path – Tiphareth to Geburah

Prayer Psalm:

"Your word endures forever, O Lord.
It is firm as the heavens.
Through all generations your truth endures;
You have established the earth and it stands firm.
Had not your law been my delight,
I should have perished in my affliction.
Never will I forget your precepts,
for through them you give me life.
I am yours; save me,
for I have sought your precepts.
Sinners wait to destroy me,
but I pay heed to your decrees.
I see that all fulfillment has its limits;
broad indeed is your command."

Tiphareth to Geburah

This is the life path for justice and karmic adjustment. The energies that are triggered and set in motion from its symbols and images create conditions and opportunities to balance what needs to be balanced. Ultimately, the balancing frees us and enables us to pursue a course that will be more beneficial. This path reveals the duality of our nature - the good and the bad. With all circumstances that arise through this path, it is important to keep in mind that we must learn to face them and forgive ourselves for them. We must remember that we are human, and we make mistakes when we are growing and learning. We must learn to love ourselves in spite of mistakes.

Libra is the astrological influence and its primary symbol is that of the scales. This reminds us to maintain balance. The scales of justice also remind as that we will ultimately be judged by others by how we judge and respond to them.The magickal images are the scales, a single feather and the elephant. In Eastern tradition, the elephant is associated with Ganesh, the god of justice and abundance. It is a reminder that when we live our lives justly, we will have abundance within our lives on many levels.

In Egypt, Maat is the goddess of truth, and she is usually depicted with a single feather (a vulture feather). One of the tales surrounding her involves the change we call death. In the tale, the soul goes before all of the gods and goddesses to have his or her life weighed. All of the gods and goddesses have large stones that they intend to drop onto a scale as they each ask you a question about the life you just left. By the time the individual gets to the end of the line the scale is very unbalanced in regards to us. The last individual in the line is the goddess Maat, and she holds no stone. Her question though is the most important, because if you can answer her question appropriately, her single feather will balance the scales - no matter how many stones are weighed against you. Her question is simply: "Is there one who is glad that you lived?" If you can answer "yes", her feather balances the scales and the individual moves on in evolution. The feather reminds us to be gentle in our judgments - of ourselves and others.

The tarot designation is the Justice card. It has ties to the archetypal energies for the feeling and hearing our own conscience. In pathworking it manifests situations that teach us that if we do not heed that inner voice, the result is chaos and disruption.To become involved with the higher self is to discover our purpose on Earth. When we realize that we are souls first, then the higher levels of awareness open to us more fully. This pathworking helps us to recognize our higher self. The influence of this card through this path manifests opportunities to apply thoughts and actions properly. It reveals the need for balance at all times. It manifests energies that help us learn to blend more practically the physical and spiritual.

This path is the path of karmic action and assessment, and so when the Justice card is used with it, the energies activated are often catalytic, setting things in motion within our life, bringing to the forefront what needs balancing. It helps release the energies for clearing debris from our life (past and present). This card can and will stimulate and/or force equilibrium.

The symbols and images of this path create crossroads within our lives. Major decisions about whether to continue with activities in different areas of our lives or to alter them manifest strongly. They will manifest the facing of consequences either way, and teach us that all choices have consequences. Sometimes the energy of this path may manifest conditions of limbo, in which we seem incapable of making decisions. This is always a sign that it is important to make some kind of decision, recognizing that either way we choose or decide, we will encounter that which will help us to learn and grow.

The energies of this path can also reveal manipulations of others or by others. It can also bring to the forefront and reveal where there is deceitfulness and superficiality. It stimulates the need for superficiality.This path helps bring out our artistic nature. It can also make us more sociable and inspiring of the talents of others. It manifests conditions that give the opportunity to balance our nature and the creative expression of the male and female within us.

Tiphareth to Geburah

Pathworking Benefits:	Justice & karmic adjustments; courage; balance; artistic creativity; forgiveness; revelation of consequences
Spiritual Experience:	Vision of Harmony and Power
Life Path Keynote:	Justice and Karmic Adjustments
Hebrew Letter:	Lamed (ox goad) ל
Astrological Influence:	Libra ♎
Tarot Designation:	Justice
Colors:	Emerald Green
Magickal Gifts:	Scales; feather; spider & elephant
Tales and Myths:	Ali Baba; Tales of Pluto & Hades; Elijah and the Prophets of Baal; Sleeping Beauty or Tale of Briar Rose; Judgment of Themis
Strengths Achieved:	Application of thought & energy; developing conscience; decisiveness; impartiality; objectivity
Weaknesses Revealed:	Duality; unforgiving; failure to make decisions; deceitfulness; lack of conscience; ignoring our disruptions; superficiality

21st Path – Netzach to Chesed

Prayer Psalm:

"My soul hath longed for thy salvation,
and I hope in thy word.
Mine eyes wait for thy word,
when thou wilt comfort me.
For I have shriveled like a leather mask in the smoke,
I do not forget thy statutes.
How many are the days of thy servant?
When wiltthou execute judgment on them that persecute me?
The wicked have digged a pit for me,
which is not in accord with thy law.
All thy commandments are trustworthy;
yet the wicked persecute me.
They had almost destroyed me upon Earth;
but I forsook not thy commandments.
Quicken me after thy loving kindness;
so shall I keep the testimony of thy mouth."

Netzach to Chesed

This is a path whose energies manifest in our life as ups and downs. As a life path, it awakens a call to the Quest and to making choices in regards to what we truly wish the reward of the quest to be. When we choose for the higher, the path is always opening and our efforts are rewarded. When we don't, we find obstacles and hindrances as if we are entirely at the whim of the Fates. The choice to hear and respond to the call of the Quest always remains with us; we can close our ears and ignore it altogether.

This path creates circumstances that offer a way to the grail - our spiritual essence and how best to manifest it within our lives. It will open the doors within our physical life, but insures that it is not too easy to follow. Many assume that the true spiritual path, once found, is easy to follow. We still must work just as hard as on any other path, the difference though is that the pursuit of our own grail path, is most enjoyable and satisfying work and so the struggle never seems as difficult.

The images and symbols activate energies that create circumstances of promise, maturity and growth. They reveal the possibilities if we put forth the right effort. The magickal images are reminders of the possibilities that open to us when we pursue our personal spiritual quest.

The open hand is the assistance that comes to us through doors opening, others lending assistance and opportunities manifesting - often out of the blue. The Grail or cornucopia, along with the Golden Fleece, is a reminder of the abundance that is our right to participate in while on the Earth. Following a spiritual quest does not mean we must do without material goods and comforts. It does not mean that we must martyr ourselves. Working this path manifests conditions that demonstrate this clearly.

Astrologically, Jupiter, the astrological influence for this path, is the planet of abundance and wealth. Its symbology and energies when used with this path can assist us in opportunities to manifest further our own wealth within our lives.

Tarot designation is The Wheel of Fortune card. When used with the 21st path of the Tree of Life, it releases the archetypal energies of wealth and fame, and their rise and fall within our lives. Through it we learn to know good and evil according to our desires.

This card with this path manifests situations that teach us the law of synchronicity. Things happen in the time and manner and means that are best for us if we let them and do what we can or must. It teaches us the flow and flux of Nature and life. It teaches us to recognize and to place ourselves within its rhythms. It teaches us that if we want a harvest, we must first plant the seeds and tend to the growing.

The 21st path is the life path of sensitive and sensible souls (both qualities essential for success in the material and spiritual worlds). It is also the path of creative souls, artists, musician, etc. who follow the Grail of their art.

The symbols and images of this path manifest opportunities to commit to the more eternal. It may bring us in contact with a group or individual who can guide or help with our more spiritual aspects of life. It may manifest as a departure from a job or city, or it may manifest as an offer that has always been a dream. It opens the doors to opportunities, but we must recognize the opportunity for what it is and walk through the doors.

Pathworking here releases energy into the physical so that we begin to recognize that divine law operates upon the earth. We begin to recognize that some universal law is governing humanity. It can also open the gift of prophecy or the opportunity to awaken that potential. It will also open the doors to expand in many areas of life.

Through this path and its symbols (and through what they manifest within our lives), we begin to recognize that there is justice in all aspects of the world - especially within the physical where we often feel it is the most lacking. This path opens the door to revealing greater philosophy, theology, religion and ritual as an integral and workable part of life.

Netzach to Chesed

Pathworking Benefits:	Unselfishness; abundance; new opportunities; hearing the call to the quest; prophecy; understanding of Divine law; practical philosophy and religion
Spiritual Experience:	Vision of Beauty and Love
Life Path Keynote:	Call of the Quest and the Fates
Hebrew Letter:	Kaph (palm of hand) כ
Astrological Influence:	Jupiter ♃
Tarot Designation:	Wheel of Fortune
Colors:	Violet
Magickal Gifts:	The Golden Fleece; the grail
Tales and Myths:	The Arthurian Tales of Quests; Jason and the Argonauts (the quest for the Golden Fleece); Moses and the Burning Bush
Strengths Achieved:	maturity; commitment; sensibleness; awakening to the Grail; greater effort
Weaknesses Revealed:	Inability to see choices; immaturity; discontent; con-committal; self-pity; chronic complaining

20th Path - Tiphareth to Chesed

Prayer Psalm:

"Thy hands have made me and fashioned me;
teach me thy law.
So that those who revere thee may see and rejoice,
because I have rejoiced in thy word.
I know, O Lord, that thy judgments are right
and that thou in thy faithfulness has
humbled me.
Let, I pray thee, thy merciful kindness be my
comfort according to thy word to thy servant.
Let thy tender mercies come to me that I may live;
for I have been taught thy law.
Let the wicked be ashamed, for they have humbled
me unjustly but I have meditated in thy
precepts.
Let those who reverence thee turn unto me,
and those who have known thy testimonies.
Let my heart meditate in thy statutes
that I be not ashamed. "

Tiphareth to Chesed

This is the path of the Hermit, the Wayshower, and the adept. Here we have opportunities to explore the teachings of all those who brought knowledge to humanity. Here we open to higher vision and for many, to greater spirit contact.

This path and its symbols and imagery place before us opportunities to become a new person. On a spiritual level this path stimulates a greater commitment to the spiritual life. We are setting energy in motion that proclaims to the universe, "I am ready to accept change in my life!"

This path and its symbols often manifest conditions where review of past situations, feelings and attitudes frequently occur. This review helps us in throwing light upon the soul, leading us to higher goals. It creates situations where we must choose without lingering or further debate.

The magickal gifts are the wand, lamp and Eucharistic host, all of which have great significance. All reflect an opening to higher inspiration. The wand opens the world of magic and mystery, the lamp sheds light and guides, and the Eucharistic host is the commitment to the more spiritual aspects of life itself.

The tarot card for the 20th path is the Hermit. Its imagery in pathworking helps us to realize and recognize the illumination that is always present for us. It helps us to realize we are never truly alone; there is life and energy on all planes around us.

This card in pathworking manifests situations where we must leave worldly cares behind, leaving the security of the ego and forget our assumed importance of our earthly endeavors. This alone enables us to light the way for others. Thus this card with this path opens the individual to many opportunities for healing and illumination.

The Hermit card and its archetypal reflections helps us to understand the Biblical words of "Ask and it shall be given..." The problem for most people is in knowing the proper way to ask, and this is what the energies of the Hermit card help teach us through the situations that manifest around us.

When we awaken the energy of this path in our life more tangibly through pathworking we find many ways of manifesting the spiritual within the physical. This is part of the influence of the sign of Virgo. Those who do this seem to always get what they want or need.

This is the path of the strong silent types who have the capacity to conquer all with their deep compassion. This path teaches the application of power and new forms of energy expression within daily life conditions.

In the physical the energy of this path manifests opportunities to learn and explore techniques for expression of our inherent talents. It creates opportunities to become more helpful. It reveals where we are helpful and unassuming, dependable and unselfish, calm and self -reliant. It can also reveal where we are none of these things.

The 20th path creates situations that reveal where we have been or are being manipulative and underhanded. It can reveal fault-finding, superficiality and indecisiveness. It also though releases energy that enables us to become selfless servants of others somewhere within their lives, doing so in complete understanding. We become the Wayshower.

Tiphareth to Chesed

Pathworking Benefits:	Spiritual guidance; ancient teaching; commitment; helpfulness; service and guidance to others; acceptance of change and spiritual
Spiritual Experience:	Vision of Harmony and Love
Life Path Keynote:	Visionary Guidance
Hebrew Letter:	Yod (hand) י
Astrological Influence:	Virgo ♍
Tarot Designation:	Hermit
Colors:	Yellowish Green
Magickal Gifts:	Lamp, wand, Eucharistic host
Myths and Tales:	Ruth of Old Testament; Ceres & Demeter; Erigone and Dionysus; Snow White and Seven Dwarfs; Persephone and the Eating of Six Seeds; the Night Journey of Muhammed
Strengths Achieved:	Dependability; unselfishness; openness to change; illumination; strong & silent compassion
Weaknesses Revealed:	Hypocrisy; false pride; non-committal; fear of past; underhandedness; indecisiveness; improper application of power; too much deliberation

19th Path - Geburah to Chesed

Prayer Psalm:

Thou has dealt with thy servant, O Lord,
according to thy word.
Teach me good judgment, grace and knowledge;
for I have believed thy commandments.
Even before I was humbled, I believed,
And I kept your word.
Thou art good, O Lord, and doest good;
teach me thy statutes.
The justice of the proud has multiplied,
but I keep the commandments with my whole heart.
Their hearts are stubborn,
but I keep thy law.
It is good for me that I have been humbled,
that I might learn thy statutes.
The law of thy mouth is better to me
than thousands of things of gold and silver."

Geburah to Chesed

This is the life path of fire. The symbols and images of this particular path release fire-like energies into our lives so that we have no choice but to clear out the dross that has been accumulating. This path creates situations that strip away our illusions and the outer faces that we present to the world. It manifests situations that place us in a position of being only ourselves - the place where we find our only true strength.

This is a path that manifests situations that reveal the height and depth of ourselves, opening our eyes to see who we truly are. We can use this path to draw upon our innate inner strength. It can also manifest situations that show us where self-pride may be tripping us up. This path reveals our personal myths and assists us in destroying them. Energy gets set in motion in a way that demands we put our true destiny into operation.

The magickal images are the lion and the serpent two of the great and mystical beasts. The lion is an ancient image for the power of the inner sun - courage and strength of will. The snake reflects the transformations that occur through growth with its shedding of the skin, outgrowing the old to be born into the new.

The cup of bitters is also one of the magickal images associated with this path. It reflects the bitter taste that fills us when we must give up something that we have been hanging on to inappropriately. The cup of bitters becomes a honeyed elixir when we drink it, accepting the new over the old. The effects of this path with this symbol are long lasting, and it can take a while for the energies to play themselves within our life circumstances. This is the path of the Cup of Sorrows that must be drunk by everyone upon the spiritual path. But it is only as bitter as what we allow it to be. It is through the trials that we gain our greatest strengths.

The tarot card for this path is Strength whose imagery stimulates the development of true strength. This card's image is a link to archetypal energies that can manifest conditions for the facing and removing of fears and doubts. This is the path of self-discovery through overcoming indecision. Its energies teach us not to allow others to take advantage of us. This card when used with pathworking stimulates the desire to overcome material and spiritual barriers.

The 19th path is the path of the Knights of the Grail in their quests. It involves the righting of wrongs and paying the price to reap the rewards. This is the path of the peace keepers, the defenders of the weak. It helps us in melding opposites and contrasts.

This path and its energies awaken the creative urge, one that manifests within our environment as a reflection of our own being. it forces a look at what we may not wish to see but must see regardless so that our true strength can manifest.

This is the path of opportunities for developing self-assurance protectiveness, warmth and sincerity - inspired by universal love. It may also create situations that will reveal vanity, self-seeking, dictatorship and egotism in us or others. it is only by facing these aspects that are hidden that we learn to truly love ourselves and transmute the lead into gold. It is here that we truly experience the serpent bite of higher knowledge!

Geburah to Chesed

Pathworking Benefits:	Strength of will; opportunity to burn out dross; self-reliance; courage and obedience to the higher; self-assurance; creativity; self-knowledge
Spiritual Experience:	Vision of Power and Love
Life Path Keynote:	Power of Strength of Will
Hebrew Letter:	Teth (serpent) ט
Astrological Influence:	Leo ♌
Tarot Designation:	Strength
Colors:	Greenish yellow
Magickal Gifts:	Cup of bitters; lion and serpent
Myths and Tales:	Theseus and the Minotaur; Beauty and the Beast; Hercules and the Nemean Lion; Tales of Richard the Lionhearted
Strengths Achieved:	Peacekeeping ability; righting of wrongs; sincerity; inner alchemy; facing of reality; defense of the weak
Weaknesses Revealed:	Burnt out attitudes; false fronts; avoidance of trials and responsibilities; vanity; indecision; cruelty; taking advantage of others

18th Path – Geburah to Binah

Prayer Psalm:

"On the Lord's business have I meditated,
that I may keep thy commandments.
I entreated thy favor with my whole heart;
save me according to thy word.
I thought on my ways
and turned my feet to thy paths.
I prepared myself
and delayed not to keep thy commandments.
The bands of the wicked have beset me;
but I have not strayed from thy law.
At midnight I rise to give thanks to thee,
and of them that keep thy commandments.
The earth, O Lord, is full of thy mercy;
teach me thy statutes."

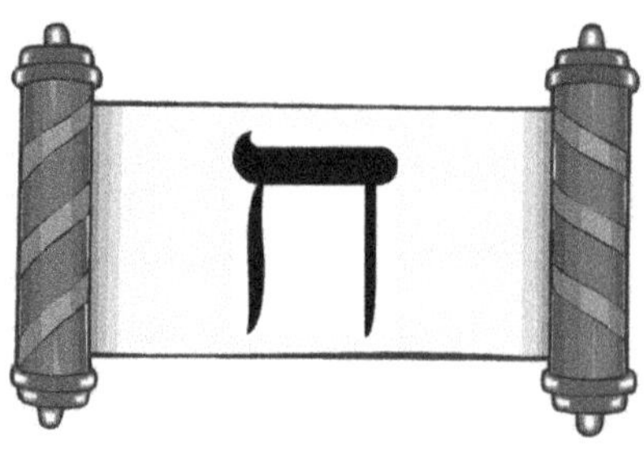

Geburah to Binah

This is a path that releases energies into our life that help us regain balance and a sense of stability. It opens energies that provide a feeling of protection and renews our will to carry on after our trials. It creates situations that let us know that everything will be okay.

This is the life path of enlightenment through discipline. It is the path of learning to concentrate, focus and discipline ourselves. When we learn this, we find that we can climb any fence (the Hebrew letter) to uncover the hidden knowledge beyond it.

This path lets us know through the circumstances in our life that discipline, determination and hard work will bring its rewards. It does not mean the work is over, but with this path, situations arise that help us recognize our progress. We find ourselves able to use our energies more effectively.

The magickal gifts of this path reflect this as well. The silver star reminds us that we can reach beyond ourselves with success if we lay the proper foundation. The sphinx is an ancient symbol of the hidden knowledge that can open to us, while the chariot reflects the discipline necessary at all times on our path.

The tarot card whose symbology reflects this path is the Chariot. It reflects opportunities for self-discipline and control. This card and its imagery activate an energy that teaches us that we are first a soul, and thus we have responsibilities as such. The archetypal forces linked to it stimulate a merging of the divine with the soul, providing opportunities to create a new consciousness.

This card is a reminder that by controlling and understanding the divine power within us all, we can realize all that we need. It is our right to explore and to realize our purpose in life. This card - with this path - reflects the energies for death and change, with resulting new control.

This is the path that on the Tree of Life crosses the abyss by the Gate of Death, but the so-called Angel of Death always comes in a friendly guise and not one of terror and foreboding. This is the path of the Dark Mother - she who brings enlightenment to darkness through proper discipline.

This is also the path of heroes, and the bridge to the Grail Castle. This is a bridge that is like walking upon the edge of a knife. It seems sharp and full of danger initially, but it widens with each step forward, forming a strong bridge.

This path teaches us to focus individual attention on the present. It strengthens psychic energy, and it will manifest situations that will bind the family together. We may find ourselves frequently caring for other's needs and wants and always able to do so.

This path can create stimulate opportunities to overcome any tendency toward hysterics and irritability. It can force a reckoning with selfishness - in ourselves or those around us. Most of all it helps manifest situations where the direction of thought, feelings and action must be focused on the present and this ultimately serves to relieve worry and pressure.

This is a path of climbing beyond and opening to new realms through discipline. This brings enlightenment and revelations and even the development of telepathy. But we must learn how to focus, climb and trust where our individual efforts take us - even if not the accepted path of the mainstream.

Geburah to Binah

Pathworking Benefits:	Protection; will to carry on; hidden knowledge; strengthens psychic energy; enlightenment in darkness; awakens hero's energy
Spiritual Experience:	Vision of Power and Sorrow
Life Path Keynote:	Enlightenment and Birth through Discipline
Hebrew Letter:	Cheth (fence) ח
Astrological Influence:	Cancer ♋
Tarot Designation:	Chariot
Colors:	Amber
Magickal Gifts:	Silver star; sphinx; chariot
Myths and Tales:	Hercules and the Lernaean Hydra; the Elves and the Shoemaker; St. George and the Dragon; Moses and the Parting of Red Sea; Grimm's Seven Ravens; Grimm's Tale of Fisherman and his Wife
Strengths Achieved:	Balance; enhanced concentration; courage; discipline; self-control; psychic energy
Weaknesses Revealed:	Instability; avarice; cruelty; depletion of energy; lack of caring; inability to focus; no control; lack of determination

17th Path – Tiphareth to Binah

Prayer Psalm:

"Remember you word to your servant
since you have given me hope.
My comfort in my affliction
is that your promise gives me life.
Though the proud scoff bitterly at me,
I turn not away from your law.
I remember your ordinances of old, O Lord,
and I am instructed.
Indignation seizes me
because of the wicked who forsake your law.
Your statutes are the theme of my song
in the place of my exile.
By night, I remember your name, O Lord,
and I will keep your law.
I have been comforted
because I kept your precepts."

Tiphareth to Binah

This is a path whose release energy is often difficult to understand. As a life path, it works to bring together the twin aspects of ourselves, the male and female. We are all a combination of both masculine and feminine energies in a variety of ways within our daily lives. This path helps us to see and realize that there is another side to us. This is also the path though of fate and discrimination. When we discriminate appropriately in our life, Fate seems to work for us. On the other hand, this is a path in which Fate also works independently to bring us choices, to help us see and utilize our twin aspects.

We are dual in nature. If we are predominately one, then situations will arise to help us see the other side of us. If we are more assertive and masculine, then we may be shown a softer, more feminine side to ourselves. If we are more feminine, then the masculine, more assertive aspects may emerge within our life circumstances. This path creates situations where we must try and unite and integrate more fully our opposite aspects - especially those we may have been ignoring or giving little credit to. When we bring the male and female together, we give birth to the Holy Child within us - that is the true us.

The magickal images of this path are ones that enhance our abilities to bring to life the benefits of the Holy Child within -in which arises the ability to control Fate herself.. The woman crowned with stars is the reflection of the blending of the heaven and earth, with the ability to move within both realms. The whale is a mammal, and while most mammals live upon the land, this great creature lives within the seas. This reflects the ability to move between and feel comfortable in two worlds. The girdle is a feminine symbol but it is used for binding, giving it a masculine aspect. It reflects the ability to control and direct Fate and love.

And of course, the double edged sword has a multitude of significances. It is the sword of Fate, which we all must learn to wield at some point - to direct and control our own. It is the sword of discrimination, of seeing both sides and choosing according to which is best. It is also a reflection of opposites working together.

The tarot card for this path is the Lovers. Its energies reflect a path and/or life of choice, discrimination and communication. This card and its imagery awaken the energies to help us listen to our own inner voice and trust in it. When we do, we are working with the Fates. Its imagery may manifest circumstances that teach us that we hold our own destiny - our Fate- within our own hands, and it releases the karmic desires of the higher self. Through this card in pathworking we learn that we cut ourselves off from blessings and guidance by using only our conscious intellect.

This path is known as the Gate of Fate across the abyss. It implies that we are fated from prebirth by what we have already set in motion - but it also teaches us that we can learn to change and direct our own fate. This path includes the serious and the funny, and its energies can help us find our own true path by listening to our inner voice. Such energies become most active when the advancement of others (including ourselves) is upheld. This is the path of gold, encased in lead. It is the path of alchemy. The bringing together of the feminine and the masculine is an alchemical process. Learning to do it in all aspects of life, makes one a true alchemist.This path shows us that we must love ourselves to be able to fully love another. It releases into our life energy that reminds us that our outer world always reflects aspects of our inner selves. Paying close attention to the actions and attitudes of people around us after this pathworking will reveal much about our own inner self - good and bad.

Through this path we learn to be more selective of whom we associate. It demonstrates that we all have a variety of aspects that must be integrated. This path will reveal more clearly our intelligence, our versatility and our sensitivity to others - including our lack of it. It can manifest situations that clearly reveals where we dissipate our energy and are aloof and indiscriminate. This path shows us through our physical lives all of the instruments of our personality that we can use for the greatest expression of our individuality. When we use them as such, we are one with Fate.

Tiphareth to Binah

Pathworking Benefits:	Discrimination; power of silence; devotion to the Great Work; alchemy; balance; love of self
Spiritual Experience:	Vision of harmony and Sorrow
Life Path Keynote:	Fate, Discrimination and Devotion
Hebrew Letter:	Zain (sword) ז
Astrological Influence:	Gemini ♊
Tarot Designation:	Lovers
Colors:	Orange
Magickal Gifts:	Double edged sword; whale; woman crowned with stars; girdle
Myths and Tales:	Castor and Pollux; Romulus and Remus; Prince and the Pauper; Beauty and the Beast; Grimm's tale of Old Woman in the Forest
Strengths Achieved:	Versatility; balance of male & female; intelligence; sensitivity; strengthens inner voice; humor
Weaknesses Revealed:	Lack of communication; lack of humor; inability to choose; rigidity; insensitivity; indiscriminate

16th Path – Chesed to Chokmah

Prayer Psalm:

"Let your kindness come to me, O Lord,
your salvation according to your promise.
So shall I have an answer for those who reproach me
for I trust in your words.
Take not the word of truth from my mouth,
for in your ordinances is my hope.
I will keep your law continually,
forever and ever.
And I will walk at liberty,
because I seek your precepts.
I will speak of your decrees before kinds
without being ashamed.
And I will delight in your commandments
which I love.
And I will lift up my hands to your commands
and meditate upon your statutes."

Chesed to Chokmah

This is a path whose symbology and imagery opens the flow of energy that triggers a probing of the mysteries of how we came to be where we are. This is the life path for vision of incoming life on all levels. It creates a need and a desire for serious introspection. Many situations arise that bring about such deep considerations for those who perform the pathworking and for those whose life path this is.

This path manifests situations that drive home the need to place the Divine Will first. it manifests circumstances that make us aware that there truly is a reason for who we are and where we are - even if it does not reveal the reason. Only time and meditation can reveal it.

This path shows the potential of the marriage of higher and lower selves. It provides a glimpse of the higher levels our life has been leading up to, whether we were aware of it or not. It reveals the creativity and fertile possibilities of our life and our life circumstances - no matter what they are or seem to be.

The magickal gifts reflect this as well. The wand is an ancient symbol of the directing the creative life force, the planting of seeds - a phallic connotation. It is a symbol of the ability to create, to imbue new life. The wedding has a multitude of symbolic applications for this path. It is the union of two to become something new. From it comes new life and ultimately birth on many levels. The bull is a symbol of fertility, of the creative seed of life.

This path and its imagery often manifest situations within the physical life that reveals the creative talent that lies within. It reveals that there is creative talent, but such talent must still be brought out and given more light once revealed.

This path may create situations that test loyalty and understanding (of us and others). It may test our individual fertility and productivity in life. It can reveals stubbornness, rigidity and overindulgence that must be overcome before the seeds of creativity can truly take root and sprout.

The tarot card for this path is the Hierophant. The Hierophant is a symbol for the upliftment of the soul. Its imagery is linked to the archetypal energies that contribute to the spirit of the Divine on Earth in any number of ways. Through the use of this card, conditions manifest that help us learn to defend our beliefs and to live by the truth.

Upon this path we learn to face all false sense of security, as well as our ancestral fears. It is a path of freedom only when released from everything that is not our own belief. This path links the archetypal rulers of wisdom and mercy, the kindly and compassionate. It is the path of the Round Table, and it leads across the abyss of the Tree of Life through the Gate of Royalty. The Hierophant opens the gate for us to know the royalty of ourselves.

Chesed to Chokmah

Pathworking Benefits:	**Initiation into mysteries; obedience / devotion to the higher; uncovering reason for our life; hidden talents; fertility**
Spiritual Experience:	**Vision of God's Love - Face-to-Face**
Life Path Keynote:	**Vision of Incoming Life and Freedom**
Hebrew Letter:	**Vau (nail) ו**
Astrological Influence:	**Taurus ♉**
Tarot Designation:	**Hierophant**
Colors:	**Red Orange**
Magickal Gifts:	**Wand; phallus; dove, weddings; bull**
Myths and Tales:	**Tale of the Minotaur; Hercules and the Cretan Bull; Tale of Europa; Grimm's tales of Water of Life and the Three languages**
Strengths Achieved:	**Loyalty; greater understanding; fertility in life; upliftment of the soul; freedom of beliefs; kindness and compassion**
Weaknesses Revealed:	**False security; ancestral fears; misunderstandings; misplaced loyalties; overindulgence; stubbornness; wishy washy beliefs**

15th Path – Tiphareth to Chokmah

Prayer Psalm:

"Teach me, O Lord, the way of thy commandments,
and I shall keep them until the end.
Give me understanding, and I shall keep thy law;
yea, I shall observe it with my whole heart.
Make me to go in the path of thy commandments,
for therein do I delight.
Incline my heart unto thine testimonies,
and not to fables.
Turn away mine eyes that they may not behold false;
and quicken thou me in thy ways.
Strengthen thy word unto thy servant,
who is devoted to thee.
Turn away my reproach,
because thy judgments are good.
Behold, I have delighted in thy precepts,
quicken me in thy righteousness."

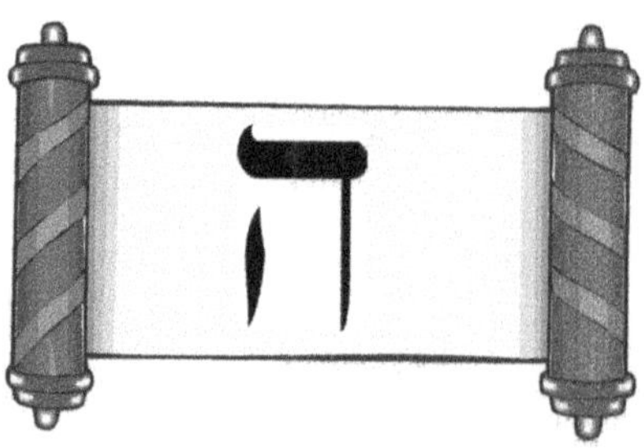

Tiphareth to Chokmah

This is a path whose symbols release energy for incoming life upon all levels. It is the life path of vision - particularly of spirits and guardians within the world. It is also a life path that opens one to the vision of the Divine (face to face), but it must be remembered that a vision is not the same as seeing the Divine first hand.

The energies operative at this level of our consciousness are subtle, and the symbols are a bit more abstract in the manner in which they reflect and manifest specific energies within our lives. They are no less intense though, and they actually may be more intense than usual.

This path and its symbols and imagery helps us to connect our own personal existence with that of all creation. The whole of our universe surfaces within our life, revealing just what is possible and what we are capable of. It manifests situations that show us we are connected to all times and all people, making us confront that aspect. Past life information and connections are revealed.

This path releases energy that shows us our life potentials, thus our awareness of ourselves and all humanity grows. We begin to realize that we are both creator and created in our physical life circumstances, and thus we must take responsibility for them.

The magickal gifts also reflect much of this. Solar symbols can be used with this pathworking to awaken past life knowledge and perceptions and their influence upon us within our present life. The spear and the chalice are both symbols for piercing and seeing in the darkness, tools for opening to vision. The hawk is a common visionary totem and animal, providing messages - spiritual and physical of our potentials and possibilities.

The tarot card for this path is the Emperor, although sometimes the Star is also used. The emperor is linked to those archetypal energies that assist us in recognizing both the divine laws and the human laws of life. When this card is used in pathworking, it releases energies that lead to respect for authorities. It manifests situations that teach us to strive for higher, more spiritual laws within our lives. It manifests life experiences which teach us that our balance is only disturbed when we are not in tune with the necessary order of things.

Through the influence of this card, the individual learns to attune to the necessary order, even if it means facing bitterness. At such times, meditating upon the Emperor card will be of assistance. It eases the bitterness and opens us to awareness of higher laws and disciplines currently at play within our life.

In pathworking, this path is known as the Angelic Gateway across the abyss of the Tree of Life. It fills our life with guiding spirits whose presence becomes more recognizable - more tangible. They help to teach us the spiritual laws and how to work with them. It is a path that manifests guardian angels and friends - calming hands within our lives. This path brings clarity of the soul. The Hebrew letter of "heh" is the window - particularly to that of spirit.

In pathworking, opportunities manifest to increase our courage, along with our ability to inspire and bring new life to others. Our intuition increases, and we have greater opportunity to initiate new activities.

We may also see the effects of past foolhardy actions and egotism. Acting without proper forethought, without subtlety or in an opinionated manner will create strong learning situations for us and those around us. We may find ourselves involved in situations that make us aware of ourselves and how we are affecting the growth of others, positively or negatively. We begin to see through the window of our lives.

Tiphareth to Chokmah

Pathworking Benefits:	Renewed life; visions of the Divine; devotion to the Great Work; spirit contact; initiative; connections to others
Spiritual Experience:	Vision of Harmony and God
Life Path Keynote:	Power of Angels and Guiding Spirits
Hebrew Letter:	Heh (window) ה
Astrological Influence:	Aries ♈
Tarot Designation:	Emperor (sometimes the Star)
Colors:	Scarlet
Magickal Gifts:	Spear; all solar symbols; hawk; chalice
Myths and Tales:	Jason and the Golden Fleece; Chinese Tale of One Honest Man; Grimm's Boy Who Went Forth to find what Fear Was; Cinderella
Strengths Achieved:	Visionary energies; revelation of life potentials; courage; ability to inspire; attunement to higher orders
Weaknesses Revealed:	Disrespect for authority; bitterness; unclear focus; disassociation from people; egotism; foolhardiness; acting without forethought

14th Path – Binah to Chokmah

Prayer Psalm:

"I lie prostrate in the dust;
give me life according to your word.
I declared my ways and you answered me,
teach me your statutes.
Make me understand the way of your precepts,
and I will meditate on your wondrous deeds.
My soul weeps for sorrow;
strengthen me according to your word.
Remove from me the way of falsehood
and favor me with your law.
The way of truth I have chosen;
I have set your ordinances before me.
I cling to your decrees, O Lord,
let me not be put to shame.
I will run the way of your commands
because thou hast made me of joyful heart."

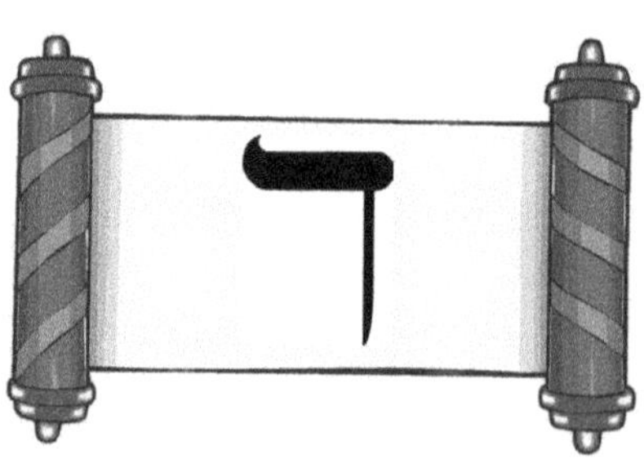

Binah to Chokmah

This is a path of great power because it unites the primal male with the primal female. It is at the level of the supernal sephiroth (the upper three) and it crosses the width of the Tree of Life, activating opposite poles of energy within one's life. It is here that we experience more directly the archetypal energies that play upon us in various forms. It is here that we activate those energies involved in the principle of life and life-force at its most intimate level.

This is the life path of new birth, where the male and female are brought together to truly give birth to the Holy Child within us or within our life. This is the life path of fertility, illumination and creative power.

This path initiates the ability to believe the impossible and to make it probable. It opens doors and opportunities that we have not seen or considered, and thus we often find ourselves looking upon the world with new eyes once its effects are fully grounded into the physical life. It joins the archetypal male with the archetypal female - and the union of these two on any level always results in a new birth.

The magickal gifts reflect this as well. This is a path that reveals that our life is pregnant with possibilities. The full moon imagery reflects this as well. The equal armed cross, is the balanced union of the male (the vertical bar) and the female (the horizontal bar), and where they unite a magnificent birth occurs. The egg and the dove are both symbols of pregnancy, fertility and new birth. These gifts help us to release birth energies into our life more dynamically.

The tarot card for this path is the Empress. She embodies the essence of blessings and new energy. The imagery of this card when used in pathworking awakens opportunities for acknowledging and giving thanks. It activates greater status within the physical life, as physical actions determine the growth of the soul. This is the card of birth and changes that can fulfill every person's dreams. It involves lessons in understanding the feminine principles of evolution and birth. It is through the feminine or the Empress, symbols of the illumined soul, that the Christ or Divine is born within.

The 14th path is the doorway (the Hebrew letter Daleth) to giving birth to our dreams. It is the doorway to recognizing the feminine in all, with its power to create. It is the path of joy and love through understanding of universal processes of reproduction - both physical and spiritual. This path unites the male and female to create new life. It brings with it opportunities to appreciate the splendor that exists in every growing thing.

This path is called "the Illuminating Intelligence". It reveals the hidden talents and potentials we can give birth to. It shows our divine potential. It can manifest many new ways to prosper within the physical. We find opportunities to merge the imagination with reality and produce something powerful and expressive within our life.

This path can stimulate attractiveness to the opposite sex, and it can awaken new sentiments of love and sharing. There occurs a polarization. Positive energy meets with negative energy to produce a new creation in our life. Like the Empress, it shows us that life is pregnant with possibilities!

Binah to Chokmah

Pathworking Benefits:	Fertility; Illumination of potentials; revelation of the hidden; devotion; birth; love and sharing; belief in the impossible
Spiritual Experience:	Vision of Divine Sorrow
Life Path Keynote:	Illumination, Fertility and Creative Power
Hebrew Letter:	Daleth (door) ד
Astrological Influence:	Venus ♀
Tarot Designation:	Empress
Colors:	Emerald Green
Magickal Gifts:	Full moon; equal armed cross; egg; dove
Myths and Tales:	All goddess tales; The Birth of Aphrodite; Tale of Tontlewald; The Tinder Box; Rumpelstiltskin; Cinderella
Strengths Achieved:	Knowledge of birth; merging of imagination and reality; attractiveness; understanding of feminine; joy, love & reproduction
Weaknesses Revealed:	Disbelief; failure to merge creative principles for prosperity; feeling unattractive; lack of femininity; lack of joy; nonappreciation

13th Path – Tiphareth to Kether

Prayer Psalm:

"Answer thy servant that I may live
and keep thy words.
Open mine eyes that I may behold
wondrous things out of thy law.
I am a sojourner with thee;
hide not thy commandments from me.
My soul is pleased
and desires thy judgment at all times.
You rebuke the proud
and all who turn away from your commands.
Remove from me reproach and contempt;
for I have kept your testimonies.
The ungodly sat and plotted against me,
I meditated upon your statutes.
Your decrees are my delight; they are my
counselors."

Tiphareth to Kether

This is the life path that opens the energies of the abyss and crosses through the hidden sphere of Daath. On a physical level it is the path of the flow of energy from the heart to the crown of the head. This path and its imagery release energy into our lives in ways that can be difficult to understand at times, even though its effects are powerfully felt. It teaches us to pay attention to the subtleties of life. No one remains untouched by this path!

This is the life path of the Dark Night of the Soul journey. This is the path of faith, and learning to use and depend upon your resources to achieve success in our endeavors. Through the energies of this path we learn to draw upon all of our resources and all of our past experiences. At some point even they may be stripped away, leaving us only with the desire to experience the Crown (Kether). This desire is what moves us on and helps us to bear the burdens of this energy within our physical life. It brings upon us a tremendous test of faith. When this test is met, the burdens are ultimately replaced by glorious blessings in all areas of our life.

The magickal gifts remind us of the possibilities and promise of what is to be when the test of faith is met. The moon is a reflection of the sun, and we learn on this path to draw upon our own inner sun, a reflection of the Divine. The moon reminds us to follow our own inner light in spite of outer darkness. The bow and arrow is the gift of direction and light. The arrow streams a rainbow hue when loosed. It reminds us to be straight and direct on our path, no matter how difficult it seems and the rewards will come.

The dog is a guide, a guardian and a protector. On this path it activates the energies that guard and guide us so we do not succumb to the test but meet it and rise on. It is a symbol of the spiritual guardianship that is with us helping us, often without us realizing.

The tarot card for the 13th path is the High Priestess. She is the one who guides us through our self-made obstacles.

The energies this card stimulates help us to remove the barriers that separate the inner and the outer worlds. This card and its imagery help us to face what opposes us in realizing our higher self. She is a reflection of the quite inner voice, the prophetess within that sees through the dark and can guide. This is the path across the abyss known as the Gateway of Knowledge, reflected by the High Priestess. She helps us learn to balance the emotions; we can hear our inner voice.

This is the life path that enables us to overcome obstacles we have created for ourselves in this life or in past lives. Part of what is experienced is the Dark Night of the Soul that ultimately brings the hidden mysteries to the surface. It manifests experiences that help us recognize the constant flow of positive and negative energies - both of which serve a purpose within our lives. This is the path of masters coming and going upon the earth. It is a bittersweet path that opens a wealth of higher intuition and illumination.

Often through this pathworking we find ourselves being alone with only our faith in the higher. We may find that what used to bring light and benefit to ourselves is taken, hindered or hidden. We learn the powerful lesson of giving birth to the light within us. We learn that what we used to rely upon was simply a reflection of our own inner light. We experience circumstances that force us to draw upon the well of truth and light within. It is here that we have the opportunity to awaken our strongest intuition and to impregnate ourselves with the light and life of the Divine.

Tiphareth to Kether

Pathworking Benefits:	**True knowledge; completion of work; true power of faith; peace; giving birth to the Light within**
Spiritual Experience:	**Vision of Harmony through Union with God**
Life Path Keynote:	**Glory of the Dark Night of the Soul**
Hebrew Letter:	**Gimel (camel) ג**
Astrological Influence:	**Moon ☾**
Tarot Designation:	**High Priestess**
Colors:	**Blue**
Magickal Gifts:	**Moon; bow & arrow; silver; dog**
Myths and Tales:	**Isis, Diana, Demeter and other Goddess Tales; Tale of Ceres; Tales of Ceridwen; Tale of Rapunzel; Tale of Artemis and Endymion;**
Strengths Achieved:	**Faith; removal of barriers between worlds; resourcefulness; self-reliance; wealth of intuition; revelation of hidden**
Weaknesses Revealed:	**Self-made obstacles; unbalanced emotions; inability to see purpose; over dependency; conflict of being alone with being lonely; unreliance**

12th Path – Binah to Kether

Prayer Psalm:

"How shall a young one be faultless in his way?
By keeping your words.
With all my heart I seek you;
let me not stray from your ways.
Within my heart I treasure your promise,
that I may not sin against you.
Blessed are you, O Lord;
teach me your statutes.
With my lips I declare
all of the ordinances of your mouth.
In the way of your decrees, I rejoice,
as much as in all riches.
I will meditate on your precepts
and consider your ways.
In your statutes I will delight;
I will not forget your words."

Binah to Kether

This is the life path for realizing our abilities - physical, emotional, mental and spiritual. This life path does not confirm through any life situations that the abilities and potentials are fully trained, but we become very much aware they are present and can be finely developed. That's why this path is the path of hopes, visions and magick.

This path and its imagery releases energy that manifest opportunities to develop seership in any area in which we have a propensity - business, spirituality, education, art, etc. It stimulates the energies, but to make the seership more than mundane divination demands dedication and work. This is the path of vision, and situations will manifest through its pathworking that help us realize that we can attain our hopes, wishes and dreams. We begin to see we are capable of becoming anything we desire, and thus this is the path for making the true magician and alchemist.

The magickal images further reflect and assist in that when incorporated into the pathworking or into life. The caduceus is an ancient symbol of healing and one of the first and most powerful forms of the magick wand. A true magician and alchemist can heal and transform his life in a multitude of ways.

The ibis was a sacred bird to the ancient Egyptians with the ability to kill snakes and serpents. The snake a symbol of life, death and rebirth is swallowed and thus part of the medicine of the ibis. The ibis is also a wading bird, and all animals that move between realms (such as dry land and into water) reflect the potentials of those who are aligned with it.

The four symbols of sword, cup, wand and pentacle reflect the four elements (fire, water, air and earth) over which the true magician in life has control. They are the symbols of all that is available - the elements themselves are within the realm of the alchemist to use and work with.

The tarot card for the 12th path is the Magician. This card when used with pathworking presents the individual with all the tools necessary for growth and higher consciousness. In pathworking opportunities become plentiful, but may go unrecognized because they are often in primal states. This card and its imagery awakens the realization that we have all that we need to achieve success, but it also reminds us that we must learn to use all of our tools - physical and spiritual.

The use of divine power is available to those upon this path or working with its imagery and symbols. it is a path that awakens energy and manifests situations that teach wisdom, truth and dexterity. it is a path for recognizing what has not been nourished. It is the energy of mother figures and womb-like settings.

This is a path whose working will manifest a separation of the physical from the spiritual. We begin to see definite distinctions, even in those areas we once believed were spiritual. We begin to see ways of integrating and making both work for us.

This path activates situations that expand our intelligence and our studies, manifesting educational opportunities - both formal and informal. Communication increases - with others and with our higher self.

This path may also stimulate restlessness within the physical life that can only be resolved by balancing the spiritual with the pragmatic. This path opens strong emotions, exposing them so they can be expressed by the mind in various forms of artistic and creative endeavors. It is the path of hopes and visions.

Binah to Kether

Pathworking Benefits:	Realization of our abilities; alchemy and magick; true vision of the spiritual; strong emotions; artistic and creative endeavors
Spiritual Experience:	Vision of Movement from Sorrow to Divine Union
Life Path Keynote:	Hopes, Visions and True Magick
Hebrew Letter:	Beth (house) ב
Astrological Influence:	Mercury ☿
Tarot Designation:	Magician
Colors:	Yellow
Magickal Gifts:	Caduceus; Ibis; sword, cup, wand and pentacle; all Seeing Eye
Myths and Tales:	Tales of Thoth, Odin and Mercury; Rumpelstiltskin; Grimm's Tale of the Riddle; East of the Sun, West of the Moon
Strengths Achieved:	Nourishment; wisdom and dexterity in life; seership; balance of intuition and rational; intelligence
Weaknesses Revealed:	Failure to recognize ability; blocked vision; restlessness; unbalanced emotions; not taking advantage of growth situations

11th Path – Chokmah to Kether

Prayer Psalm:

"Blessed are they whose way is blameless,
who walk in the way of the Lord.
Blessed are they who observe His decrees,
who seek him with all their heart.
And do no wrong
but walk in His way.
You have commanded
that your precepts be diligently kept.
Oh, that I might be firm in the ways
of keeping your statutes.
Then should I not be ashamed
when I behold all your commands.
I will give you praise with an upright heart,
when I have learned your just ordinances.
I will keep your statutes,
do not utterly forsake me.

Chokmah to Kether

This is the last of the actual paths, the last of the links between the various sephiroth. It is a life path whose keynote is simplicity - the becoming again as a child. Its symbols and images activate and manifest within our lives in a powerfully simple manner.

This path manifests situations where we must simplify our life and reclaim what we lost in childhood - innocence, wisdom and joy. Here is the energy of all manifestation. This is the path followed by Enoch and Elijah of Biblical lore, the prophets who walked with God and were no more. On this path we are often left to find our own meanings and correspondences.

On a more mundane level, its energies manifest experiences that are as varied as the people upon the Earth. It may create a foglike status - walking and acting as if not knowing what to do next. It may also make the mind clear as to how to initiate new work or continue more effectively with the old.

The magickal gifts remind us of the simplicity of manifestation and creation in life. The fan is an old symbol for the element of air, and the winds of inspiration and abundance that can open to us. An old myth speaks of how the Gate of the East winds is the gateway to abundance and prosperity.

The hat with the feather and the staff with the rose, are symbols of new journeys and paths that can open to us. Children possess an openness and trust in the universe that is reflected by these symbols - that we need nothing other than our hat and our staff. The rose is the rose of life that lives within the heart of every child and those who keep the child alive within them.

The tarot card for the 11th path is the Fool. This is the card of complete trust. For those whose life path it may be, this card's imagery will stimulate the development of poise within the universe. It is linked to the archetypal energies of renewed innocence. It activates a more childlike response to the world - learning to keep wonder and simple wisdom alive within our physical lives.

This path teaches that each day must be seen as new and approached without fear. It is the path for those who will be or are becoming true teachers of wisdom, often merely through the example of their lives. This is the path of the high temples, retreats and monasteries - filled with scrolls of ancient wisdom and teachings that can be passed on to others.

For some this pathworking will stimulate gregariousness and a cooperative attitude within life. We may find ourselves more inventive and inspired, full of workable ideas. On the other hand, it may manifest a predisposition to repetition, hyperactivity and coldness - which must be balanced for true productivity. At its best expression, this path creates situations that stimulate the intellect, the intuitive faculties and the artistic mind. It reveals the simple wisdom of the child within!

Chokmah to Kether

Pathworking Benefits:	Simplification of life; completion of work; initiation of new endeavors; stimulation of intuition and artistic abilities; prophecy
Spiritual Experience:	Vision of Union with God
Life Path Keynote:	Simplicity and Becoming Again as a Child
Hebrew Letter:	Aleph (ox) א
Astrological Influence:	Air 🜁
Tarot Designation:	The Fool
Colors:	Bright Pale Yellow (sunshine)
Magickal Gifts:	Fan; hat with one feather; staff and a rose
Myths and Tales:	All tales of rebirth; Grimm's tale of Devil with Three Golden Hairs; Grimm's Tale of Foundling and Thumbling
Strengths Achieved:	Innocence and trust; mental clarity; cooperation; poise in the universe; wisdom teachings
Weaknesses Revealed:	Over complications; foglike perspective; repetitive; hyperactivity; coldness; distrust

PATHWORKING ENERGIES AND SYMBOLS

Path	Sephiroth Linked	Virtues & Vices of the Linked Sephiroth	Energy as a Color	Hebrew Letter	Astrology	Tarot Card	Magickal Tool of The Path
32	Malkuth to Yesod	Discrimination & Independence/ Avarice & Idleness	Indigo/ Black	ת TAU the cross	♄ Saturn	The World	The T-cross, a cauldron, a girdle.
31	Malkuth to Hod	Discrimination & Truth/ Avarice & Dishonesty	Orange Scarlet	ש SHIN tooth	△ Primal Fire	Judgement	Flint and steel.
30	Yesod to Hod	Independence & Truth/ Idleness & Dishonesty	Orange	ר RESH head	☉ Sun	The Sun	All solar symbols; lion; sparrowhawk.
29	Malkuth to Netzach	Discrimination & Unselfishness/ Avarice & Lust, Impurity	Crimson	ק QOPH back of head	♓ Pisces	The Moon	The scarab or the beetle; dolphin.
28	Yesod to Netzach	Independence & Unselfishness/ Idleness & Lust/Impurity	Violet	צ TZADDI fishhook	♒ Aquarius	The Emperor or Star	Cup; grail; a star; the apple; the eagle.
27	Hod to Tiphareth	Truth & Unselfishness/ Dishonesty & Lust, Impure	Scarlet	פ PEH mouth	♂ Mars	The Tower	Lightning; wolf; bear; rubies.
26	Hod to Tiphareth	Truth & Devotion to the Great Work/ Dishonesty & False Pride	Indigo	ע AYIN eye	♑ Capricorn	The Devil	Yoni and lingam; goat and the ass.
25	Yesod to Tiphareth	Independence & Devotion to the Great Work/ Idleness & False Pride	Blue	ס SAMECH prop	♐ Sagittarius	Temperance	Rainbow; bridge; bow and arrow; the centaur.

PATHWORKING ENERGIES AND SYMBOLS

Path	Sephiroth Linked	Virtues & Vices of the Linked Sephiroth	Energy as a Color	Hebrew Letter	Astrology	Tarot Card	Magickal Tools of The Path
24	Netzach to Tiphareth	Unselfishness & Devotion to Great Work/ Lust, Impurity & False Pride	Green/ Blue	נ NUN fish	♏ Scorpio	Death	Scarab; death boats; stinging insects & plants to soaring eagles.
23	Hod to Geburah	Truth & Energy & Courage/ Dishonesty & Cruelty	Deep Blue	מ MEM water	▽ Primal Water	The Hanged Man	Cup & sacramental wine; clay pot; asbestos.
22	Tiphareth to Geburah	Devotion to Great Work & Energy & Courage/ False Pride & Cruelty	Emerald Green	ל LAMED ox goad	♎ Libra	Justice	Scales; single feather; spider & elephant.
21	Netzach to Chesed	Unselfishness & Obedience/ Lust & Impurity & Pride and Hypocrisy	Violet	כ KAPH palm of hand	♃ Jupiter	Wheel of Fortune	The open hand; Grail; the Fleece; all quests.
20	Tiphareth to Chesed	Devotion to Great Work & Obedience/ False Pride & Hypocrisy	Yellow	י YOD hand	♍ Virgo	The Hermit	Wand; Lamp; Eucharistic host;
19	Geburah to Chesed	Energy & Courage & Obedience/Cruelty & Pride & Hypocrisy	Greenish Yellow	ט TETH serpent	♌ Leo	Strength	Lion and serpent; vinegar wine; cup of bitters.
18	Geburah to Binah	Energy & Courage & Silence/ Cruelty & Avarice	Amber	ח CHETH fence	♋ Cancer	Chariot	Silver star; the sphinx; chariots;
17	Tiphareth to Binah	Devotion to Great Work & Silence/ False Pride & Avarice	Orange	ז ZAIN sword	♊ Gemini	Lovers	Doubled-edged sword; woman crowned with stars; whale; girdle.

PATHWORKING ENERGIES AND SYMBOLS

Path	Sephiroth Linked	Virtues & Vices of the Linked Sephiroth	Energy as a Color	Hebrew Letter	Astrology	Tarot Card	Magickal Tools of The Path
16	Chesed to Chokmah	Obedience & Devotion/ Pride and Hypocrisy	Red Orange	ו VAU nail	♉ Taurus	Hierophant	Wand; phallus; dove; weddings; bull.
15	Tiphareth to Chokmah	Devotion to Great Work & Pure Devotion/ False Pride	Scarlet	ה HEH window	♈ Aries	The Star or the Emperor	The spear; solar symbols; stars; chalice; hawk.
14	Binah to Chokmah	Silence & Devotion/ Avarice	Emerald Green	ד DALETH door	♀ Venus	Empress	Girdle; full moon; equal-armed cross; egg; dove
13	Tiphareth to Kether	Devotion to Great Work & Completion of Great Work/ False Pride	Blue	ג GIMEL camel	☽ Moon	High Priest	The moon; bow and arrow; silver; the dog.
12	Binah to Kether	Silence & Completion of the Great Work/ Avarice	Yellow	ב BETH house	☿ Mercury	The Magician	Caduceus; Ibis; all-seeing eye; sword, cup, wand & pentacle.
11	Chokmah to Kether	Devotion & Completion of the Great Work/ (No vices)	Bright Pale Yellow	א ALEPH ox	🜁 Primal Air	The Fool	The fan; hat with one feather; staff and a rose; nakedness.

KETHER
CHESED
HOD
YESOD
MALKUTH
(Kingdom)

Part Three:

Touching Greater Power

"The voice sounded a bit like mine so I was inclined to trust it. The voice told me some things about myself that needed changing for my own good. I knew these things; I had just never done anything about them. The voice told me it was now time to stop procrastinating. It reminded me that if I continued to wait for tomorrow to make needed changes in my life, tomorrow would never come. Tomorrow is only a convenient scapegoat for refusing to face reality today. That little voice was very convincing. It promised me if I would heed its advice, something very good would come of it. I listened, I heeded and something unusually good came of it."

- Joseph Whitfield
The Eternal Quest

Chapter Six

Pathworking and the Tree of Life

"Contrary to popular fantasy, magical arts are not employed to 'get what you want', but to unlock whatever you are not, thus revealing and releasing whatever you may be."

- R.J. Stewart
Living Magical Arts
Blandford Press
(New York, 1987, p. 20)

This book is about working with images of the Tree of Life - paths and sephiroth - and learning how to enter into them in a sympathetic manner. To do so, we must be able to loosen the restrictions of the mind. Any creative person, artist or inventor has already learned to do so. Through the imagickal techniques of the Qabala we are learning to use the imagination in a productive manner. We are developing the ability to see the significance and interrelatedness of all things. Such skills take time and practice, but once accomplished, they grant us power, strength and control over our life and destiny.

Keep in mind that there will always be elements that we cannot control as long as we are in the physical. This play of "free variables" in life is what forces us to become ever more creative and productive. Through imagickal techniques such as pathworking though, we become more active within our life, and we unfold our own power and magick. We realize that we can take a creative and active role in life circumstances. Working the paths on the Tree of Life helps us with this.

There are 22 paths that connect the temples of the Tree of Life in its traditional teachings. There are other paths that are hidden, and which will be the subject of a future work. These are not of concern to this text. The 22 traditional paths are bridges between the various levels of the subconscious - the sephiroth. Ideally, they enable us to access any level of the mind at any time to any degree we desire. The problem is that these bridges may be blocked and not fully functional, inhibiting a full and powerful access to various levels of the consciousness. When unblocked, they become the paths of wisdom.

One of the most effective means of developing our potentials is through *PATHWORKING.* Pathworking is the process of using archetypal symbols and images in an imaginative (and sometimes mythologized) journey to elicit specific effects within our daily lives and to open the psychic and spiritual planes more consciously. It can be accomplished through a variety of meditative and ceremonial techniques. Pathworking is *"the magical application of story telling, yet another aspect of creative visualization, and an important key to effective magic"*. (Marian Green, *Experiments in Aquarian Magic*. Wellingborough, Northamptonshire: The Aquarian Press, 1985 p.26.)

Most creative visualizations are a type of pathworking. Daydreams can be a type of pathworking as well. Pathworking is the use of the symbols and images in an imaginative journey for a wide variety of purposes. We can walk a magickal path or take a magickal journey for healing, for divination, for enlightenment or even to examine symbols and images for clarification.

The problem though with many types of pathworkings is that the effects they elicit within our daily life are not easily defined. They are atavistic, - uncontrolled. Rarely are there guidelines or maps that reveal how the energies and symbols we focus upon are likely to play out within our lives.

This is what makes pathworking with Qabalistic imagery so powerful. The symbols and images have been used in very similar ways by great numbers of people for a great many centuries. Because of this, we know what effects such meditations and workings are likely to have within our life. We can then work with them to elicit specifically what we wish and need.

Qabalistic pathworking is an imaginative (imagickal) journey between two of the temples on the Tree of Life. On this journey various symbols, images and magickal gifts are encountered, according to the effects we wish to elicit. This activates and releases specific archetypal energies into our daily life. These energies manifest life situations that bring rewards, tests, enlightenment that accelerate our own spiritual development.

There has developed in modern times a great mystique surrounding this occult practice of pathworking. For many groups and individuals it is perceived as the be-all and end-all of metaphysical skills. The truth is that there are variations of pathworkings performed at some time by most people who meditate and who practice spiritual development in any of its many forms.

Pathworking is simply a tool for opening and expanding awareness. It is a meditation technique that incorporates very specific guided imagery, archetypal symbols, creative visualization and imagination to open new dimensions and realities. Pathworking is sometimes viewed as the means to manifesting our most wonderful innate gifts - as the epitome of spiritual unfoldment. It is seen as the pot of gold at the end of the rainbow, but this is somewhat misleading. It is a technique that merely opens a pathway to the pot of gold. That pathway must still be traveled. We must also remember throughout the journey that the Qabala will show us our greatest potentials while also revealing our greatest weaknesses. It will manifest our greatest rewards and bring upon our greatest tests.

Pathworking is a dynamic method of undertaking and accelerating our personal spiritual quest. Qabalistic pathworking clears the bridges between the different levels of consciousness represented on the Tree of Life, giving us access to any level of consciousness at any time to any degree we desire. It is a powerful tool for those who wish truly to be the creators and heroes of their own life journey. Through Qabalistic pathworking we become the mythic hero in our individual spiritual journeys. We write and star in our own heroic tale.

Hero tales provide pictures of the journey we each must take if we wish to open to higher initiations, mysteries and energies of the universe. Almost every major myth or heroic tale starts with a younger individual leaving home to seek a fortune in any of a multitude of forms. These tales often have older characters who, when met along the road, offer advice and assistance. These elders represent those who work as mediators between the physical and spiritual worlds and who become available (showing up in our life) as we expand our awareness and open to new possibilities. In the ancient tales and myths, it is how the advice is acted upon that determines the future of the young seeker and how progress is made.

One of the common forms of the hero's quest is the entering into service of a mighty king or queen, symbolic of a greater force - or even our own higher self. For many the call of the quest in tales and legends (and in real life) is a call to adventure and excitement, but it is not always recognized for what it truly is: *a time of growth and emergence into responsibility and maturity!*

It is a time of transition and a time of dynamic growth - growth that can entail some very strong emotional highs and some very intense emotional lows. It is a time of serious self-assessment (sometimes forced). The individual must examine the circumstances, people, situations and beliefs of his or her life. The individual must examine what has been lost, stolen, broken and/or no longer necessary, so that it can be cleaned out once and for all. This makes room within the hero's life for that which is more beneficial. It is a time for cleaning the attic.

Many enter into metaphysical and occult practices as a means of escaping their daily lives. They look for these mystical practices to solve their problems. Many see the spiritual path as leading up into some blinding light into which all of their troubles and problems will be dissolved. In reality metaphysical and mystical practices are paths to find the light within so that we can shine it out into our lives. If an individual has difficulty handling the situations daily life, invoking spiritual energies will not necessarily make things easier.

More likely, the spiritual energies will serve to intensify the daily, mundane circumstances of life - forcing a reconciliation or resolution of daily troubles and problems. Our own fears, doubts, limitations and perspectives - whether self created or imposed upon us by society - create barriers to accessing and expressing all of our highest capacities. Qabalistic pathworking shows us not only what our barriers are but where they are as well. It brings them to the surface so that we must do something about them. This forces a reckoning that ultimately makes us more responsible and stronger. At the same time it manifests other wonderful rewards for us.

When we start our journeys, everything may be goodness and light which is as it should be. This is the strengthening process, preparing us for greater tasks and mysteries to be undertaken. When we use pathworking, we are proclaiming to the universe: *"I am ready to take on greater work and responsibility, and I am taking it on in full awareness of what that entails!'*

Paths on the Tree of Life

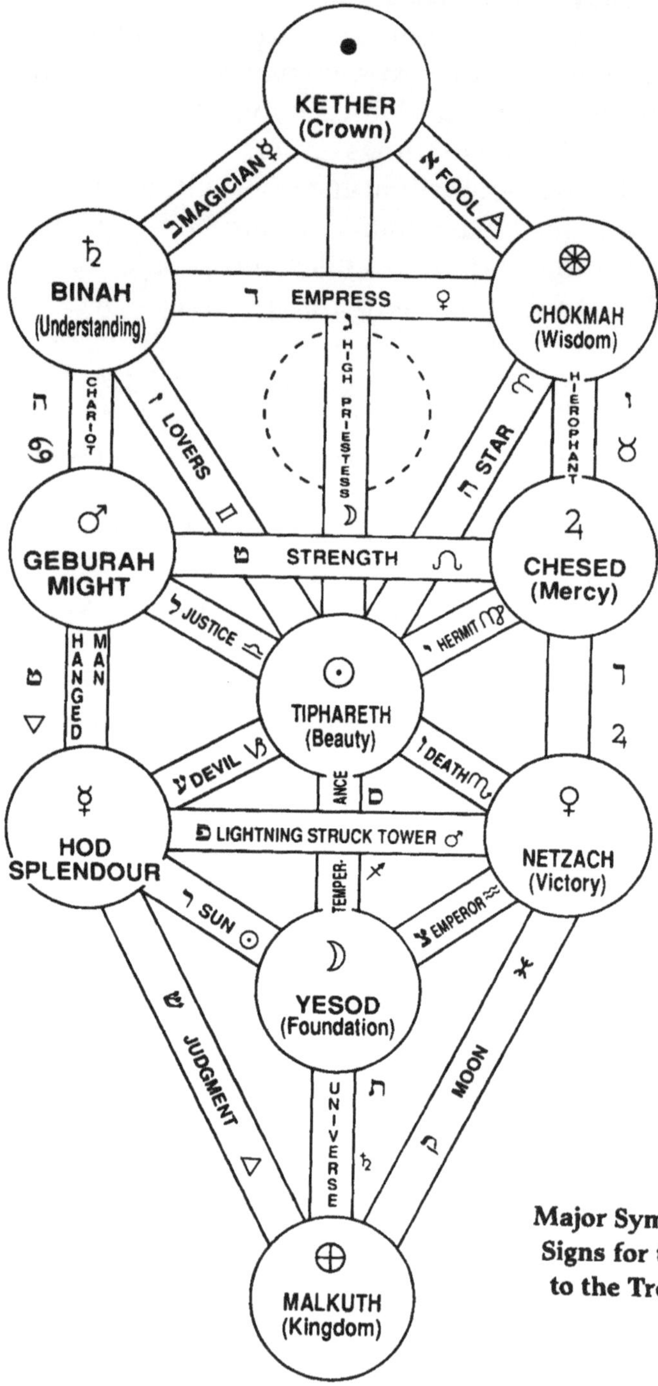

Major Symbols and Signs for the Paths to the Tree of Life

Pathworking and the Ancient Mysteries

Pathworking accelerates the meeting of karma and it accelerates the release of our higher gifts. This makes it easier to manifest them into our daily lives. Instead of seeking some light to shine down upon us, through pathworking we develop our own light to shine out from us.

The paths are bridges that link the various sephiroth on the Tree of Life. These bridges between the various levels of our consciousness become congested with outworn ideas, attitudes and perceptions. They become clogged with our fears, our doubts and a multitude of hindrances that we accumulate throughout life. Pathworking is a means of clearing the bridges. It is comparable to clearing out clogged water lines. Doing so enables the water to run more freely and more powerfully throughout our house.

When we tap the specific sephiroth, as we learned to do in part one, the result is *ILLUMINATION*. Illumination is a higher form of consciousness which changes the mind, enhancing all of our perceptions. When we begin to bridge more strongly the different levels for even greater growth through pathworking, we institute *INITIATION*. We open ourselves to the Mysteries of Life.

All work with the Qabala sets energy in motion that will play itself out within our daily lives - through the people and situations that are in it. This is why working with the Tree of Life demands continual watchfulness. Nothing is insignificant and what we experience may be manifesting due to our work with a particular Qabalistic exercise. Remember that thro ugh the Qabala and its associated images and symbols, we learn to control what manifests within our life and the degree of intensity. Its symbols and images activate archetypal forces that in turn manifest and play themselves out in our daily lives. We must realize that everything in life can have a hidden message and lesson within it (if we choose to see it), and that it may be related specifically to a particular exercise that we performed.

The Lesser Mysteries

The bottom four sephiroth (Malkuth, Yesod, Hod and Netzach) and their corresponding paths comprise what are called THE *LESSER MYSTERIES.* They activate energies for the unfoldment and the development of the personality. They are linked to forces that involve searching for and awakening more than just a physical existence. Through these paths and sephiroth, the seeker learns to look beyond. The tests activated by these paths involve the development of good character, which form the foundation of higher development. They also involve learning to open and access the subconscious more easily.

Everything associated with the Lesser Mysteries involves other people and our relationships with them. Our greatest learning comes through the groups we encounter, formally and otherwise. The Lesser Mysteries involve learning to maintain a sound mind and body, to control instincts and passions, and to strengthen the mind.

The Greater Mysteries

THE GREATER MYSTERIES involve the middle three sephiroth (Tiphareth, Geburah and Chesed) and their corresponding paths. These mysteries involve learning to awaken and develop individuality - those unique creative energies and abilities that last more than a single lifetime. These are the qualities that we strengthen and manifest more each lifetime. Within the Greater Mysteries is the lesson of true faith which opens the veils to true spiritual insight. The lessons at these levels change our focus from the outer world to the inner world. Th2rough these levels, our inner principles are focused and dedicated to higher service.

The Greater Mysteries always involve probationary periods in which our dedication to the higher is tested. It is when working with these that we meet what many occultists refer to as *the inner plane adept* - who will guide us in greater teachings and the development of dedication.

Dedication, however, does not imply neglect of the physical for the spiritual because it is only by our work in the physical that we learn to apply our lessons. Dedication involves recognizing that some duties in the physical will have precedence over work in the mysteries. It is here that we learn that the fulfillment of our daily obligations to ourselves and to others demonstrates our dedication to the higher and that our ability to fulfill these obligations creatively and positively may be part of our probationary testing. And sometimes this means we must put aside specific, personal metaphysical studies in order to fulfill our obligations.

Through the sephiroth and paths of the Greater Mysteries, we learn to act upon our own resources, without reliance on others. The personality is sacrificed for the spiritual. This involves facing debts and duties within our life and learning to take responsibility for our thoughts, feelings and actions. It involves learning to be alone without being lonely. It requires learning to consciously work out our individual destiny.

The Supreme Mysteries

THE SUPREME MYSTERIES are those that deal more specifically with teaching us the path of our true spiritual essence, its effects upon our physical life and the understanding of how spiritual life and energy is structured. These mysteries involve the upper three sephiroth (Binah, Chokmah and Kether), along with their corresponding paths.

The energies of the Supreme Mysteries often play themselves out in our lives more abstractly. Many times they involve great leaps of faith. It is through them that we begin to understand how everything works together, and we learn to set it in motion for the benefit of all - not just for ourselves. We begin to recognize and understand the universal rhythms and how to align ourselves with them.

All of the mysteries and lessons associated with the sephiroth and the paths are of equal importance in our lives and our evolution. They simply serve different functions. They are simply different expressions of energy to help us.

We work on all of these levels simultaneously, and most people are not even aware that the experiences within their lives are reflections of these mysteries. Through work with the Qabala and especially through pathworking, we attempt to become more cognizant of these energies and to more consciously control and direct it. We learn to be active within our life, stimulating and setting the energies in motion around us consciously rather than being passive and letting the universe play upon us. By learning to set the energies in motion, we accelerate our teaching and our learning. We learn to control them without being overcome by them.

The Mysteries upon the Tree of Life

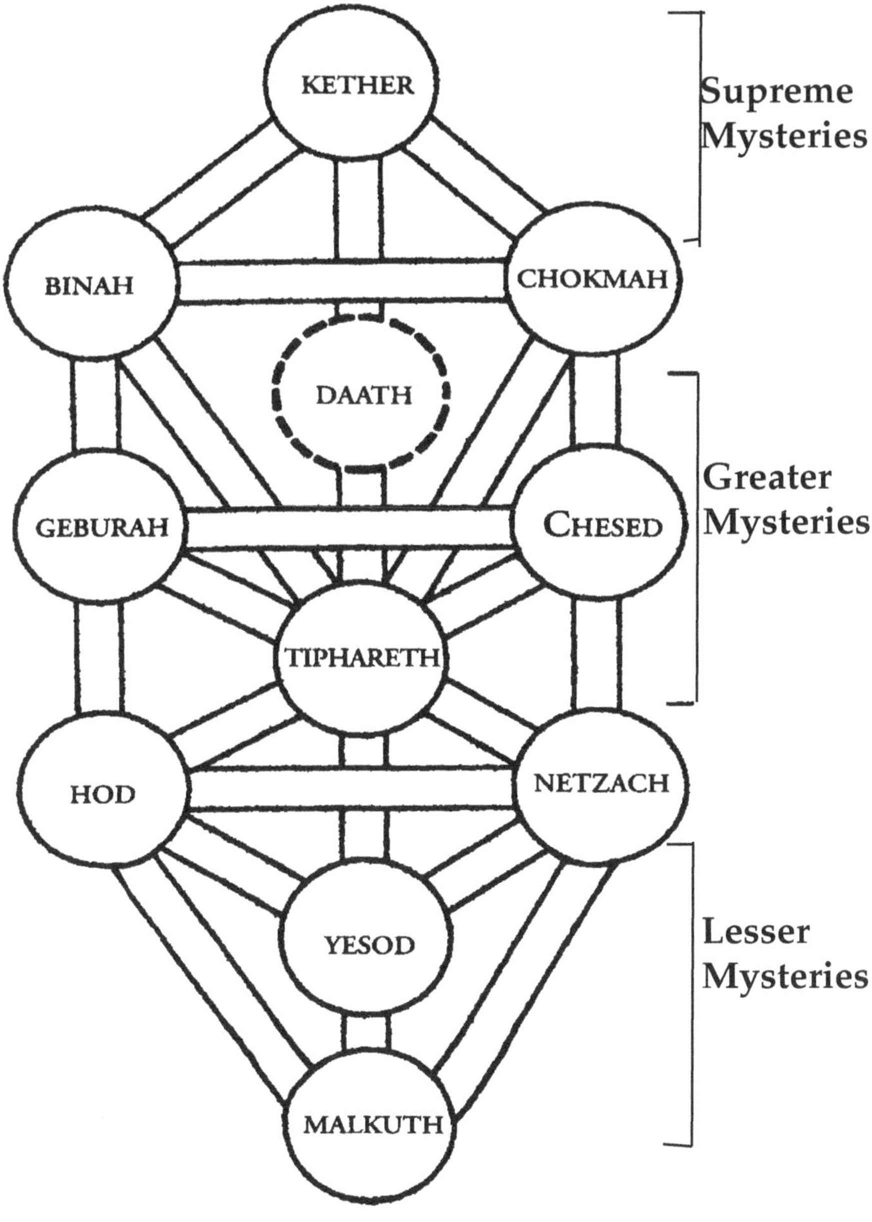

The Benefits of Pathworking

It is very easy in the modern world to think we know all about the world and its various realms. After all, explorers have touched the four corners of the Earth. We have ventured into space and into the ocean depths. Others are just now beginning to explore the more subtle realms and dimensions of life, realms that have served as the inspiration to most of our ancient myths, legends and archetypes.

Reading about these realms and experiencing them are two entirely different things. We cannot truly know something until we have experienced it. Theory and knowledge without application is impotent. To most people our legends, myths and ancient teachings are merely words, but there is a means to discovering the truths and realities upon which they are based. One of the most powerful means of discovering the truths is through pathworking.

The paths on the tree of Life are keys for astral travel, scrying in the spirit, past life exploration, healing and more. They traverse the mind and the various planes of existence. By traveling or working the paths, we awaken dormant and untapped resources of the mind.

Although pathworking may seem like a fantasy of the mind or an innocuous daydream, it is dangerous to assume they will have little effect upon our lives. We are working with powerful symbols which generate and release archetypal forces. The paths contain symbols that will act upon the subconscious mind and awaken what is hidden there. And although the situations, experiences and workings may be symbolic, they will strongly affect the physical world in which we operate daily.

We must remember that whatever we do on one level of our consciousness will flow down and manifest similar expressions on a more mundane level. We are learning to use symbols and images to activate and experience specific energies within our life. This occurs through the normal, day-to-day circumstances. Those who doubt that such connections and relationships exist have only intellectualized the process, and these individuals will come face-to-face with what will be for them a harsh reality of the interrelationship.

The Qabala is a system of evolvement. Through pathworkings we instigate energies that will in turn manifest situations and experiences that hasten our growth. It makes us face what we have not faced. It brings to the surface our hidden fears so that we have no choice but to confront and overcome them. In this way we open more fully to higher and stronger knowledge and spiritual experiences. Because of this, those who approach the Qabala lightly or wish to dabble will experience a strong awakening.

It has been said that the Qabala will show us our deepest fears, but it will also show us our greatest potentials. Through pathworking we become the catalysts of our own lives. By working the paths, we begin the process of consciously and willingly finding the dross of our lives and then clearing it out to reveal the light within. Pathworking brings upon us situations and activates those stresses that must be dealt with for change to occur.

The Qabala is an agent for transformation between the inner and the outer, the upper and the lower, the past and the future and for all levels of consciousness. The raising of matter and awareness from an ordinary level to one that is extraordinary is the task of the true Seeker. And although difficult at times, the epiphanies that come from each activation and working are worth every difficulty.

Without techniques like pathworking, the tasks and the successes of the seeker are often random and atavistic. The conscious work upon the Tree of Life enables us to have a system that we can adapt and use effectively for ourselves.

Pathworking Benefits

Increased enjoyment (gives the conscious mind and opportunity to relax).

Enhances concentration.

Stretches and improves the imagination.

Develops your ability to work with symbols.

Stimulates awareness of the significance and continuity of life's circumstances and events.

Awakens hidden skills, ideas and inspirations.

Invokes testing to lead to higher perceptions and realms.

Intensifies communication between levels of our consciousness.

Integrates more subtle levels of consciousness with our normal waking consciousness.

Stimulates greater self-control.

Manifests a facing of ourselves on all levels.

Precautions for Pathworking

Pathworking is a powerful tool of invocation. The symbols and images serve to activate and manifest the play of universal energies more strongly upon the physical life and our mundane world. It is easy to underestimate pathworking's ability to affect our outward life in the physical world. Its effects can be felt for long periods of time.

The invoking of energies through pathworking may become too intense for those who have difficulty handling the stresses and energies of daily life. The energies awakened – along with their ensuing life situations – will intensify normal life experiences so that the individual has no choice but to transmute them. It will force reconciliation.

Some individuals may not like having to face and experience the aspects and situations brought into play by these techniques. Remember though that the Qabala shows us our greatest fears and weaknesses, but only so we can face them, transmute them and shine more brilliantly as a result.

In addition, the subjective world may grow too real for those who cannot cope with the physical world. Pathworking is not an escape. Those who use it as such will find themselves lost in all areas of their life.

It is easy to become "fairy charmed" and disappear into the world of uncontrolled fancy within the mind. Other realms are there for us to explore and to learn and grow from, but only so they can enhance our physical world. They are not escapes from reality on any level.

The energies invoked and stimulated and their corresponding physical life experiences must be synthesized. Discrimination and discernment is ever important to avoid being led astray. Everything that occurs in your life will take on greater significance.

I must stress though that some preparation is needed. We should at the very least be somewhat familiar with the energies of the individual sephiroth and worked with each one of them several times before undertaking pathworking. Remember that the sephiroth hold traces of energies from all paths that enter or leave them. Thus every level of consciousness - every sephiroth - contains not only its own unique aspects, but it also contains influences from all of connecting paths to them.

Pathworking links two sephiroth, activating both of their individual energies, along with the path's own aspects. Thus, before a pathworking is performed, the work on each individual Sephira should precede. When it comes to the Qabala, more is not better, and the goal is to learn how the energies will play out within our life without being overwhelmed by them. In this way all of the benefits are achieved more easily and more successfully.

Monitor and Record what Manifests

The Tree of Life Journal can be a invaluable tool when working with pathworking. It can enable us to monitor more effectively what we set in motion through the work and how it manifests within our life. In this way we can soften or intensify the effects, adjusting them as we may need them.

The journal is a manual to assist us in assimilating and synthesizing what we set in motion within our physical, daily lives by our work with the Qabala. It will also help us to learn and remember the symbols and images that are our tools, along with one of the most important keynotes or "tricks" to working with the Tree of Life:

IMPORTANT NOTE:

The more symbols, images and other associations (i.e. fragrance, meditation stone, color candle, etc.) that we use with a Sephira or path, the STRONGER the effects will manifest within our daily life. Thus if they manifest too strong, or become overwhelming, then we know the next time not to use or incorporate so many of them in one working. In this way we learn to control what we set in motion, along with learning to control the intensity.

The journal enables us to keep track of what path we worked, what technique we used, when we performed it, what symbols and images we incorporated into it, what aids (fragrances, candles, etc.,) we employed, and what ensued in the week or two following the working. In this way we can then determine how much more or less to include the next time, for results within our daily life that are more to our liking and closer to our particular goal or purpose.

As stated earlier, the form you use for your journal is entirely up to you, but it should be a format that includes all of the necessary information of the pathworking (what and when performed, etc.) and it should also allow for space to list events or occurrences from the week or two that follows. It should also allow for easy periodic review and additional notes.

This journaling also serves to ready the mind for the pathworking, ultimately facilitating the process. By taking time to record, prior to the working, what your purpose is, along with the basic information of the path, you create a shift, sending a message to the appropriate level of the mind, telling it to get ready. It is an important and powerful preliminary to a successful pathworking.

The following are some guidelines to recording your pathworking in the journal. Don't be afraid to adapt them and adjust them:

1. Before each pathworking review the symbology and qualities of each path, as well as the two sephiroth we are trying to bridge together more strongly.

This creates the proper mindset, facilitating your pathworking efforts. It also begins the process of activating the corresponding energies, reflected through the symbols.

2. Write down the path, the sephiroth and the benefits you hope to achieve, along with the magickal gifts that most reflect those particular benefits.

You may even choose to draw the Tree of Life, coloring

the path you will be working. Again, the physical activity of writing and even coloring sets the tone for bridging the inner to the outer life.

3. It is always good to write down what you hope to achieve with this imagickal pathworking.
What energies of the path and the sephiroth are you hoping to set in motion within your daily life? Where do you want to see them manifest most strongly? ***This is important! If the purpose is not suitable for the path you have chosen, your teachers upon the path itself (the archangels, magickal images, etc.) will let you know, and the energies may manifest in an obscure manner.***

4. Writing the hopes for the pathworking and a review of the symbols will activate the energies more fully and in a more appropriate manner.
It sets an etheric, mental guideline for the energies. Remember that with pathworking we are trying to bridge more dynamically and tangibly the subtle archetypal energies within the physical life.

5. Take time after the working to write down your experiences.

Often pathworkings take their own course, varying from what we set forth. Jot down what you feel and what happened. Write down your impressions, imaginings and anything that came to your mind through the pathworking.

Some people find it effective to write a stream-of-consciousness for ten minutes following the pathworking, writing anything and everything that comes to mind. Every pathworking releases energies that need to be grounded. This initiates that grounding.

6. Leave a space in your journal for assessment.

At the end of a week, go back and review what you wrote. Look over the week's events. Reflect and meditate upon the correlation. You will begin to see the ties.

Take time to re-read what you have experienced and assessed. Soon you will recognize the creative aspect of your work and life, and how much control you have over both. You will begin to see connections between, all things, all people and all dimensions.

Recording the pathworking experience in your journal strengthens your knowledge and awareness of what you set in motion. It assists you in recognizing the archetypal energies as they affect you individually and uniquely. You will begin to more clearly recognize how they play within your life, and thus you will be able to more fully synthesize them.

EXERCISE:

Discovering the Personal Life Path

Benefits:

- uncovering the mystery of your birth
- understanding of our life path

Almost all of the esoteric sciences can be applied to the Qabala. Numerology - the mysticism of numbers - is no exception. Archetypal energies are reflected in many forms. They are reflected through symbols and images, colors, sounds and even numbers. All energy and life is vibration, and numbers are the mathematical correlation of those vibrations in relation to us or to any aspect of life.

Numerology is an ancient science that dates back almost 10,000 years BC. The masters of the fourth root race (Atlantean Epoch) recognized that everything in nature was geometrically formed. All of the world's scriptures - such as the vedas, the Zohar, the Torah, the Bible and others - cannot be understood in their most esoteric sense without an understanding of vibration and the significance of numbers.

The masters of Israel were well versed in the Law of Vibration and how archetypal forces were reflected through it. The 22 letters of the Hebrew alphabet were considered the 22 steps the soul had to take to mastership and as the 22 paths that bridged and united all the levels of our consciousness. Each letter and its numerical correspondence indicates an initiation - a path we must walk to develop mastership.

We each come into life to learn certain lessons and develop certain capacities, and we bring natural abilities to assist us in our life path. Because of the density of physical life, we often lose contact with the soul and its purpose for this incarnation. In its wisdom though, the soul chooses a time, a date, a place, and a name - all with numerical and archetypal correspondences. They play upon us subtly and unconsciously, creating situations in which we undergo lessons we have chosen. We are not controlled by these influences, but becoming aware of them can increase our understanding of what we hoped to accomplish in this lifetime. They can help us understand why we have appeared on this planet at this time, what lessons we have to learn and how to use our innate tools to assist us in overcoming obstacles.

Our name is one of our key energy signatures and can reveal much about our potentials. This has been the subject of two previous works - *THE SACRED POWER IN YOUR NAME* and *THE MAGICKAL NAME.* Although there are applications of our name to the Tree of Life, we will not be examining such within this text.

Our primary focus will be on our birth date and how it reflects the energy of our path in life. We will use some basic numerology techniques with our birth date, to determine two things:

1. The particular path on the Tree of Life that reflects the path we have chosen to walk and learn from most strongly within this particular incarnation and

2. The particular Sephira or level of consciousness that we can draw upon most strongly to help us in our life path.

Our birth date can be translated into numbers which can be correlated to the Tree of Life. It can be a link to a particular Sephira and a particular tarot card, thereby indicating a specific path for us. In other words, if we know which tarot card our birth date relates to, we can discern which of the paths on the Tree of Life we have come to work with more strongly. This in turn helps us to put into perspective many of our past life experiences.

Our birth date is a dominant energy signature. It reflects the keynote of our existence. When applied to the Qabala, it can reveal which level on the Tree of Life can be used more easily to realize our true happiness and success. It can also indicate exactly which path - with all of its tests, initiations and rewards - we must walk to achieve mastership in this lifetime.

Our birth date corresponds to our life path - our destiny. In traditional numerology, this is the school of life lesson, what we have come to learn in this lifetime. It reflects the lessons that the soul wants to complete here on Earth, along with the path of experience necessary for our further development. It indicates the path we walk, the strengths and weaknesses we are more likely to encounter, the archetypal symbols and images most effective for us and what we are ultimately striving for.

The birth date, when translated to the Tree of Life, provides two powerful keys to our unfoldment. It will tell us the Sephira, that level of our consciousness which can most easily reveal and illumine aspects of our life more fully. Through this Sephira we can discover the archangel who will often serve as a predominant teacher and source for our illumination upon the spiritual path.

The second key involves translating the birth date to a specific path to determine where and how our tests and initiations are more likely to occur. This requires translating the birth date into a corresponding tarot trump, which then determines our life path. The tarot trump also serves as a bridge to the archetypal forces of that path.

1. Converting the birth date to numbers

To discover the specific Sephira and the specific path, we must reduce the birth date to numbers. The digits are then added individually. From this, they are reduced in two fashions to help us determine our personal Sephira and life path.

Begin with the month in which you were born. Use the number for the month rather than the name. For example: January = 1, February = 2, March = 3, etc. Add to this the day and the year. For the year use the complete designation - no abbreviations (i.e. 1962 rather than '62).

SAMPLE:

March 1, 1960 = 3-1-1960 = 3+1+1+9+6+0 = 20

When the total is achieved, we will reduce it in two ways to determine the individual Sephira and the specific life path.

2. Determining your Sephiroth from the birth date

There are only ten Sephira upon the Tree of Life, each with its corresponding number:

1/10	**Kether**
2	**Chokmah**
3	**Binah**
4	**Chesed**
5	**Geburah**
6	**Tiphareth**
7	**Netzach**
8	**Hod**
9	**Yesod**
10/1	**Malkuth**

(Note that for both Malkuth and Kether, the numbers 1 and 10 both apply. Those whose birthdates reduces to 1 or 10 should work with both levels. Both Kether and Malkuth will be important in the life of these individuals.)

In the sample above, the birth date of March 1, 1960 numerically becomes 20. This number must be reduced to become 10 or less. Thus the 20 becomes 2+0 which equals 2.

SAMPLE:

March 1, 1960 = 3+1+1+9+6+0 = 20 = 2+0 = 2 = Chokmah

In this sample, the number 2 represents the Sephira which the individual has come to awaken and use throughout his or her life for greater illumination. And as we can see from the chart, the number two applies to the Sephira of Chokmah. It is through the second Sephira or Chokmah that the individual will find the archangelic and angels teachers most influential. It is through this level that assimilation and understanding of the individual's life experiences will occur most strongly. Reading and meditating more about our particular and individual Sephira will yield much more insight into our life experiences.

3. Determining the Life Path from our birth date

To determine the specific life path on the Tree of Life, our birth date must be correlated to a tarot card. Although there are 22 paths, the numbering of the actual paths begins with 11. For this reason, we do not apply the birth date number directly to the path number. For example, with the birth date we have used above (March 1, 1960), we cannot apply the number 2 to a specific path because the paths actually begin with the number 11.

NOTE:

Do not apply the birth date number directly to a path number. It must first be applied to a tarot trump, from which we determine the actual path our birth date relates to!

The birth date must be related to a tarot trump in order to determine the specific life path on the Tree of Life. The tarot trumps number 22 cards total (corresponding to the 22 letters in the Hebrew alphabet). The tarot trump, like the Hebrew letters, are associated with specific paths, thus by linking our birth date to a tarot card, we can determine our specific life path.

Birth Date and Life Path

Birth Number =	Tarot =	Life Path on Tree of Life
1	Magician	Binah to Kether (12th Path)
2	High Priestess	Tiphareth to Kether (13th Path)
3	Empress	Binah to Chokmah (14th Path)
4	Emperor	Tiphareth to Chokmah (15th Path)
5	Hierophant	Chesed to Chokmah (16th Path)
6	Lovers	Tiphareth to Binah (17th Path)
7	Chariot	Geburah to Binah (18th Path)
8	Strength	Geburah to Chesed (19th Path)
9	Hermit	Tiphareth to Chesed (20th Path)
10	Wheel of Fortune	Netzach to Chesed (21st Path)
11	Justice	Tiphareth to Geburah (22nd Path)
12	Hanged Man	Hod to Geburah (23rd Path)
13	Death	Netzach to Tiphareth (24th Path)
14	Temperance	Yesod to Tiphareth (25th Path)
15	Devil	Hod to Tiphareth (26th Path)
16	Tower	Hod to Netzach (27th Path)
17	Star	Yesod to Netzach (28th Path)
18	Moon	Malkuth to Netzach (29th Path)
19	Sun	Yesod to Hod (30th Path)
20	Judgment	Malkuth to Hod (31st Path)
21	World	Malkuth to Yesod (32nd Path)
22	Fool	Chokmah to Kether (11th Path)

We begin as we did above, by translating our birth date into numbers. In determining the personal Sephira, we kept reducing the number until it was 10 or less because there are ten sephiroth on the Tree of Life. In determining our personal life path, we reduce only until the birth date number is 22 or less because there are 22 tarot trumps, each corresponding to one of the 22 paths of wisdom.

SAMPLE:
March 1, 1960 = 3+1+1+9+6+0 = 20 = The Judgment Card = Path of Malkuth to Hod (31st Path)

By using the table on the previous page, we can determine which tarot card applies to our birth date. From that tarot card, we can determine the path we have come to truly work with. By examining that path we can discern which energies will play upon us more strongly throughout our life. We can explore more fully the path our soul has chosen to walk towards mastership in this lifetime.

The imagickal techniques, pathworkings and meditations on that path will reveal much insight into our life experiences. It can even reveal how close or far off we are from our soul's original intentions. Work with this life path can also reveal to us how best to get our lives back on track.(Keep in mind though that we always have free will, and even though we may have chosen a particular path prior to our incarnation, we do not have to hold to it. It can be more difficult when we change our course though, and it can explain many of the circumstances we have experienced.)

One other method that can reveal further insights into our soul's potentials and tasks is by examining the path associated with our astrological sign. It is not as specific as the path of the actual birth date, but its energies will also be reflected within our life to some degree.

Remember that we use the Qabala - the sephiroth and the paths of wisdom - to expand our awareness of who we are and what we can do. We use it for revelation and transformation. Connecting them all, finding and exploring all of the various correspondences, will provide much to assist us in our own great alchemical changes in life.

Chapter Seven

Creating Astral Doorways

"...in your own Bosom you bear your Heaven
And Earth and all you behold; tho' it appears Without it is Within,
In your Imagination of which this World of Mortality is but a Shadow."

- William Blake

When we first begin to work with the Qabala and all of its inherent energies, some tremendous benefits come to us. First and foremost, it shifts our attention away from the physical world and its problems to the magnificence and wonder of the Divine within ourselves and our lives. We begin to recognize that there are many wonderful dimensions to life - some much less tangible than what we may have ever experienced, but just as real.

The symbols we use to bridge and create doorways between the levels of our mind, also serve to create bridges and doorways to other realms of life. Thus, in the process of working with the Tree of Life, we begin to experience a great increase in psychic and astral phenomena. Dreams become more colorful, lucid and even prophetic. Our own psychic sensibilities will become heightened, manifesting in a variety of ways.

As anyone who works with the Qabala for any length of time will soon learn, the paths linking the different levels of consciousness are also paths to other planes and dimensions. We will not be exploring these other dimensions to any degree within this text, but the methods of opening doors between our levels of consciousness and the methods of opening the doors to those other realms are very similar.

As we learn to create astral doorways for our individual pathworkings, we are also laying the foundation for opening consciously the doorways to other planes and dimensions at the same time. As a result, we will increasingly experience phenomena associated with those more subtle dimensions. In fact, pathworking can be a wonderful exercise for developing the ability to explore those ethereal realms of life. Through pathworking we learn to open and close doorways to those more subtle realms at will.

Many terms have been given to the exploration of these other planes - particularly that which in the Western world has come to be known as the astral plane. Some of the more common terms for the exploration of those subtle realms are astral travel, astral projection, scrying in the spirit, and rising on the planes. The terms are not always synonymous, but they are techniques for opening to and exploring the subtle realms of life.

The one commonality among all of them is that they all involve at least two primary steps. The first involves energizing and strengthening our own subtle energies (our own astral body) through clearing out and accessing other levels of consciousness. The second step they all have in common is learning to use our subtle energies as an independent vehicle for expanding our consciousness.

Working with various symbols and images (such as the Qabalistic ones) and using meditation techniques (such as pathworking) starts the process of energizing and strengthening. And there is as much to manifest in our lives just through intense energizing as there is through trying to develop an independent vehicle of consciousness. The psychic/ astral phenomena listed on page 254 is but a small sampling.

The second, which involves such things as astral projection, is often sought before the first one has occurred. Usually because there's a bit of glamour attached to it. When this is done though without proper preparation, it leads to imbalances on all levels. It is comparable to attempting intricate gymnastic movements without proper stretching, training and practice. it will result in injury that can prevent participation of any substantial degree throughout the rest of this incarnation period.

Fast is not always better, and when it comes to working with the more subtle realms of life and the more intricate energies of our essence, taking our time and learning proper techniques is most essential. The techniques and tools provided in this book will enable you to develop increasingly greater capacities that will ultimately lead to conscious out of body experiences.

3 Forces that Impact the Astral Plane

The astral plane and other subtle dimensions are very fluid, changeable realms of existence. Unless we are able to discriminate (the lesson associated with Malkuth in the Tree of Life), we will find ourselves blown hither and yon by all of the subtle manifestations of those realms. The Qabala - with its well-established sign posts - enables us to open to those subtle realms with the least danger of delusion and deception. The proper use of these symbolic signposts requires practice and persistence.

This is why pathworking is so powerful. It not only bridges the various levels of consciousness within us, but it opens bridges between our mundane world and the less substantial dimensions (the spiritual worlds) operating around us. When this occurs, we cannot deny the reality of some divine force within the universe.

This process also opens us to three of the most powerful expressions of that divine force. Through pathworking with the Tree of Life, we discover that these three forces are predominant within *all* dimensions, if we learn to open to them in a controlled and balanced manner. Through our work with the Qabala we will learn to wield them within our lives. These forces are:

1. The Force of Imagination

Through thought and/or action, the imagination opens us to higher realms and levels of consciousness, enabling us to make contact with those beings who can serve as our teachers and provide us with assistance.

2. The Force of Light

There arises increased awareness of how light manifests within all realms and dimensions to bestow greater wisdom, perception, love and bliss.

3. The Force of Sound

We begin to realize that everything that the Divine is and does in all worlds manifests through the creative expression of sound. We learn to create through the power of words, music and sounds.

Psychic and Astral Phenomena of Pathworking

1. **Mediumship**
2. **Apportation**
3. **Materialization**
4. **Precipitation**
5. **Clairvoyance**
6. **Clairsentience**
7. **Levitation**
8. **Spirit Lights**
9. **Firehandling**
10. **Transmutation of metals**
11. **Production of fire**
12. **Psychic and spiritual healings**
13. **Spirit communications**
14. **Animal and nature communication**
15. **Lucid dreaming**

Astral Keys and the Spiritual Explorer

The ancient Qabalists knew that if we tried to explore the subtler dimensions, we could open ourselves to wide barrage of energies that might not be controlled. Because of this, they explored the universe in a very controlled and directed manner, using the Tree of Life diagram as their map. The various images and symbols became road markers, guiding you from one level of consciousness to the next, assisting you in finding your way through it. The images and symbols are keys to the astral dimension and the subtle forces that permeate all of our lives - often without us being aware.

These images, symbols, colors and various correspondences will help us in several ways as we become spiritual explorers through the Qabalistic Tree of Life:

1. They exercise our spiritual muscles.

Many times our spiritual and psychic "muscles" - just like our physical muscles - will atrophy if we do not use them. The work with the various symbols and images, along with exercises like that which follows in this chapter, serve to exercise these abilities. They stir our psychic muscle circulation. They stretch our abilities, loosening them and strengthening them. They restore the flow of blood, so to speak, so we can awaken, use and control our spiritual and psychic muscles and potentials more effectively.

2. They open and close astral doorways, prevent our getting lost among the subtleties and ever-changing energies of the astral dimensions.

When we open to the Tree of Life and the other dimensions permeating it, the symbols, images and correspondences help us to keep track of where we are. They protect us from accidentally wandering off our path or work with the Tree. Sometimes new images will show up, but if they are not in conjunction with those with which we are familiar and with which we are working, it is very often an indicator we have wandered off track. By focusing upon the image and symbol we have chosen - or by using the divine names of the path we are working - we dissipate any intrusive forces, and we create a doorway back to our correct location. They provide a built in safety line to our normal state of consciousness. (Specific techniques for doing this will be provided later.)

3. They also help us to open and clear the pathways between the different levels of consciousness.

The symbols and images often act like faucets by which we can control the flow of energy into our normal, waking consciousness. Through them, we learn to turn the energy on and off at will. The exercise "Creating Astral Doorways" - which follows in this chapter - is one that applies specifically to this process.

Working with the symbols and images can be compared to cleaning out clogged pipes or pruning out the dead limbs and leaves of a Tree. Our own psychic and spiritual pipes may be clogged with misconceptions, misinformation, fears, doubts, and limitations (self-imposed or otherwise). We, as a living Tree, may find ourselves smothering from stunted growth and dead limbs because of it. By working with the Tree and its images, we clean out the pipes and shake loose the debris - the dead limbs and leaves - to restore to the Tree (ourselves) greater flow. In turn we then have more and freedom and ability to stretch and grow fuller.

4. They assist us in accessing specific forces within ourselves and the universe.

The symbols and images open doors to ever-deepening levels of consciousness and ever-increasing new realms and dimensions. The various correspondences for the sephiroth and the paths are ways of controlling and directing the manifestations of these energies and dimensions within our lives.

The techniques in this book enable us to access all the levels of consciousness represented by the Tree of Life. They are designed to increasingly bridge the various levels to each other and our normal waking consciousness. In order to gain the greatest benefit from all of the exercises, we must become familiar with the symbols and images before we employ them. It is important to understand how they operate if we are to use them for our greatest benefit.

At first the symbols and images may seem too complicated and intricate, there being so many symbols and images associated with the Tree of Life. This is where the journal becomes an invaluable tool. The initial work may seem cumbersome, but eventually the use and understanding will grow. We begin to see increasing correspondences, and they begin to teach us aspects of the universe beyond the mundane teachings we have had.

Keep in mind throughout that the work with the symbols (whether using them to open astral doors or as reflections of spiritual gifts) reflect powerful archetypal energies. They will stir those archetypal forces up and release them into our daily lives. Through them, we begin to realize that the individual sephiroth are storehouses of our potentials, and the pathworking becomes a generator for setting the energy into motion so we can unfold those potentials.

As we work with the pathworking exercises within this book - whether preliminary or the actual working - energies will be released that will clean out our inner channels. It will point out where the bridges need to be repaired. *The energy will manifest in a myriad of ways according to how we use the symbols and images.* The symbols and images are keys but we must still find our own way of using them within our life. That is part of the responsibility of the true spiritual explorer. And it begins with learning to use them as keys to open the spiritual doors to human potentials and other dimensions.

EXERCISE:

Creating Astral Doorways

Benefits:

- **develops visualization and creative imagination**
- **ability to form and empower images for psychic and spiritual use**
- **opens and closes doors between levels of the mind and other dimensions**

This exercise will make all of the pathworking exercises of the following chapters more effective. It helps strengthen our visualization and creative imagination skills to more dynamically activate the energies of the various symbols. And there are a number of tools and techniques that can assist us in this.

All of the paths connect two levels of consciousness. Because of this, there must be a door exiting from one level and a door opening into the next. The exercises in this chapter will teach you to use specific symbols to create astral doorways. They will also enable you to open and close the astral doors at will. Ultimately this will help you if you encounter energies while pathworking that make you uncomfortable. If that happens, then you can create an appropriate astral doorway and leave the pathworking scenario, closing the door behind you.

In the next chapter we will explore a variety of pathworking techniques that we can use or adapt. Before working with them though, it is much more effective to first learn to open and close the doors between the levels of the mind and the various dimensions. This is where the symbols and images of the various sephiroth and the paths come into play.

It is for this reason, that every Qabalistic student should study and develop at some point a basic knowledge of symbology - specifically of the Hebrew letters (including their meanings), astrological glyphs and the tarot images. These three can be tremendous aids to meditation in general, but more importantly, they are powerful tools for releasing the energies of the Tree of Life. For the purposes of this work, we will learn to use these symbols to create the primary astral doorways for exploring the paths and making the entire tree more dynamic within your own life.

Keep in mind though that all of the symbols (Hebrew letter, astrological glyph, the color, the tarot card, etc.) can be used to create the doorways between the sephiroth. Our focus will be primarily upon the primary ones. Familiarizing yourself with these basic symbols and images of the path is most beneficial before attempting the actual pathworking. It will enable you to achieve better results.

Take time to develop the visualizations of this exercise so that the astral doorways can be effectively used throughout the rest of this work and your life. Visualize, imagine, taste, touch, smell, hear and feel everything! Focus only upon the images and ideas of this exercise. These are the warm-ups. They loosen your psychic and spiritual muscles for the greater pathworkings ahead.

Preliminary Preparations:

1. Find a comfortable place where you can perform the exercises undisturbed.

Remove the phone from its hook, and let others in the environment know not to disturb you.

2. Choose the two sephiroth that you wish to bridge.

Initially, I recommend that the pathworking be done in order from the bottom of the Tree of Life up. In other words, begin with path 32, Malkuth to Yesod, and work up to path 11, Chokmah to Kether. Leave at least a week or two between pathworkings, so that you will be able to more clearly discern their effects within your daily life. Then once the entire Tree has been worked, feel free to "mix and match", according to your desires or goals.

3. Having chosen the two sephiroth and the path, review and familiarize yourself with the symbols, colors and other images associated with each, and the path that joins them.

4. Using the quick reference chart on the following page, light a candle for the color of each sephiroth.

Also light incense or create a blend of essential oils for each of the two sephiroth. The candles and incense will set up a vibration in the area that will facilitate a triggering of the energies from both levels of consciousness. They will stimulate and awaken both levels of consciousness within us, making it easier to join them through the pathworking. To further enhance this, you may wish to use a meditation stone from each of the two levels.

Some fragrances won't seem to blend well together. This varies from individual to individual, from time to time, and from path to path. When they do not seem to blend together well for us, it is significant. Often these are signals times tells us that some levels of our consciousness are more difficult to harmonize than others. Some may need more work than others. The more often we work the paths throughout the Tree of Life, the mixed vibrations will become less discordant.

5. Once these preparations have been made, close your eyes to eliminate visual distractions. Then slowly perform a progressive relaxation.

Focus upon each part of the body, from head to toe and back again. Imagine and feel warm, relaxing feelings filling and soothing each part of the body in turn.

This exercise for creating the astral doorways should take no longer than 20-30 minutes. As you develop your abilities, you will find that this time will be shortened tremendously. Do not hurry it. And do not get upset if the mind wanders. Just bring your attention back to the image you are supposed to be focusing upon. Remember that we are training the subconscious mind to work for us and to focus its energies upon what we want.

You may have to repeat the refocusing, if you mind wanders a lot. Each time you do though, you send a message to the subconscious that trains it to follow your directions and your will even more fully. Eventually you will develop through this exercise the ability to form, empower and then dissolve images and energies of the archetype to which it is linked.

6. The following exercise will work with any two sephiroth. We are simply using Malkuth and Yesod.

Through this exercise, we will learn to open the door that leads from Malkuth to Yesod. At some point in our work with the Tree of Life, we will start in Yesod and open the door leading down to Malkuth.

Energy ascends and descends, and we must learn to work with the Tree from both directions (bottom to top and top to bottom) because the energy and effects within our life differ according to the direction. Everything within us and within our world is polarized, and we must learn to work from both poles to be complete. Each direction opens a flow of energy into manifestation with its own intensity. This is why it is important to learn to use the symbols as astral doorways. We can then open and shut the flow as we desire to any degree we desire.

Candle and Fragrance Chart

Sephira	Color of Candle	Fragrances
Kether	white	frankincense, ambergris
Chokmah	gray	eucalyptus, musk, geranium
Binah	black	myrrh, chamomile
Chesed	blue	bayberry, cedar, nutmeg
Geburah	red	cinnamon, tobacco, cypress
Tiphareth	yellow	rose, jasmine, lily
Netzach	green	patchouli, rose, bayberry
Hod	orange	rosemary, frangipani, mints
Yesod	violet	wisteria, lavender, honeysuckle
Malkuth	citrine, olive russet or black	sandalwood, lemon, carnation

Creating Astral Doorways

We begin as always outside the Tree of Life. You step through the small opening and into the inner darkness of the tree. The feelings are warm, comfortable and familiar. This truly is your Tree of Life. And you know that there is nothing in it that can harm you as long as you do not give into your own doubts and fears.

You breathe deeply and begin the process of calling the temple into life. Into the blackness of the inner Tree, you softly intone, "Adonai ha Aretz."

The blackness shifts around you, becoming an olive green.

Again you speak the divine name.

"Adonai ha Aretz."

The olive green shimmers, becoming the color of russet and autumn. Now you begin to see the inner temple. You can make out the large stone alter, with its lamp. You can see the three baskets and the statue of the young maiden.

A third time you speak the divine name for the Temple of Malkuth.

"Adonai ha Aretz."

The russet shimmers, and a soft citrine, sunshine fills the inner temple and everything within it stands out clearly. You are still amazed at your ability to call forth form out of what seemed nothingness.

You stand within the temple. The baskets are overflowing. The lamp shines brightly upon the altar. The pillars stand strong on either side of the altar. You know that you are in the temple of Malkuth. You know that you are home, and you breathe deeply.

Suddenly, the sound of stone grinding against stone fills the temple. It penetrates you like fingernails scraped against a chalkboard. You turn to see the entrance through which you entered the tree closing behind you - sealing you into the temple. For a moment you panic, frightened, but then you remember that this temple is yours. If opened once, then surely you have the power to open it again.

You turn once more to the altar, and from behind it steps the young woman, crowned as if stepping down from a throne. The magickal image of the Temple of Malkuth has come to life. About her is the fragrance of new mown hay, of spring flowers and summer innocence. There is an air of quiet confidence about her, as if the entire world belongs to her. The world and all of its treasures are her inheritance.

She smiles and says, "All that you need to move anywhere within the Tree has been given to you. But knowing and doing are often very different. The two must be brought together if true understanding is to come forth."

She steps back from the altar and fades from sight as if melting through the walls. It is then that you remember the symbols that open the paths, leading to others levels within the Tree of Life.

Yesod is closest to Malkuth. It runs straight up the middle pillar. You pause, bringing to mind the symbols governing that path. You bring to mind the Hebrew letter tav. You visualize it, projecting its image against the back wall, behind the altar. You see the energy flowing out from you and gathering against the wall, like heat off a road on a hot summer's day.

Then it stops.

You must concentrate harder. Again you visualize the Hebrew letter tau. You visualize it as if it is carved or engraved into the wall itself. It begins to take form. It grows in clarity, and as it stands out against the wall, a door forms around it! As you concentrate, holding the focus upon the symbol and the newly formed door around it, the door swings open. Through the open doorway you see a path leading out from the Temple of Malkuth. Far in the distance you see the violet Temple of Yesod with the symbol of the moon shining upon it. The path itself is a crystalline indigo, and you smile, thrilled by your accomplishment.

Mentally, you close the door. The Hebrew letter and the door begin to fade, and you feel the energy drawing back into you. And you are standing once more, looking at a blank wall.

Next, you bring to mind the astrological glyph of Saturn for this path. You project it against the wall, seeing it engraved upon it. You focus upon it until it stands out clearly, and when it is fully formed, a door manifests around it. As you concentrate on both, the door swings open to reveal that same crystalline indigo path leading to the distant Temple of Yesod.

Then you close the door, allowing the astrological symbol and door around it to dissolve. You feel the energy moving back into you, reabsorbed by you.

You smile broadly, amazed at what you are doing. You are beginning to see the power of your own thoughts.

Now you decide to try the tarot card. This you know may be a little more difficult, requiring a little more concentration because it is a more intricate image. You focus upon the back wall again, and you begin to visualize the World card as a life size image against that wall. You concentrate, focusing, and slowly the image begins to take form upon the wall.

As you focus, the card begins to shimmer, melting into the wall itself. It takes on three dimensional proportions, as if you could just step up to it and just walk into the scenery of the card itself. In the distance, behind the primary image of the card you see again the Temple of Yesod.

You realize triumphantly that you have found the doorway to the path leading from Malkuth to Yesod. Slowly you allow the picture to dissolve. It loses its three dimensional form and appears like a simple painting hung upon the wall. Then it too begins to dissolve, and you feel the energy moving back into you.

You realize that now you can create the doorway through any of these keys - the Hebrew letter, the astrological glyph and even the tarot card. You now understand that this is the way to open the doorways between all of the temples. And you understand the young maiden's words more fully. With practice, it will become easier to use any and all of the symbols - not only to bridge levels of the mind but to link other dimensions with our more mundane life.

You look around the temple of Malkuth, and you see that there is still no doorway out of the Tree. It is still sealed. You are puzzled. You now understand and know the symbols and images that open the doorways to allow you free movement with the Tree of Life, but how do you get out? What symbol or image opens the doorway to exit the tree and return to your normal state of consciousness? Maybe the divine name?

You step to the altar, pause and take a deep breath. Slowly you intone the divine name for Malkuth again.

"Adonai ha Aretz".

The bowl of water sitting upon the altar begins to bubble. You look down into it, and it is like looking into a deep well. The water settles and an image begins to form at the bottom. it is simple. It is personal. For some it is a color, for others a geometric shape. For some it is a flower, and for others it is more intricate. It can be a design of anything, but it is a symbol which has significance for you. And as you look upon that image in the bottom of the bowl, you begin to understand why you have been drawn to it most of your life.

The image in the bowl fades, and you turn to face where the entrance to your tree used to be. Just as with the symbols for the paths, you visualize this symbol and you project it against the back of the Tree of Life. It begins to take shape, manifesting clearly as if engraved into the Tree itself. Slowly a door forms around it and it opens to the outer world. You smile, amazed.

You turn back to face the altar and offer an expression of gratitude for what has been revealed. You take some nourishment from each of the baskets, and then stand back to close the temple. You tone the divine name three times, watching as the temple goes from citrine to russet to olive and to black - until you call it into being once more.

You turn and step from the tree into the outer world, bringing with you the gifts and a greater realization of your own growing abilities and power. You turn to the Tree and you see your personal symbol upon the doorway to the inner Tree.

This is your image, your personal symbol of power for the inner workings of the mind and the various dimensions. It will provide protection, and you know that if ever lost or confused while working in your Tree of Life, this symbol will create a doorway that will allow you to exit safely. It will allow you to return to your normal state of consciousness.

It is a private symbol of power for you and you alone. The more you learn about it and use it, the more it will do for you. Realizing this deeply, you allow the image and the doorway around it to dissolve and become reabsorbed back into you - into your heart. Your Tree of Life is sealed shut, until you open it - which will be your task from this day forth.

You breathe deeply, and you feel yourself returning to your normal state of consciousness, more alive with possibilities than ever before!

This technique for creating astral doorways should be practiced for each level upon the Tree of Life and for each path. It can even be done as a prelude to the actual pathworkings described later. It will help empower them and manifest even more dynamic results.

Practice entering into the Tree - into each individual Sephira and practice forming all doors that lead to other sephiroth from it. This will serve several distinct functions. It demonstrates that we each can - through the symbols - open doors that lead to every level of consciousness. It reveals that we each have the ability of opening and closing astral doorways in a controlled and concentrated manner.

It also manifests our own individual, creative power symbol for protection and balance throughout all of our work with the Tree of Life. In essence, it becomes a power totem to serve us while working with the energies of the Tree, especially ion the very changeable level of the astral plane and other dimensions.

As we grow and expand our own consciousness, this personal symbol may change from time to time. Usually this occurs when it is time to work with the energies of the Tree of Life on a much higher level than we have done previously.

All
pathworkings
have a
guardian aspect
for security, safety
and balance.
These are the divine names, the
archangelic energies and your
personal symbol.
The divine names will
dissolve inappropriate
energies and images.
The personal symbol
will provide for you
an emergency exit.

Chapter Eight

Pathworking Techniques

"Things will happen in the time, manner and means that is best for us if we allow them to - in other words - if we do what we can and must and then allow the events to play themselves out appropriately."
- Law of Synchronicity

When we begin to bridge the various levels of our consciousness through pathworking, we are inviting a whole series of initiations. These will manifest through the normal experiences within the day to day life. This is why most of the ancient masters taught their students and disciples to "be ever watchful". Our greatest growth does not always come with easily recognized spiritual beeps and buzzers, alerting us to pay attention.. Our growth occurs through daily life circumstances. When we work with the Qabala, we are developing the ability to observe the subtle interplay between our spiritual activities and our mundane life circumstances.

Pathworking shows us both common and uncommon relationships in our lives. In order though to recognize them for what they are and to assist our expanded awareness through them, watchfulness is absolutely necessary. This is why the pathworking journal can be such a powerful tool. The symbols on the paths and throughout every aspect of the Tree of Life reflect specific energies of the universe. When we learn to consciously use them in a specified manner, those abstract energies come into very tangible expression within our lives. Remember the axiom: *"All energy follows thought!"*

Pathworking triggers an awareness of synchronicity within our lives. *"Synchronicity, as described by Carl Jung, is when events coincide relatively within the same period and cluster around a central dynamic or value which gives meaning to the whole. It is not quite simply events occurring at the same time that creates synchronicity, but rather events occurring in simultaneous relation to each other to produce meaning. It is present when extraordinary coincidence is experienced within a larger context of meaning - both in terms of a person's own life journey and in terms of universal principles."* (Strephon Kaplan-Williams, *Jungian-Senoi Dreamwork Manual.* California: Journey Press, 1985; p. 268.)

With pathworking, as in life, experiences with the good and bad will occur and should be expected. Greater power will be given to see how we handle it. Temptation in many forms will arise. Tests of character and stress will be encountered, and our values will be challenged both inwardly and outwardly within our life. By working the paths on the Tree of Life, we are inviting the tests so that we can attain the rewards.

And rewards of both the spiritual and mundane should be expected. Both will manifest clearly and strongly. Greater power will be given in all situations of life. Our vision and perceptions will increase tremendously. We will find that which we thought beyond our control is no further from us than we allow it to be. We will see the reality of our dreams, and we will know the joy of setting them in motion and re-creating our life along any lines we desire. We discover that we are never given a hope, wish or dream without also being given opportunities to make them a reality. That is the journey of life.

The Pathworking Journey

Most pathworking techniques are meditations of journeys. The journey reflects the archetypal energies of growth within our lives. The function of the meditational journey and its symbols determine the specific manifestations within our lives.

The use of magickal and mythical journeys in our meditational and imagickal processes enables us to take a more active role in our own growth and unfoldment. It enables us to learn how to align ourselves with the forces of the universe, rather than be at odds with it. It enables us to work directly with the principle of correspondence that we discussed earlier.

When we create a magickal journey, we create a series of images and actions empowered with specific symbols. These are then played out within our minds in an altered state of consciousness. The relaxed state enables us to activate greater inner energies, which are empowered by the symbols.

We use the power of our imagination - controlled, directed and enhanced through the use of specific symbols - to elicit specific results. The journey becomes then a symbolic representation of that which we are wishing to manifest, overcome or grow within our day-to-day life. This can include greater clairvoyance, higher tests and initiation, prosperity, love, encounters with those of like mind, the overcoming of obstacles and pretty much anything we desire.

Imagination is one of our greatest assets, but we must learn to use it in a consciously controlled manner, or it becomes little more than uncontrolled fancy. It is a human potential that can be developed to enhance and augment our lives. It is not an escape tool but an unfoldment tool. It is a powerful means to directing specific images to manifest what we need. Through pathworking journeys, we develop this ability.

Through the imagickal journey, we build a story much like a normal daydream. The difference is though that we are a part of it and it follows a prescribed pattern. It also is infused with specific symbols. There are a variety of ways of doing this. We can construct our own or even use traditional myths and tales as the backbone.

As we will discus more fully later, many times archetypal energies impress themselves upon and within myths and tales to elicit higher learning and consciousness. The ancient figures, images and actions within them are steeped in this energy. They have a powerful thoughtform connected to them. When we use a particular tale, or create a pathworking similar to it, we align ourselves with that energy. This triggers a powerful release of it into our lives.

The four exercises that follow within this chapter build upon each other. We begin with a simple temple-to-temple journey that we can adapt and infuse with greater creative imagination. This empowers it and its impact within our lives. From there we move to more intricate scenarios, such as with tarot pathworking, ultimately leading to the use of ancient myths and tales which in turn leads to creating our own pathworking rituals. Utilizing these formats, we develop greater capability with handling and directing the subtle energies within our lives. They are powerful training tools that we will use time and again through the rest of our lives.

Preliminary Considerations to any Pathworking

In the beginning of pathworking, do no more than one per week. In fact you may wish to wait two weeks in between in order to see how the energies play out in your daily life. Sometimes it is even more effective to repeat the path several days in a row to intensify the experience, but remember that the energies of the path and the two sephiroth will all be activated. And make sure that you have familiarized yourself with the symbols and images prior to the working.

Do not work two paths together. For example, don't do the path from Malkuth to Yesod and continue right on to Tiphareth. We need time to synthesize the experience and discern clearly how the energies are playing within our life. If we activate too much, we won't be able to determine what set what in motion. Working two paths will complicate the situation.

As mentioned earlier in the text, we are each touching the paths at different levels based upon our own personal growth and development. These paths though are also links to astral and other dimensions. The more we use them and their symbolic keys, the easier it will be to recognize and move consciously within those dimensions. Also the more we use them, the stronger the effect they will have upon our physical life. The astral world though is a world where things change and dissolve as soon as the mind is taken off of them. This is why familiarity with specific symbols is so essential. It is why focus and concentration are important to develop when working with them.

Other people will be using these symbols and these paths. Sometimes people and images appear that are out of context or with which we are not familiar. When this happens, leave them alone until you can test them and find what relates to you and what does not.

IMPORTANT NOTE:

All pathworkings have a guardian aspect for security, safety and balance. These are the divine names, the archangelic energies and your personal symbol. The divine names will dissolve any inappropriate energies and images. The personal symbol will provide for you an emergency exit. It is also good to visualize yourself in the company of the archangel of the temple you begin with.

All meditations, journeys, and imagickal pathworkings have a beginning, middle and end. Most will begin inside the Tree where the Temple of Malkuth is found most easily. Malkuth is one step removed from our day-to-day consciousness and life. If our work or exercise is interrupted, simply visualize the Temple of Malkuth. From it you can easily step from the Tree, and you will be brought back to your normal state of consciousness - safely.

There should be no interruptions when performing your pathworkings. Make sure the phone is off the hook and that you will not be disturbed. Pathworking is a form of deep meditation, and all altered states of consciousness induce a hyper aesthetic state in us. We become highly sensitive. Sounds are more shattering, and lights are more penetrating. Unexpected interruptions are upsetting to the nervous system.

Use as many aids as you find comfortable to help you. Incense, candles, crystals and music set a tone and energy that facilitates our work. Guidelines for their use were given earlier. The atmosphere in which we operate is extremely important to a successful performing of the imagickal pathworking exercises.

Every path contains milestones or markers to help you identify the right path once you have started. This is why previewing the symbols and images of the paths helps. If you do not see them in any form along the path, or if the path changes color, it usually indicates that you have wandered off track. Returning your focus by visualizing the path in the appropriate color or by visualizing it into existence as you did in the exercise "Creating Astral Doorways" will keep you on track. If that becomes difficult, focus on the Temple of Malkuth, return to it, and exit the Tree. It may be that this is not the time to attempt that particular path.

It is good to plan on seeing the symbols of the path somewhere along the path itself. It is easy to do, especially if you use the methods of creating the pathworking scenarios yourself. These are described later in this chapter. The symbols are the key to a successful pathworking. They relate to the energies of the path itself and they serve as a catalyst for the archetypal forces. They keep us connected to those spiritually subtle energies of the path.

There may arise a time along the path when you feel you cannot complete the working. Maybe you are uncomfortable with the energies. Maybe you are feeling a little fearful or doubtful. Do not be upset by this! *And above all, honor that!* Ultimately you know what you can handle and at what rate. There is no sense in traumatizing yourself. It won't help you grow any more. Simply visualize the Temple of Malkuth, and allow yourself to return to it. Then exit the Tree. Work on the sephiroth or other paths until you feel comfortable working the one that created the distress. Emotional upset can occur during a pathworking, and although it often reflects that we have successfully accessed the archetypal forces there, part of our development requires that we honor ourselves by not traumatizing ourselves in the growing process.

Some pathworkings will have immediate effects upon your life. Others may take weeks or even months before their manifestation and impacts will be fully recognized. *Be assured, they will have an impact. They will affect your life on all levels.*

Initiation involves change and growth. Through pathworking, we hasten that process. The phrase, "Be careful what you ask for because you may receive it" is quite appropriate. When you work with the Qabala and imagickal pathworking, you are asking for a complete awakening - not just enough to satisfy curiosity or a need for psychic thrills. The energy released and its effects are often stronger than we imagined.

Some of the more abstract paths and levels can be the most powerful and the most effective. Some that we would expect to have the least impact may have the most. Not everyone will be affected the same way. We each are progressing and developing in our own unique manner. The energy released will play within our lives in a unique manner. But every word, phrase and picture can trigger chain reactions which rise to the surface within our life.

There is freedom within the paths and the visual images created through the workings. This is why the most powerful and effective pathworkings are those in which we create the scenario in accordance with the energies and symbols of the path itself. This technique is described later in this chapter, and through it the archetypal energies will play more dynamically and uniquely within our lives. This is what makes it such an individual and yet vital growth process. It will amplify the effects.

Most importantly, do not make the mistake of thinking that these techniques are an excuse for daydreaming and psychic thrill-seeking! They are so much more than mere fantasy, and such assumptions will be devastated by the truth of their power being driven home!

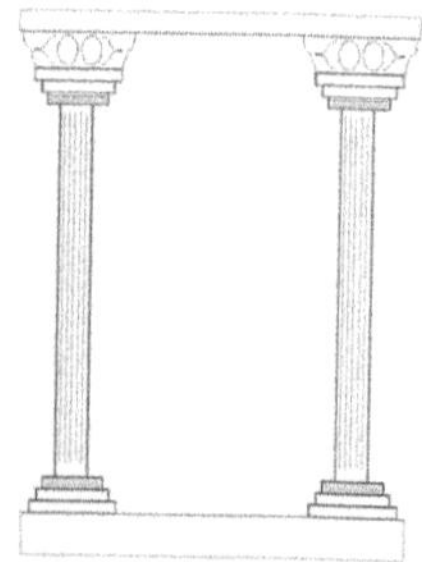

EXERCISE:

Temple to Temple Visitations

Benefits:

- bridges levels of the subconscious
- opens up hidden talents
- opens up the astral plane

Each Sephira is actually a temple of consciousness in which our more universal capacities reside. In this imagickal pathworking, we use these temples of the mind as starting points and destinations, thereby bridging the energies of two levels of consciousness more strongly.

In the past we learned to activate different levels of consciousness for greater *illumination.* We are now linking the levels that will release the energies and manifest conditions for *initiation.* We will manifest situations that will help us to apply that illumination more fully within our life.

We always start by entering the Tree of Life. Once inside, we awaken the temple and, as we learned in the last chapter, we create a doorway that opens to the path that leads to the next temple. For this exercise, we will use the Hebrew letter of the astrological glyph for the path. (All techniques in this book build upon each other. If we have been consciously exercising this creative ability, there should be no difficulty at all.)

Through the doorway, we step out onto a path of the appropriate color, leading to the second temple. As we step onto the path, we are met by the archangels of the two sephiroth. We may choose to be met by the magickal images as well or instead of. These are our escorts. As you walk along the path, discuss with your escorts the purpose and function of the path and how its energies are likely to manifest within your life.

Along the way, various things may be encountered. These will vary somewhat from individual to individual, but the things encountered are markers that let you know that you have not wandered off the path. **THIS IS IMPORTANT!** We need the markers. On some paths there may be no companions. We may need to walk them alone - experiencing and synthesizing the energies for ourselves. Often in such cases, the archangelic influence may not appear until the destination is reached.

These markers should be planned for ahead of the actual working. If they are not seen, then it is important - as in the method of "Creating Astral Doorways" - that we visualize them into being. By doing so, we link ourselves back to the path if we have wandered. If we have not, it serves to make our connection to the path stronger.

The first marker is the **color of the path.** No matter how long the journey may seem, as long as you stay on the path of the appropriate color, we will ultimately reach our destination. I often visualize myself, dressed in the colors of the path with my clothing trimmed in the colors of the two sephiroth. It's just an added precaution.

Plan to encounter **a road mark** of some sort approximately halfway through the pathworking. This is the second marker. The road sign or marker should have the Hebrew letter for the path or the appropriate astrological symbol. This helps activate the energies and anchors us more strongly to the pathworking. I sometimes visualize a necklace with a medallion hanging from a tree, halfway through the working. Engraved into the medallion is one of the symbols for the particular path I am working. Sometimes I visualize the gifts of the path waiting for me at the halfway point.

Individuals other than your guides and escorts may appear upon the path. The more you learn about the path and its energies, the more significant they will become. There are many symbols and images that reflect the forces of the path.

With time and practice, you will learn to recognize when others that show up have something to do with the path itself.

Usually, **the individuals that are appropriate to the path will have insignias of the path on them.** Often times the insignias are the Hebrew letter or the astrological glyph. It may appear as an insignia upon the individual's attire or even upon the individual's body - such as a tattoo.

Guidelines for Temple to Temple Visitations

1. Fill in the journal for the path.

Review the basic symbology associated with it. Make sure to review the energies associated with each of the two sephiroth as well.

2. Set the appropriate atmosphere.

Choose appropriately colored candles and fragrances. Use them both simultaneously. Remember that pathworking is a linking of two distinct levels of consciousness. You may even wish to use a colored candle for each sephiroth and place between them a third candle of the color for the path, as a symbolic link between the two. If the appropriate color for the path can not be found, using a simple white candle will suffice very well.

The burning of incense and the use of candles sets up an energy vibration around you that resonates with the specific levels of consciousness. This facilitates tapping the energies within ourselves. If the fragrances do not seem to blend well, it may reflect that bridging the two levels may require a little more effort than expected. With the Qabala nothing is insignificant. As you work with the energies, the blending will become less discordant.

Having a place that you can use as an altar upon which to set the candles is very effective. Encircle them in some manner - such as with rope - to symbolize the tying together of these levels of our consciousness. This adds to the room's vibrations. The more significance and effort we put into preparations, the stronger the impact the pathworking will have upon the physical life.

3. Use stones and crystals to help you.

Earlier, I provided a list of stones and crystals whose energies are appropriate for the various levels of consciousness. Pick and hold a stone from each of the sephiroth in each of your hands. If a Sephira with which you will be working is located on the right-hand pillar of the Tree of Life, hold the appropriate stone in the right hand. If it is located on the left hand pillar, hold the stone in the left hand. Use the other hand for the other stone and its Sephira.

Another effective way of using the stones is to cup the hands upon the lap, holding both stones within them. There are also other ways of using crystals and stones, including using gem elixirs associated with the various Sephira. These are merely examples, and you should not limit yourself to them exclusively.

4. Use movements and physical activities to enhance the effects.

We can powerfully effect a change in consciousness through the use of movement in conjunction with our pathworking. This can be done to create a mindset before the working and to ground the energies solidly upon completion. Techniques for this will be described in Part Four. Some of the more basic movements are provided in my book *Secret Paths of the Qabala*.

5. Then begin your imagickal pathworking.

As in the previous imagickal workings, enter into the Tree of Life, creating a doorway into the Tree with your personal symbol. Call the temple into being. Remember that the temple should have basic accouterments:

- An altar standing between two pillars.

- An ever-burning lamp upon the altar.
- Stone statue of the magickal image of the temple
- Magickal gifts on or near the altar.
- Any other more individual aspects of the temple.

The temple will eventually become uniquely yours. In time it will take on a more personal feel with symbols and images that are unique to your own level of consciousness.

6. Create your astral doorway.

Using the Hebrew letter, the astrological glyph or even both, create an astral doorway at the back of the temple that opens and leads to the path and other Sephira. See the path in the appropriate color, and the second temple in the far distance.

7. Step through the doorway and out onto the path.

As you step through the doorway, pause to allow the archangels of the two temples to appear and greet you. The archangels should always greet you as you step through. They may not always accompany you on the path, but they should always greet you at the beginning and at the end. They are the guardians of the seekers, and even if it is a path that you must walk alone, they will always greet you first. (Sometimes the magickal images will do the greeting.) If they do not, step back into the temple and close the door.

As the figure of the archangels and/or magickal images step up, use the divine names to test them. If they are not truly your guardians for this path, their images will dissolve from view as you project the divine name of the temple. If they are the guardians, their images will become more distinct. The archangels expect this testing, and they will not be offended by it. Remember that other beings exist in this dimension, some of whom may not have your best interests at heart.

Having tested, begin to walk with the archangels along the path toward the second temple. As you journey, allow them to speak to you of your own life as it is reflected within this path. Allow them to tell you how the energies are likely to manifest within your daily life upon completion. As you walk with them, be sure and watch for your road markers. You may even wish to have the archangels provide insight into the significance for this path when you come across them.

Imagine them asking you questions as to why you wish to travel from one sphere to the next. Allow the teachers of this path - be they the archangels of the magickal images - to inform you of what you can expect. Allow them to lead you to the second temple.

When you arrive at the second temple, allow the archangels to present you with a gift that represents the energies of this path that you can take into the outer world with you. Sometimes you may find this gift waiting for you by the door of the second temple.

Using the Hebrew letter or astrological glyph, create a doorway into the second temple. Step into the darkness of the temple, and using the divine name for it, bring it to life, just as you did with the other temple. At this point you may wish to have the magickal images from both temples melt into you.

Thank the teachers, whether the archangels of the magickal images. Ask permission to return. Courtesy operates on all planes and dimensions!

Alternate toning the divine name of the first temple with that of the second. Repeat each alternately three times, to close both temples and the pathworking down. Then using your personal symbol, create a doorway to leave the Tree of Life, taking with you the gifts of the pathworking. Exit the Tree and allow the inner vision to dissipate so that it may manifest within the outer life.

8. Ground the energies.

At this point you may wish to repeat the physical movements or perform the "Banishing Ritual of the Pentagram" as described in Part Four to ground the energies and to seal tightly all doors. At least performing the balancing postures will help rid yourself of the "spacey" afterglow that often occurs with altered states of consciousness.

9. Wrap up the exercise.

Extinguish the candles. If the incense is still burning, allow it to burn out. As it does it carries your wishes for the pathworking to the heavens to work for you more fully. Make note of anything special that occurred or that you experienced in your pathworking journal.

10. A special reminder.

At your destination temple, pay attention to how the archangels and the magickal images relate to each other and to you. It is also good to take a few minutes at the end to contemplate and reflect upon what you have experienced. This will help you to put it in perspective more easily in the days ahead. Using the journal to write these reflections helps to bridge the inner world to the outer, ultimately eliciting greater insight!

EXERCISE:

Tarot Pathworking

Benefits:

- **develops tarot as a tool for divination and scrying**
- **helps strengthen astral plane connection**
- **strengthens the use of images for magickal processes**

There are forces in the universe that we barely understand or even recognize. Because we so often do not understand, we are afraid or hesitant to work with them. Given the correct information though, and by approaching such with common sense, we begin to realize that the physical world in which we are so strongly focused is just a minute part of all words that exist. Few of us realize until we consciously step out upon our own spiritual path that many of these worlds interpenetrate with our own.

This is why the Qabala teaches how to connect with beings who are companions in our journeys. These beings are the archangels, angels and the archetypal thoughtforms manifesting through such the magickal images and the tarot. Most of these guides and beings are disseminators of information. They help to illumine us about ourselves and our lives.

They are also protectors and companions. With the Qabala there is a built in safety check to insure that those forces we encounter are helpful and beneficial. This is why the divine names are so important. They represent the highest, most spiritual force at that particular level of consciousness, and thus they will dissipate anything that is not appropriate to the level at which we are working.

The names of the archangels and our ability to open and close doorways also serve to protect us. This includes the use of the tarot images for creating and exiting from the Tree of Life.

The tarot has a great mysticism about it. The images reflect specific archetypal forces that can be related directly to the Qabala. The exact date and place of the tarot's origin is not truly known. One theory holds that it arose out of ancient Egypt. Although the tarot may incorporate some archetypal images, many of which have correspondences to distant antiquity, the tarot as we know it today seems to have actually arisen around the time of the Renaissance.

And regardless of its origins, its applications and correspondence to the Qabala can not be denied. It is a tool that has great application to pathworking and divination through the Tree of Life. The tarot is a structured system of magical images.

In tarot pathworking, we bring the images within the tarot to life for pathworking purposes. This is part of the power of creative imagination. Magickal use of the imagination involves a practiced blend of deliberate and concentrated visualization. At the same time there must be spontaneous allowance of other images and symbols to arise in association with our primary scenario. This takes time and practice, but it is the work with the tarot images that develop this skill.

Work with the tarot cards in pathworking may be different from other pathworkings in several distinct ways. As with the other techniques, we converse with the character(s) in the cards. We may also hear other voices as well. File these other voices away for future meditation.

It is not unusual to discover that the scenery in the picture is different when you step into it. If after testing it with the divine names and it still remains different, don't assume you did anything wrong. This is actually a common experience.

Archetypal energies play upon each of us differently. It is what makes us each uniquely creative. If the color of the path is correct, and if the other symbols of the path are visible, and the image remains after testing it with the divine names, do not be concerned. It is the Tree of Life simply adapting itself more personally to you.

On the other hand, if there are no indications that you are where you are supposed to be, just step back into the temple. If the images dissolve when using the divine names, just return to the temple and try it again at another time.

Guidelines for Tarot Pathworking

The previous exercise is the basis for all of the pathworking techniques within this text. Before doing the others, it is beneficial to review the steps in it. Most of the others will follow the same format, with some unique variations and some special reminders.

1. Choose the starting temple and the path.

2. Set the tone for the Pathworking.

As before, choose the appropriate candles, fragrances, stones, etc. that will assist in shifting to the levels of consciousness appropriate for the working. Use candles for the two temples and for the path. A good technique is to hold the card in your lap or even place it between the two candles representing the two sephiroth with which you will be working.

3. Review the path.

Familiarize yourself with the tarot card and the primary images of the path you have chosen. You may wish to get a text on the tarot, and read what has been taught about the imagery of the tarot card you will be using for your pathworking. Become familiar with the card, its meaning, and its image. You should be able to bring to mind and hold the image of the card with your eyes closed. Record this information in your pathworking journal, along with all of the other basic information of the path.

4. Begin the pathworking.

Enter into the Tree of Life and bring the temple alive through the use of the divine name. See all of the aspects of the temple form themselves - i.e. the altar, the gifts, the magickal image, the pillars, etc.

Visualize the image of the tarot card, hanging like a picture against the back wall, behind the temple. As you focus upon it, see it becoming three dimensional, as if you can step into it. (Sometimes using the archangelic and divine name help the picture become more three-dimensional.

5. Step into the picture.

As you step into the picture, wait until the figure comes forward to greet you. See, feel, smell, and hear everything that you can within that scenario. When the figure approaches you, use the divine names to test it. If the figure dissipates, continue waiting. If the figure becomes more clear and distinct, then proceed.

6. Walk the path.

The figure from the tarot card walks the path (in the appropriate color) with you. This figure teaches you how the energies of this path through this card are likely to play within your life. The images of the tarot trump and the thoughtform energies built around them, become teachers to awaken your awareness. Let the figure at the end of the pathworking present you with a gift from the path to take into the outer world.

7. Look for your markers.

While walking the path, be sure to use your markers. Remember the astrological symbols and Hebrew letters all serve as markers to insure you haven't wandered off track. See these symbols imposed upon the scenery periodically as you walk the path.

8. Enter the second temple.

As you approach the second temple, visualize the tarot card as a doorway into it. Thank your guardian/teacher and step into the second temple. Call it into life, using the divine names. There you encounter both archangels. Allow them to present you with any special gifts or information from the pathworking.

9. Conclude the pathworking.

Using the divine names from both temples,, as taught in the previous exercise, allow the temple to close down. Then using your personal symbol, create a doorway out of the Tree of Life, bringing your gifts out with you.

10. Ground the energies.

Absorb your personal symbol back into you so that the door to the inner Tree is closed. Then perform some of the grounding exercises, the physical movements or postures described in Part Four. You may even wish to perform the banishing exercise to more strongly seal the Tree of Life. Fill in your journal, noting what you learned, felt and experienced through this pathworking.

EXERCISE:

Pathworking through Tales and Legends

Benefits:

- **reveals hidden mysteries of myths and tales**
- **awakens magic of mythical imagery**
- **prepares us for astral journeys**

As you become familiar with the various energies and associations of the paths, you begin to realize that there are certain myths, tales, and legends that strongly correspond to these same energies. Some of these were listed for each path in part two.

Many of the ancient myths and tales contain keys to understanding the mysteries of the universe. These mysteries were often veiled in myths so that anyone who desired could seek them out. The images, the characters, and the actions within the tales often reflect archetypal energies and lessons. We can use these tales in pathworking to release those same energies into our lives.

Often people are drawn to a particular culture, and if that is so, the stories and tales of the culture are a wonderful starting point. We may in fact be drawn to that culture because it may have been one that opened up esoteric teachings to us in a past life.

Begin by examining any culture and its tales that seem to reflect what is going on within our life. Different cultures all have their own unique aspects and often the tales will reveal an approach to life that is similar to our own or to what we are experiencing. For example, the Greek tales are often centered around the hero's journey - *"the hero or mortal who, in pursuit of his divinity, is subjected to a series of personal initiations which take the form of mythological deeds...and simply represent the trials of the aspiring human soul..."* (Murry Hope, *Practical Greek Magic.* Northamptonshire: Aquarian Press, 1985, p.10.)

African traditions reflect a powerful, instinctive response to nature and the world around them as a Mother with her children. The tales frequently involved the testing and development of human values within daily life. The Celtic tradition was one of artistry, nature worship and matriarchy. The Germanic tradition was one of developing strength - often through war and struggles. The traditions of Central and South America often reflected and focused upon the duality that exists within all life -learning to live with opposites. Among the native peoples of North America, the tales reflect a strong tradition of developing and understanding a personal relationship with all of Nature - nothing was separate and any aspect of Nature could be a brother or sister. Only by working with Nature could harmony be achieved.

These are, of course, generalizations. There is a great diversity reflected within the tales and myths of every tradition. But the tales and myths can provide a powerful starting point. We do not have to stick with a particular tradition. Keep in mind that many of the ancient traditions used their folklore to mask deeper teachings. By working with those that seem to coincide with your particular purpose, you amplify its effectiveness with pathworking.

We often find the Greek tales being used in pathworking techniques. The tales of the Greek heroes lend themselves well to most Qabalistic imagickal journeys. On the other hand, the hero tales of any tradition will do so as well. If, for example, we have reached a point where we are ready to take upon ourselves greater initiations, we can use the tales of Hercules and his twelve labors. We could just as easily use the tale of Odysseus or the travels of Jason and the Argonauts. In other traditions we would use the hero tales and quest myths as well.

We simply substitute ourselves for the hero or heroine. We hold to the basic structure of temple-to-temple pathworkings, but as we step through the doorway onto the path, we enter into the tale itself. Then depending upon which character we are aligning with, we see ourselves encountering and experiencing all that the character experienced.

For this technique explicit directions and guidelines can not truly be given. Each must adapt the tale to himself or herself. This allows for our own creative input, and it allows us to awaken the energies in our own unique manner upon the paths. There is no right or wrong adjustment of the tales, as long as we hold to the basic tenets and guidelines of pathworking (i.e. keeping the symbols upon the paths somewhere within the tale's structure.

One of the ways we can do this is to have all of the characters of the tale in dress that has the symbolic insignias of the path upon them in some fashion. Remember that the symbols keep us in the proper place and enable the pathworking to be more effective. By doing this, the entire tale becomes the core of our pathworking.

Guidelines for Pathworking with Myths and Tales

1. Enter the Tree of Life and bring to life the first temple.

2. Then create our astral doorway that opens onto a path that leads to the second temple.

3. As we step through the doorway, we enter the scenario of the myth or tale.

4. At the end of the tale, we enter the destination temple, with what we attained through the adventure of the tale.

5. There we are greeted by the archangels, who also provide some extra commentary on the working.

6. We close the temples through the use of the divine names

and we exit the Tree of Life.

7. We ground the pathworking through the physical movements and through recording in our journal.

This may all seem like some kind of fanciful daydreaming, but when applied in this manner, it becomes a powerful force. Daydreams are also much more important in our lives than is often believed. Dreams, whether of the night or day, are much more than just a stress-release mechanism. Dreams put us in touch with other realities and planes of life that we do not always consciously recognize or acknowledge. Our dreams must be translated through the reality of the flesh, and with pathworking, this is what we are attempting to do.

We are using mythical dreams as an arena for developing a greater relationship between our physical self and the divine consciousness. They are ways to foster practical connections between outer and inner awareness. They are a means of fostering a relation to the divine.

They are powerful, which is why this technique and the one that follows will stimulate greater activity of nighttime dreams as well. Paying closer attention to our dreams when we are pathworking will help us to recognize the effectiveness of our Qabalistic work. Dreams though do not always provide answers. They often are questions, invitations to explore relationships. They are callings to the spiritual journey.

IMPORTANT NOTE:

When using the ancient myths and tales, remember to use your own imagination and construction. Do not hold to the letter of the tale. Adapt it according to your own purpose. A degree of spontaneity is vital in pathworking. Know ahead of time what you wish to happen with the journey. Construct it and adapt it so that the outcome meets your own personal purposes, even if the outcome is different than that of the tale's outcome.

EXERCISE:

Creating the Life Adventure

Benefits:

- **creating our own life experiences**
- **develops ability to manifest rewards and tests**
- **enhances ritualistic abilities**

Having worked with the tales and myths, we can then take the pathworking process to an even more dynamic level. We can learn to perform the pathworking in a much more personalized, ritualistic manner. This technique builds further upon the mythic work of the previous exercise, but instead of following the myths scenario, we completely create our own.

This is a much more advanced pathworking. It requires a familiarity with all of the paths and the basic qualities and characteristics. I recommend that the paths have been worked all the way through prior to performing this particular type of pathworking.

To accomplish this, we begin by contemplating and deciding what we wish to accomplish through the pathworking. In the journal give this more creative working a title, just as if you were titling a short story. In essence we are translating our purpose into a dramatic or story scenario. We will empower it with the appropriate symbols, and then play it our in the traditional pathworking format.

Putting the purpose into dramatic form, as if to act it out, is extremely powerful. It gives your purpose structure and animation through the imagery that you create. The ancients used such ceremonies, mystery plays and rituals to stimulate energies and to resolve problems. Theater was an important part of the ancient mystery schools. The symbolic enactment of universal energies brought about a dynamic release of them within the participant's physical lives. This has been a form of sympathetic magic used throughout the world.

Trust your own intuition in creating the pathworking scenario, but you must employ the basic symbology of the path. The symbols serve as the catalysts, and without them our efforts will be impotent. Consciousness is awareness joined with the appropriate action.

Guidelines for Creating the Life Adventure Pathworkings

1. Choose the area of your life that you wish to impact.

2. Choose the path that has the energy most appropriate for your pathworking purpose.

3. Review the path and fill in your journal.

Make note of the purpose for this working, and why you have chosen to perform this with the designated path.

4. Play through the scenario in your mind.

Determine the ideal manner you would like to see the energies manifest. If the pathworking is to resolve a problem, visualize yourself meeting it, facing it and resolving it. If it is to accomplish a goal or achieve something, visualize the easiest and best way this could unfold for you.

Use the ancient tales and myths as a guideline. See yourself upon a quest, searching out gold or something valuable that represents your goal for the pathworking. if the purpose is to overcome something within your life or to move past an obstacle, make that obstacle mythical in proportions. Some visualize their obstacles as monsters that must be slain, etc.

Use your own creative imagination!

When we use this particular technique, we are trying to release energy into our life that has been blocked or hindered, so that we have full access to our resources at any time. This activation intensifies situations to the point where they can no longer be ignored. We are forcing resolution so our energies are free to pursue more creative and productive endeavors. The gift is sometimes hidden within the problem, so that only by facing what is hindering us, can the gift be released.

5. Use the symbols of the path in the scenario.

Make sure that you use the appropriate colors, fragrances, Hebrew letter, , etc. within your pathworking. These may be a part of the scenery or even the dress of the individuals you incorporate into your pathworking. You decide. Part of what you are learning to do is to use your creative imagination in order to manifest conditions that will benefit your life.

6. Enter the Tree of Life.

Bring to life the temple and open a doorway. Walk through the doorway into the path and your adventure.

7. Walk the path, allowing the drama to unfold.

It is a good idea to work into your adventure some assistance from someone else. I personally like to have the archangels show up to provide guidance, strength or general assistance in my scenarios. It also serves as extra protection. Make sure you encounter the symbols of the path about halfway through as always.

In time you may want to enact this scenario out. It is a type of magickal role-playing, but not of the dungeons and dragons variety. In an earlier work, *MAGICKAL DANCE,* I described a variety of ways in which dance and theater can be used ceremonially. I discuss this a little in Part Four, but it is one of the most powerful tools for activating dynamic forces to play within our lives.

8. Enter into the second temple.

As the drama concludes and your purpose is accomplished, create a doorway into the second temple and bring it to life. There allow the two archangels to comment and clarify your experiences and what you may expect to unfold in the days ahead as a result of it.

9. Close the temples and exit the Tree of Life, bringing your gifts out with you.

10. Ground the energies and record impressions within your journal.

IMPORTANT NOTE:

We have created a scenario according to our own unique purpose. Visualizing it being enacted is the same as daydreaming. The only difference is that now we are empowering the energies with specific symbols and then we are grounding the energies. We chose specific images and clusters of images, placing them within a scenario that reflected our personal purpose. We then linked them to archetypal forces.

With this kind of pathworking we are recommitting powerfully to our spiritual goals. This implies that we must transmute what we are now to create something greater. Resolution of present situations brings change, and change brings growth.

If conflicts and imbalances arise or intensify, it is only so we will be forced to look at new possibilities. We are resolving our life experiences by consciously working from the outer to the inner and back to the outer again. We are bridging and expanding our resources. We are learning to weave together the elements of our physical life with our spiritual life. Rather than remaining passive creatures, we are becoming conscious *creators* of our own life experiences!

Part Four:

The Holy of Holies

"The Light was in the world,
and the World was made by it,
and the world knew it not."

- John 1:10

Chapter Nine

Amplifying The Effects

"Thou carriest within thee a sublime Friend whom thou knowest not. For God dwells in the inner part of every man, but few know how to find Him...For one who finds his happiness and joy within himself, and also his wisdom within himself is one with God. And, mark well, the soul which has found God is freed from rebirth and death, from old age and pain, and drinks the water of immortality."

- Bhagavad-Gita

Working with the Qabalistic Tree of Life is a creative process. This is why incorporating physical ritual behavior can be so powerful with it. Ritual movement and posture helps us to direct and focus our consciousness. Directed physical behavior helps us to align physiological responses with our spiritual goals. It enables our physical energies to touch with higher forces.

The purpose of ritual movement is to make the world of energies and powers more physical. We attempt to re-express the energies upon the physical plane. Sacred movement was a means of transcending our humanity. Through it we gain control over normally automatic responses by evoking emotions and energies and then channeling them through the movement. Sacred movement involves improvisation and individual creativity. Every movement is linked to a particular purpose.

There are physical movements and postures that correspond to every level of the tree of Life. There are ways of using movement and dance that set the energy of the Tree in motion without us meditating upon it. Most of these are examined in my book, mentioned earlier – *Secret Paths of the Qabala.*

We will be focusing upon those simple physical activities that will activate the energies more dynamically within our life and that will also ground them. Keep in mind that we are physical beings, and as such, everything we experience must ultimately be expressed and experienced through the physical. When we incorporate physical movement and postures within our Qabalistic work, we pull those archetypal energies more powerfully and release them more dynamically into our lives.

Physical movements enable us to move from the outer world and all of its hassles to the inner realm much more easily. It creates a mindset. The physical activity stimulates nerves that subtly cause the mind to shift gears. The movements employed throughout the rest of the chapter are designed to help us make that transition from the outer to the inner and back again more easily.

Gestures, postures and movements express the inexpressible. They utilize both aspects of the brain, especially when we are aware of their significance. They are direct and powerful ways of communicating with the divine within us. They assist our concentration and they help us to ground the energies that we awaken.

The postures and movements are kept simple throughout this chapter, but do not let their simplicity mislead you into believing they are not effective. When we incorporate physical movements with pathworking, the impact will increase by 3-4 times.

The postures can be done both before and after the actual pathworking or they can also be incorporated into the entire working itself. Doing them before will help us open more fully to the Tree of Life energies. Performing them after will help ground the awakened energy into our physical life more strongly.

Movement and sacred dance is more powerful when employed with music. Thus these exercises that follow, when incorporated with pathworking, are even more effective when music is employed with them. On the following page is a list of music appropriate to use in pathworking or when working with the individual Sephira. (They are guidelines only, but the music listed reflects the energies inherent to the Sephira.)

When we attach special significance to our movements, especially when delving into the universe and attempting to touch the divine, we are praying through movement. It has been said that prayer is a state of heightened awareness and communication. Prayers can be simple or complicated; either way they can work for us. Their style is dependent upon the import we attach to them. When we pray the Tree of Life through movement, we are using all aspects of ourselves for growth and enlightenment. In our present time, the physical aspects are often ignored in spiritual studies.

It is not the movement, but what we believe of the movement, that gives it power. Physical movement with intention is freeing and strengthening. It awakens our bodies to the spiritual, while freeing the spiritual to nurture the body. Heaven and Earth. The roots and all of the branches. We dance the Tree of Life every day, but our movements have no power. When we dance our prayers - and pathworking is a form of prayer - we empower our lives. We climb the Tree to become nestled within its arms.

MUSIC FOR THE TREE

Sephira	Corresponding Music/Composers
Malkuth	Anything of the home and hearth; Brahms *Lullaby*; Dvorak; Puccini.
Yesod	Handel's *Water Music*; A Chopin *Nocturne* (anything that evokes deep feelings).
Hod	Woodwinds and horns; Mozart; Gershwin (rhythmic variety); Bach; Mozart's *Magic Flute.*
Netzach	Beethoven's *Pastoral Symphony*; Zamfir; Schumann; Mendelssohn.
Tiphareth	Handel's *Messiah*; Haydn's *Creation*; Pachelbel's *Canon in D*; Berlioz; sacred hymns.
Geburah	Marches of any kind; strong rhythms; Wagner's *Ride of the Valkyries*; Verdi's *Grand March*; *Pomp and Circumstance.*
Chesed	Franck's *Panis Angelicus*; Beethoven's *Fifth Symphony*; Tchaikovsky.
Binah	Bach-Gounod, *Ave Maria*; Schubert's *Ave Maria*; Brahms' *Lullaby*; Debussy's *Clair de Lune.*
Chokmah	Haydn's *Trumpet Concerto*; Rachmaninoff; Haydn's *Creation*; Vivaldi.
Kether	Wagner's *Pilgrim's Chorus*; Theme from *2001: A Space Odyssey*; Pachelbel's *Canon in D.*

Playing these or other pieces of music that you choose in relation to the sephiroth adds even greater depth and power to the dance!

EXERCISE:

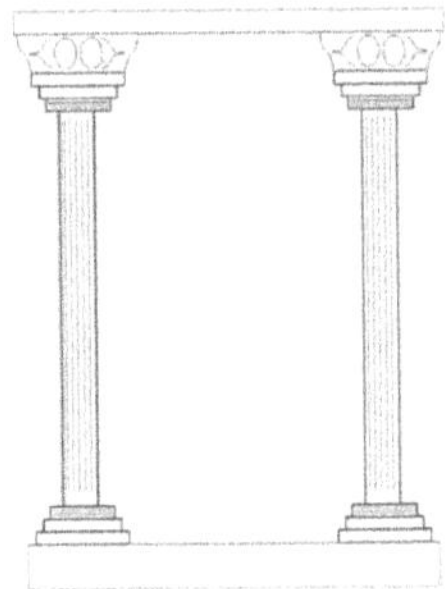

Balancing Postures

Benefits:

- grounding and balancing
- manifestation of energies

The movements for balance are especially effective before and after meditation upon any level of the Tree of Life. They insure a more balanced experience of the energies. Through the use of these postures, we manifest energy in a more balanced manner.

IMPORTANT NOTE:

Right Leg = Pillar of Severity (Binah, Geburah, Hod)
Left Leg = Pillar of Mercy (Chokmah, Chesed, Netzach)
Both Legs = Middle Pillar (Kether, Daath, Tiphareth, Yesod, Malkuth)

In trying to determine which pillar is associated with which leg, we must see ourselves as backing into the Tree of Life diagram. The Middle Pillar becomes the spine. The left leg becomes the Pillar of Mercy and the right leg becomes the Pillar of Severity.

The right and left legs symbolize the right and left pillars of the Tree. If we have more difficulty balancing on one leg than on the other, the weaker leg indicates a greater difficulty with the sephiroth that correspond to that pillar. It indicates that we may have more difficulty balancing the related areas of our life.

The first of these postures depicted on the following page is the pose of the dancer. This is what we are becoming - the dancer of the Tree of Life! We are learning to choreograph our life and our personal resources for greater manifestation. It is a preparatory posture. It awakens the inner Tree of Life.

In postures B and C we are learning to balance the flow of energies down the pillars. Many people have difficulty balancing upon one foot and leg. This is significant. Using the principle of correspondence, an inability to maintain balance in the physical reflects an inability to balance the more subtle spiritual energies of the Tree of Life. As we increase our ability to balance on one leg, we increase our ability to balance the energies we activate and manifest.

Most people find it easier to balance on one leg than the other. This is also significant. It indicates the ability to balance the energies of one pillar more easily than the other. This provides clues as to where extra work is needed. Keep in mind that the Qabala shows us our greatest weaknesses and our greatest strengths, but we have to become aware of them. How we balance provides us with insight.

Postures D and E are for balancing and grounding the energies of all the pillars. Posture D brings all three pillars into alignment and balance. Posture E grounds the energies into the physical. It is representative of Malkuth, where all energies of the Tree of Life must express themselves at some point. All of these balancing postures train us in focusing our energies. They activate the energies of the Tree in a more balanced manner.

Hermeticists used similar postures in developing balance. Many practiced the Hanged man posture, as depicted upon the tarot card. The Hanged Man is hung upon the Tree of Life.

Keeping the arms folded during all of these postures force us to concentrate and work for even greater control. With the arms folded across the chest, we have a symbolic gesture of balance at the heart of our growth and evolution!

A.

This position enables you to awaken the energies of the Pillars so that you can become the Dancer in the Tree of Life.

B.

C.

Postures which balance the Pillar energies of the Tree.

D.

Middle Pillar of Balance.

E.

Grounding the energies of all three Pillars, before touching the specific sephiroth.

EXERCISE:

Walk to Nowhere

Benefits:

- **induces altered states of consciousness**
- **shifts perceptions**
- **intensifies pathworkings**

The Walk to Nowhere is a series of steps whose purpose is to induce an altered state of consciousness. It involves repeating a set rhythm of steps: four steps forward and four steps backward. Forward. Backward. Inner. Outer.

These steps should be taken with full attention in a sure, slow and deliberate manner. With each step, place the heel down first and then the toes. This serves as a reminder to maintain a sure footing in our journey of life and upon the path we are treading.

The number of forward and backward steps can vary. One method of determining them is to base the number upon the Sephira with which we are working or the number of the path. For example, if we are working with Binah, we could use three steps forward and three back because Binah is the third Sephira. If we are working with the 14th path, we could perform 14 steps forward and fourteen steps back. To some this may seem like a lot of steps, but it is just another way of aligning our physiological responses to the Tree of Life, amplifying the effects.

This technique for pathworking is extremely powerful

and energizing. It releases the energies of the path more intensely into the physical. It also helps to develop concentration and creative imagination.

Do not be afraid to adapt this exercise. It can be used as a prelude to the pathworking meditation or as the pathworking itself. Experiment. You will be rewarded for your efforts.

Walk to Nowhere Technique

1. Choose the Sephira or the path, and review the correspondences.

2. Set the atmosphere.

3. Perform the balancing postures.

4. Enter the tree and awaken the temple.

5. Merge with the magickal image of the temple.

6. Create an astral doorway, and as you step through, begin the Walk to Nowhere.

Visualize stepping upon the path of the appropriate color.

7. About halfway through the series, visualize yourself merging with the magickal image of the second Sephira. Now you are a combination of both.

8. As you complete the path, create a doorway and enter into the second temple. Awaken the second temple.

9. Gather the gifts for the pathworking, and close the temples as described earlier.

10. Exit the Tree of Life with your gifts, and perform the balancing postures to ground the energies.

EXERCISE:

Dancing to the Stars

Benefits:

- **awareness of heavenly influences**
- **empowering pathworking results**
- **align our rhythms with universal ones**

In more ancient times, the students of the mysteries were very cognizant of the heavenly energies playing upon the earth and themselves. The imprints of the stars were a strong part of their life. If we are truly to awaken our highest consciousness, we also need to become more cognizant of this. We can use movement with the Qabala to re-imprint our souls with the influence of the stars. We will thus become more aware of their often ignored effects.

There are constellations, astrological glyphs and such which we can use to decipher and understand the various levels of our consciousness. The star and planet patterns are associated with the sephiroth and the paths. We can use them in a powerfully ritualistic manner to align ourselves more fully with them.

On the following pages are the constellation patterns and the astrological glyphs for the paths on the Tree of Life. If we employ physical movements that mimic those star patterns, we awaken their influence more strongly within our life. We become more sensitive to their subtle influences, and we draw out from our subconscious archives our ephemeral memory and attunement to the stars.

Stepping off the constellations and astrological glyphs

heightens the impact of the pathworkings. We become more sensitive to celestial movements within our lives. It heightens our awareness of how astrological configurations affect us - often without being recognized. The movements awaken us to their gravitational impact upon us on all levels.

By physically dancing the constellations, we place ourselves back within their rhythms, aligning our personal energy systems with the more celestial. The movements reflect the energies that will be released through the pathworkings, making them more powerful.

Focusing upon the pathworking and the stellar patterns at the appropriate time of the year for the appropriate astrological sign elicits dynamic effects. For example, if we perform the pathworking for the sign of cancer (path 18) while the sun is in that particular sign - using the physical dancing of the constellation - the effects are amazing. If we only work the twelve paths associated with the astrological signs, we can dance to the heavens in the course of one year.

The techniques that follow open a broad avenue for aligning the physical with the celestial. Ultimately, we can even dance the entire astrological chart, enhancing those aspects that are more beneficial. This can be used to smooth over those aspects of our chart that are more difficult. It can heighten those aspects that are more beneficial.

The movement of the stars are so intimately connected to life in the physical that great strides can be made by anyone wishing to choreograph it.

Technique #1

1. Choose the path you will be working and review the energies associated with it.

2. Set the atmosphere.

3. Perform the balancing postures to activate the Tree of Life.

4. Step off the constellation in the area in which you will perform the pathworking meditation. As you do so, visualize its pattern formed upon the floor in the appropriate color for the path. For example, if you are performing a pathworking for the 24th path (Netzach to Tiphareth), you would step off the pattern for the Scorpio constellation, visualizing it in the color ofgreen-blue.

5. Then sit and relax. Begin your pathworking meditation then as you have learned to do.

6. At the end, when you leave the Tree, perform the balancing posture to ground the energies you have set in motion.

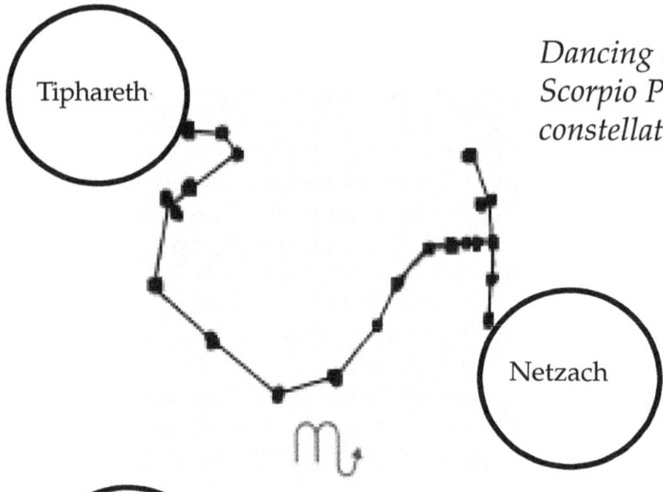

Dancing the Scorpio Path - constellation

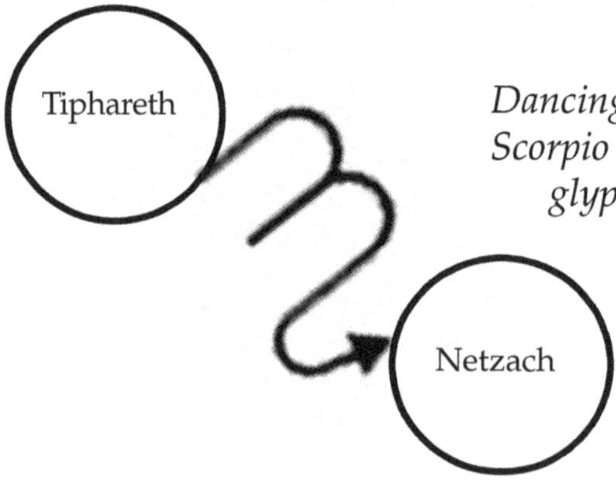

Dancing the Scorpio Path - glyph

Technique #2

1. Choose the path you will be working and review its correspondences.

2. Set the Atmosphere.

3. Perform the balancing postures.

4. Visualize the Tree, enter it and awaken the inner temple.

5. Assume the magickal image and create an astral doorway.

6. As the door opens, see the path in the appropriate color and in the pattern of appropriate glyph or constellation.

7. Begin to step off the pattern, imagining yourself on the path. Make sure that you encounter the road markers and the gifts of the path. At the halfway point assume the magickal image of the second temple and continue on.

8. Create a doorway into the second temple and open it with the divine names.

9. Close both temples and exit the tree of Life with your gifts.

10. Perform the balancing postures to ground the energy and anchor it to the physical.

Technique #3

This is an excellent exercise to perform outside at night - under the stars themselves. If you can find an area (pasture, field, woods), it is extremely effective for accelerating the play of archetypal forces in your life.

1. Choose a path and review the correspondences.

2. Having arrived at your outdoor location, set the atmosphere.

3. Perform the balancing postures, and then visualize yourself entering into the tree and awakening the inner temple.

4. Assume the magickal image and create an astral doorway.

5. Now you begin to walk in that field or woods - physically walking a path in the pattern of the appropriate constellation or astrological glyph. Feel yourself in the presence of the archangels. Carry on a mental conversation.

6. About halfway through your 'stroll to the stars" assume the second magickal image. Continue on, visualizing the path in the appropriate color and with the markers.

7. Visualize the second temple and create your doorway. Enter and bring the temple to life.

8. Close both temples down and exit the Tree, bringing with you the gifts.

9. Perform the balancing postures to ground the energies.

10. This is especially effective when performed in a wooded area. The trees become antennae to link the more celestial energies to you personally. The effects can also be enhanced by intoning the divine names periodically into the night air while walking the path.

Astrological Glyphs

SATURN—Path 32
Malkuth to Yesod

PRIMAL FIRE—Path 31
Malkuth to Hod

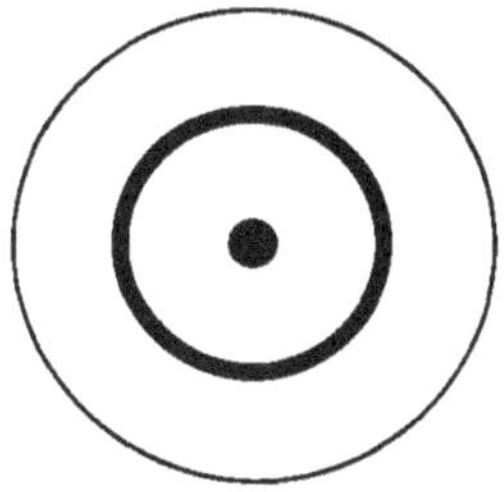

SUN—Path 30
Yesod to Hod

MARS—Path 27
Hod to Netzach

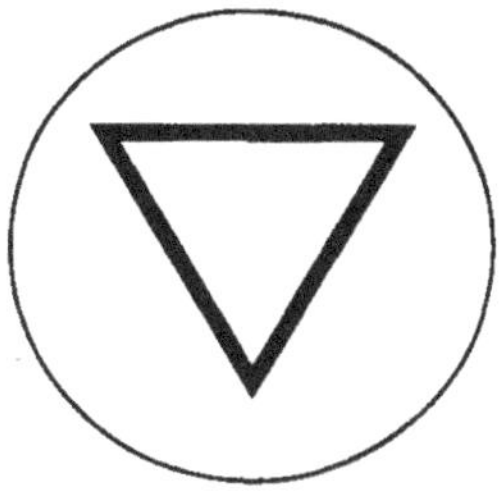

PRIMAL WATER—Path 23
Hod to Geburah

JUPITER—Path 21
Netzach to Chesed

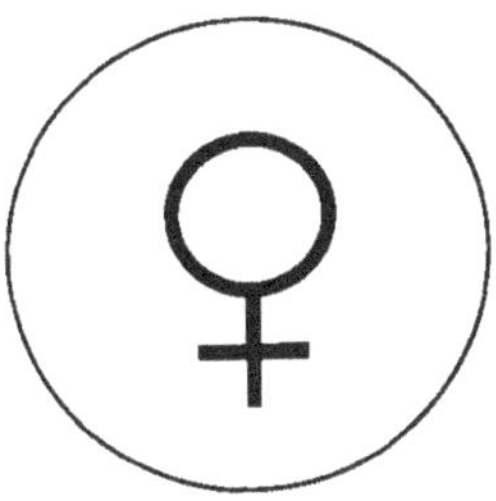

VENUS—Path 14
Binah to Chokmah

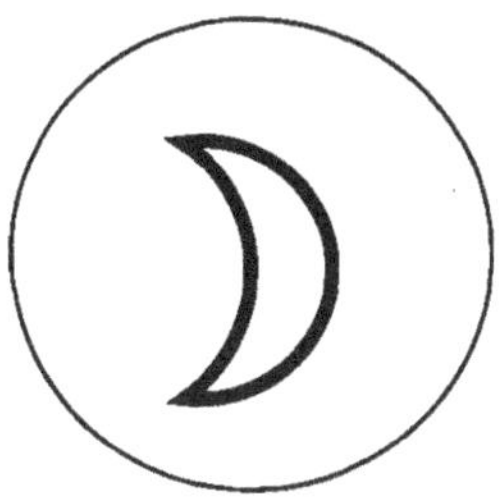

MOON—Path 13
Tiphareth to Kether

MERCURY—Path 12
Binah to Kether

PRIMAL AIR—Path 11
Chokmah to Kether

Constellations

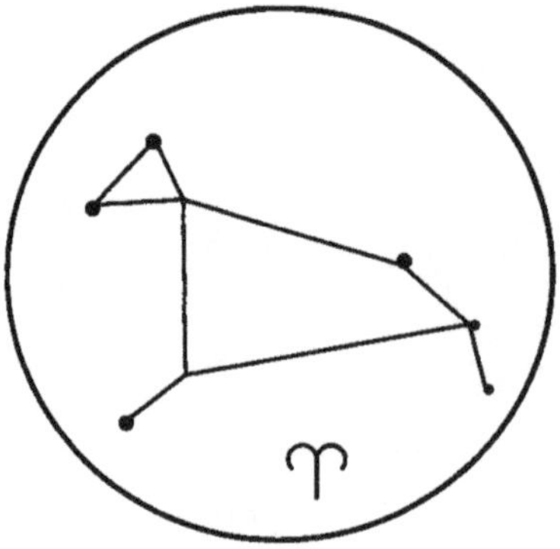

ARIES
(Path 15—Tiphareth/Chokmah)

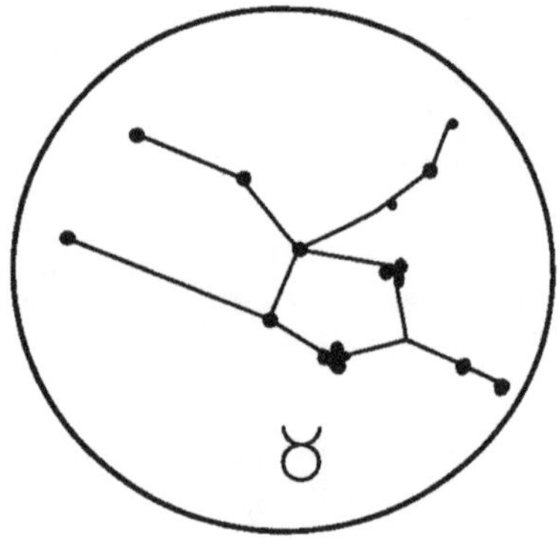

TAURUS
(Path 16—Chesed/Chokmah)

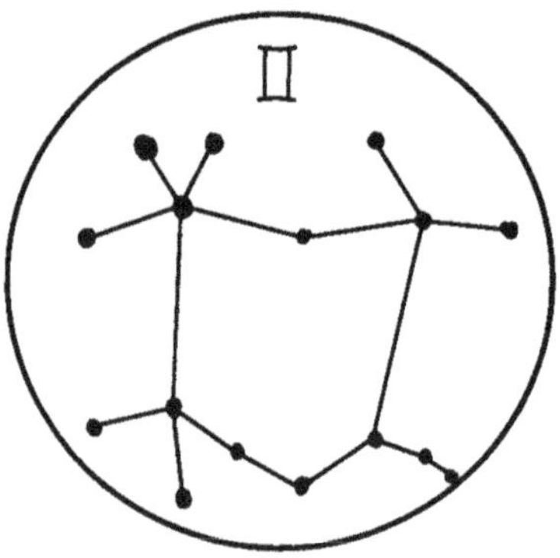

GEMINI
(Path 17—Tiphareth/Binah)

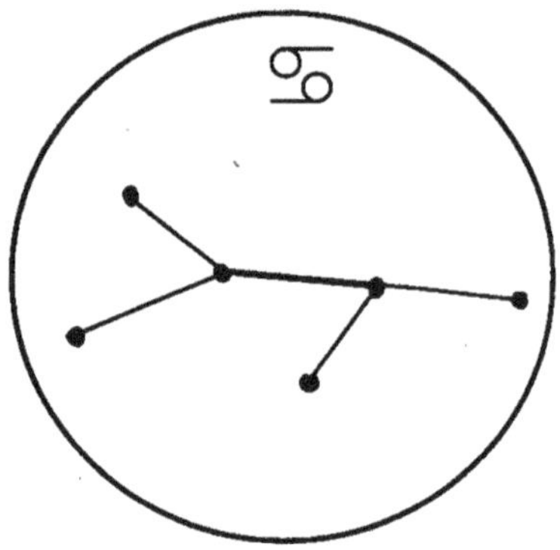

CANCER
(Path 18—Geburah/Binah)

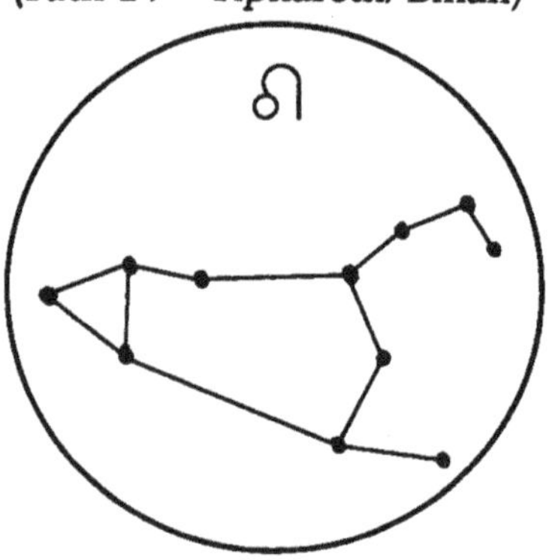

LEO
(Path 19—Geburah/Chesed)

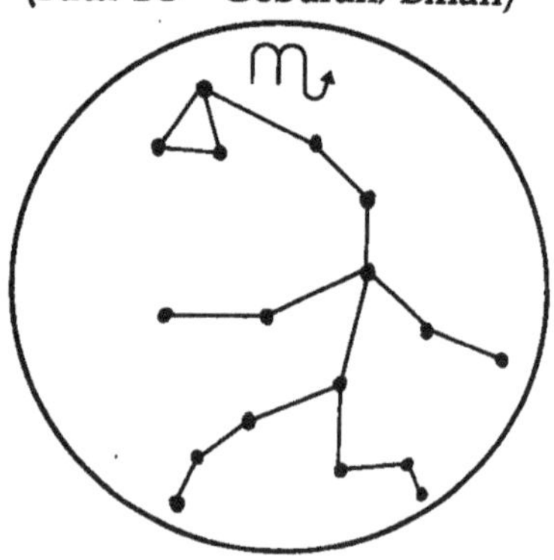

VIRGO
(Path 20—Tiphareth/Chesed)

Constellations

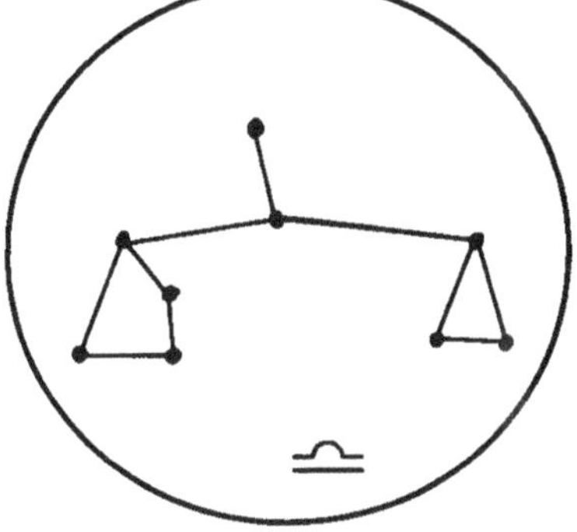

LIBRA
(Path 22—Tiphareth/Geburah)

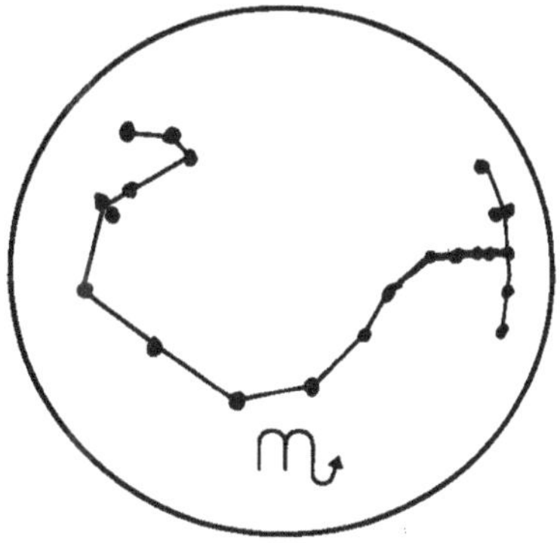

SCORPIO
(Path 24—Netzach/Tiphareth)

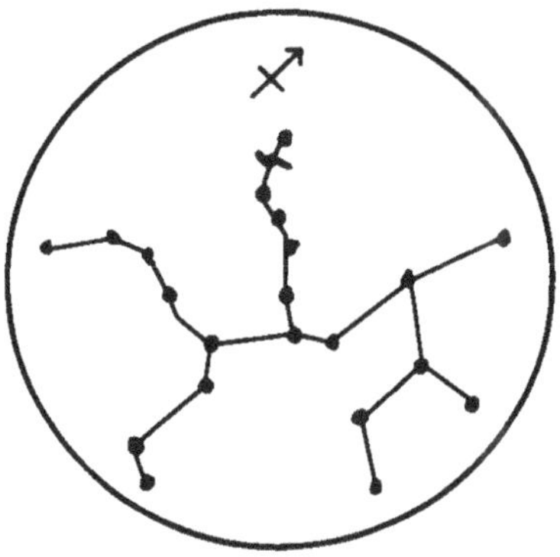

SAGITTARIUS
(Path 25—Yesod/Tiphareth)

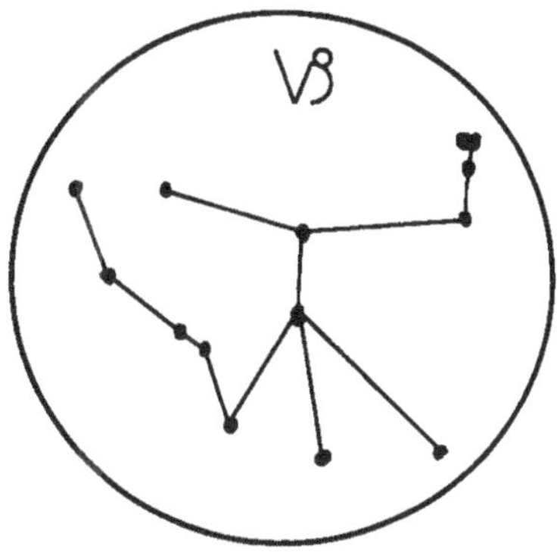

CAPRICORN
(Path 26—Hod/Tiphareth)

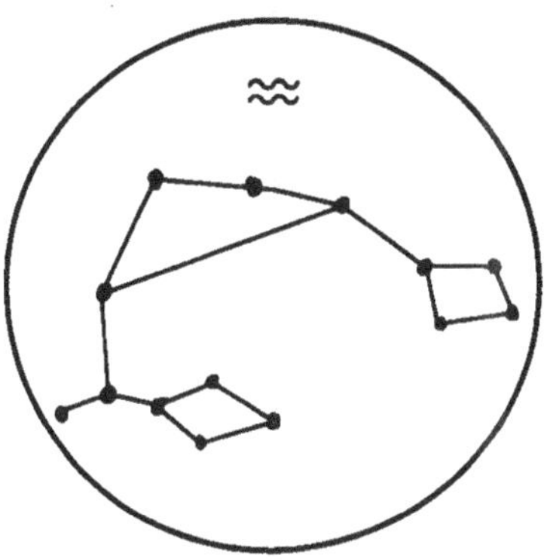

AQUARIUS
(Path 28—Yesod/Netzach)

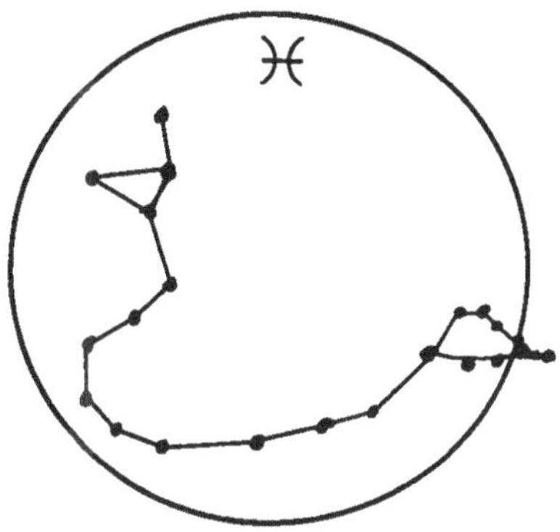

PISCES
(Path 29—Malkuth/Netzach)

All
pathworkings
have a
guardian aspect
for security, safety
and balance.
These are the divine names,
the archangelic energies
and your personal symbol.
The divine names will
dissolve inappropriate
energies and images.
The personal symbol
will provide for you
an emergency exit.

Chapter Ten

Grounding and Protection

"O blind soul, arm yourself with the torch of the Mysteries and in terrestrial night you will discover your luminous reflection, your heavenly soul. Follow this divine guide, letting him be your Genius. For he holds the key to your past and future lives."

Call to the Initiates
THE BOOK OF THE DEAD

All of the methods in this book deal with learning to open the doors that are closed. It does not matter who closed them; what is important is that we allowed them to be closed. We each have the ability to open the doors that will shed light into the dark corners of our life. In this way we see exactly what needs to be cleaned.

Much has been written about meditation and its various practices. There are, in fact, as many methods of meditation as there are people. As to which method or combination of methods is best, no one can answer that but the individual. What is important is that the method chosen be an active one.

It is not enough to simply quiet the mind and allow pleasant images to arise. Over time, this can lead to self-deception. We need to act upon what we are stimulating. We operate predominantly within the physical dimension, and thus all energies activated on other levels need to be grounded into the physical.

The imagickal techniques are not truly magickal. They may seem so to the uninformed, but they are simply techniques for developing our innate potentials. They help us to solve problems, achieve goals, open ourselves to higher capabilities and re-instill color and a joy of life.

Their application to daily life is work, as any active form of development is. That work though can be enjoyable. As it is often said, it is not the destination, but the journey itself that holds the treasures. If we are to maximize the effects of our work, we must actively use whatever knowledge, inspiration and awareness within our daily lives.

There are quick methods to open our psychic energies, but they alone do not propel us along our spiritual path to a higher destiny. Neither do they reflect a higher evolution. Only by bridging the psychic with the spiritual archetypes and then grounding them into the physical do we create opportunities for higher evolution.

Many wish to open doors because of a "power" they hope to demonstrate. This, in and of itself, is not wrong, but it is limiting. It is also a natural by-product of opening and clearing the bridges between the levels of consciousness. It unfolds as we grow in knowledge and experience, and it can be developed by anyone. But it does not reflect any higher evolution or a more moral or spiritual character.

Attainment of psychic power as an end in itself was described in the East as the *laukika method of development.* The abilities and powers are obtained only for the present personality. This occurs usually when true spiritual safeguards are not employed. In such cases it is highly likely that the powers are or will be misused.

The entire purpose of working with Tree of Life and the imagickal techniques within this book is to increase our awareness of the interplay of other dimensions with our physical life so we can learn to control them. This involves removing tunnel vision approach to life and overcoming reliance only upon the five senses.

. We must learn to use altered states of consciousness to

recognize and understand how energies play upon us in all aspects of our life. We must learn to synthesize the inner realm experiences with the outer reality.

Through imagickal pathworking we look at the patterns of our lives. We begin with the inherent capabilities and our present proficiency with them. We must look for the patterns and relationships between our lives and the lives of others. Are we repeating the same situations and experiences? We must retrain ourselves to look at life and people from all levels.

Working with the Tree of Life means opening up the intuition and ability to perceive our life in new dimensions. We will no longer be able to perceive people and things from a limited, physical perspective. Everything is affected by us, and everything affects us. Control of our environment begins with control of our self. Until we cease to be influenced haphazardly by surrounding conditions, we cannot hope to exercise influence over them.

This means that we must learn to grow and extend ourselves in an environment that promotes growth and provides protection. Through the Qabalistic Tree of Life, we achieve both. The exercises prior to this chapter have provided tools and techniques that will aid our growth. Those that follow will show us how to use the tree of Life in a manner that will assist our unfolding and provide protection for us as we open to new potentials and new dimensions.

Putting it into Perspective

Many people claim that because they have their visions and spirit contacts and because they know that all knowledge lies within, there is no reason to use strong techniques of protection. The truth is that the knowledge of protection techniques in higher-consciousness exploration, enable us to keep our vision unimpaired. They protect us against dangers of which we may be unaware.

It is easy to misuse energies awakened through the techniques provided within this book. It is easy to express them in an unbalanced fashion. Development and unfoldment release energies that can affect the mind, leading to subtle difficulties if care is not taken. The increased sensitivity alone can render the individual suspicious and quarrelsome. It can result in a form of hyper-sensitivity with a loss of discrimination.

We are not trying to dominate the universe. We are trying to learn how to work within its rhythms. Those who "dabble" with a little bit of knowledge and experience are the ones most likely to find themselves in difficulty.

Contact with non-physical states of existence has a powerful effect upon us. It tends to draw the living from the plane of objective, physical life - which is where we are supposed to be focused. This occurs even when higher energies are contacted - even more so. This is why slow, careful integration with the physical is so important. It is why we must also work to maintain the health and balance of the physical body. It is essential to staying grounded.

Work with the spiritual should never imply neglect of the physical. If the physical is unbalanced, then the expression of the spiritual through us will be also. This is why stronger techniques of protection are necessary for those opening to higher initiation. It closes the doors strongly behind us and seals them so that we learn to express the energies we have touched in a more balanced manner. The two exercises that follow are recommended to everyone for their overall health and well-being!

A third is also highly recommended, but it is not included here. It has been provided in several of my other works, including ***Simplified Qabala Magic*** and ***How to See and Read the Aura.*** It is one of the most powerful Qabalistic healing exercises. It is called the "Middle Pillar Exercise", and it is one that I teach to anyone involved in healing or spiritual/psychic development. It strengthens and pumps tremendous amounts of energy into the human aura, making the individual a living pillar of light.

The "Middle Pillar Exercise" and the "Banishing Ritual of the Pentagram" are available on audio cassette and CD, and can be attained through your local store or through the publisher of this book. A promotional advertisement is provided in the back of the book for this cassette.

Recognizing Imbalances and Difficulties

1. We find ourselves becoming self-centered. Other things and people within your life seem to be increasing intrusive.

2. You may find yourself motivated more and more by greed, lust and a desire for knowledge and power.

3. You find yourself wanting to always be out in front of people. This includes wanting to make sure everyone knows how knowledgeable you are. It also includes feelings of knowing better than anyone else.

4. You may find yourself working with speedier and less troublesome methods of developing psychic faculties. This includes focusing solely on psychic phenomena, and even psychic thrill seeking.

5. You may find yourself expressing the new energies and abilities in a misplaced manner, i.e. sexual gratification, power over others, etc. This may even involve ancient, inappropriate methods to attain effects.

6. You may develop premature trance, premature in that you do not have the development of accurate intuition, clairvoyance and a solid knowledge base to discriminate what and who works through you.

7. You display increasing hypersensitivity in many areas of your life.

EXERCISE:

The Qabalistic Cross

Benefits:

- stabilizes the aura
- balances and calms
- strengthens our focus

The Qabalistic cross should be used before any meditation, pathworking, imagickal technique and even ritual. It stabilizes the aura and protects. It should also be used to close your activity. It helps to seal off other planes and dimensions, grounding you and the energies you have activated in a balanced manner. With time and practice, through this exercise we become more conscious of the overshadowing presence of our own higher divine genius.

This exercise incorporates the Biblical words found at the end of The Lord's Prayer: "for thine is the kingdom, the power and the glory forever and ever. Amen" The Hebrew version of these words in conjunction with the physical action of forming a cross over the body, is very powerful.

1. Stand straight (or in a seated position), feet together, shoulders back and arms at your side. Face east if possible.

2. Take several deep breaths from the diaphragm. As you inhale and exhale slowly, visualize yourself growing and expanding into the heavens.

Do this until you can visualize and imagine yourself

standing upon the earth, with the entire universe surrounding you.

3. With the thumb (spirit), the index finger (fire) and the middle finger (earth) together, touch the forehead between and above the brows. Slowly intone the Hebrew word:

"Ateh" (ah-tOh)

Give equal emphasis to each syllable, and visualize the sound carrying to the ends of the universe. In English, this translates as "thine is".

4. Drawing the hand with the joined thumb and fingers downward, as if drawing the light of the universe down and through the body, touch the solar plexus and tone the word:

"Malkuth" (mahl-kUth)

This means "the kingdom". As you tone the word, imagine the light passing through the body down through the feet, so that you see a column of light that extends from the heavens through you and into the heart of the Earth.

5. Bring the right hand, with the thumb and fingers joined to the right shoulder and tone the words:

"Ve Geburah" (vuh-guh-bU-rah)

This translates as "the Power". As you tone this, touching the shoulder, see and explosion of light, that releases a stream of crystalline light that extends to infinity to the right.

6. Move the thumb and fingers from the right shoulder across the body to the left shoulder. As you touch the left shoulder, there is another explosion of light, and you tone the words:

"Ve Gedulah" (vuh-guh-dU-lah)

This translates as "the glory". As you tone them, a stream of light issues forth extending to infinity to your left. You now have a vertical stream of light passing through you from the heavens to the Earth. You also have a horizontal stream of light passing through you, extending to infinity at shoulder level.

7. Raise both arms out to the side, palms upward, and then

lay the hands over each other at the heart. Tone strongly the words:
"Le Olam Amen" (leh-O-lahm-ah-mehn)

This translates as "forever, Amen". As you tone them, see yourself a living equal-armed cross of light.

The visualization that enhances this exercise to see a brilliant crystalline white light descending from on high, through our head, down through the feet and into the heart of the planet. The light extends vertically through the body to infinity in both directions. Then we visualize a second shaft of light from shoulder to shoulder, extending in both directions to infinity. As we make the cross of light, touching each of the points on the body, visualize brilliant explosions of light. They should engulf each of the four directions, filling the body and extending into the lines of light.

Vibrate or tone the names / words strongly and clearly. If need be, tone them several times. This not only improves concentration, but it can help us to formulate the cross more clearly and vividly. We want the cross to be so brilliant that it is blinding in its intensity and actually lights up the universe. We become a living cross of light within the universe and all dimensions.

When visualizing, the idea of divine white brilliance should be focused upon. The vibrations of the words and the visualization attract a certain force to you. The nature and intensity of the force rests largely on the condition the mind is in. Thus we want to focus on the highest, most brilliant and most divine.

As we breathe in, breathe in the brilliance. As we slowly emit the breath, we should slowly pronounce the words. See and feel them vibrating and ringing throughout the universe with glory and power. At the end, visualize yourself assuming normal size, absorbing the brilliance into yourself as you return. In this way, it becomes a part of the light for your physical world.

EXERCISE:

Banishing Ritual of the Pentagram

Benefits:

- **intensely purifying to self and environments**
- **very grounding**
- **cleansing on all levels**
- **especially effective with negative thoughtforms and psychic attack**

This simple ritual involves using the power of the divine names associated with the Tree of Life, along with the power of the Archangels, for protective purposes. It is a protection against impure magnetism and influences. It cleanses the aura, as well as the environment in which it is performed.

This exercise builds a field of positive, protective, brilliant energy around you and your environment. It can be used to get rid of obsessive thoughts, protects against psychic attack, shields against lower astral entities, dissipates negative thoughtforms and seals the doors of other dimensions. It can cleanse the aura of negativity accumulated throughout the day, by our contact with others, and it seals the home against negativity projected towards it.

This banishing ritual should be practiced by anyone within the metaphysical or spiritual field. Those doing ritual work, or those just beginning to open to other energies and dimensions, those in psychic development and even those in healing work should practice it everyday to build a force field to prevent unwanted intrusions.

This exercise builds a ring of spiritual fire, studded in four directions with five-pointed stars of flame. It prevents anything other than the highest from entering into the environment. The more this technique is used, the more protective it becomes. It will set up a seal around your environment that dissolves negativity before it can reach us or after we have been touched by it.

The banishing ritual prevents a bleed through of subtle energies from other dimensions. Through it only the highest and truest vibrations can pass through the ring of fire, unless we invite it.

Once it is established, the sphere of sensation is purified, exalted and made impenetrable to disturbing influences. With such a purified aura, we can go anywhere, do almost anything, and visit most other dimensions without a fear of problems or attack. We must realize though that it is not a cure-all for a lack of temperance, patience or common sense.

IMPORTANT NOTE:

Initially this should be practiced everyday. It should also be performed at the end of pathworkings or ritual, for sometimes the doors do not close entirely. In time, it builds up permanently within your environment, so that only occasional reinforcement is necessary.

1. Stand, facing East. Perform the Qabalistic cross.

2. Step forward with the left foot, symbolic of "entering within".

3. Using your finger, a dagger, athame or slighted stick of incense, draw in the air before you a banishing pentagram.

Begin at the left hip and draw a fiery line in the air before you to a point just above your head. See the line as a blue flame. (This is a lot like creating the astral doorways.) Without stopping, continue the line down to outside the right hip. From the right hip, draw upward to just outside the left shoulder. Then continue the line of fire across the front of you to the right shoulder. From the right shoulder, bring the line back to the left hip, where you started. Envision a fiery blue pentagram in the air before you.

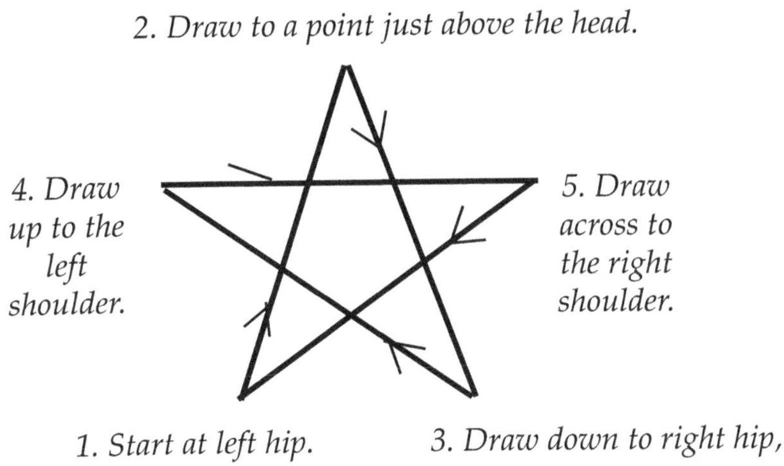

4. Thrust you finger (dagger, athame or lighted incense stick) into the heart of that pentagram and tone the divine name: "Yod He Vau He" (yOd-hA-vOv-hA)

Do this slowly and fully. Keep the finger pointing in the center. Visualize and feel the pentagram expand and explode with an intense blue heat and energy, engulfing you, your aura and all of your surroundings to the East. Visualize the pentagram continuing to grow, its heat and fire burning out all impurities and cleansing the entire eastern quarter of the world. Then it lodges in the East, burning strong and steady with purity and permanence.

5. Still holding the arm extended, pointing toward the heart of the pentagram, slowly rotate to the south (a quarter turn to the right).

As your arm moves with the body, see a stream of fire arc from the pentagram in the East to a point in the south. See this as the beginning of a protective wall or ring of flame. When completed, it will seal you within that ring of purity - sealing out negativity.

6. Drop the hand to a point outside the left hip, and just as you did in the East, inscribe in the air before you a second flaming pentagram in the South. Then thrust your finger into the heart of that pentagram and intone the divine name:

"Adonai" (ah-dOh-nI)

Visualize the same effects as with the star in the east, only now the South is being purified and cleansed, and the pentagram lodges itself permanently in the South. There are now two fiery pentagrams with an arc of flame connecting them.

7. With finger still extended, rotate another quarter turn to the West. See that arc of flame continuing, now to link the pentagram in the South with a point in the West. Inscribe in the air, a third pentagram, and as you thrust your finger into it, you intone the divine name:

"Eheieh" (A-huh-yAh)

The pentagram expands, growing, purifying everything to the West. You have now established the third pentagram and they are connected with a growing arc of flame.

8. Holding the arm straight out, you turn another quarter turn to the North, so that the arc of flame now extends from the East to the South to the West and to the North. Visualize and inscribe in the air, a fourth pentagram of fire. Thrust your finger into the center and intone:

"Agla" (ah-gah-lah)

This is not a divine name like the others. It is an abbreviation for the words "Ateh Gedulah le-Olam Adonai".

This translates as, "Thou art mighty forever, O Lord." As the fourth pentagram expands, it burns and purifies everything to the South.

9. With arm still extended, rotate to the East, completing the arc of flame and fire.

This is the protective ring of fire, studded in the four directions with flaming pentagrams. As you complete the circle, an explosion of purifying fire passes through you, around you - further cleansing and protecting the environment. This ring of fire and the pentagrams now burn upon the ethers and within the universe.

10. Drop your arms as you face the East, and breathe deeply of the purified air. See and feel everything around you cleansed and protected. Then still facing East, extend your arms out to your side, palms upward, and speak the word:

"Before me, Raphael."

Intone the name of the archangel strong and clear. Visualize a column of blue and gold light forming before you. From this column of light steps a powerful being whose energy seems fan the air around you. You feel a rush of air which revitalizes the aura. It is contact with great healing and protection. This being nods to you and then faces away from you, to protect you against any intrusion into your space - to guard the East for you.

11. With arms still outstretched, you intone the words:

"Behind me, Gabriel!"

Visualize a column of emerald green light forming behind you. From it steps a figure of those same colors with flashes of light. This being is electrical in nature, and you can feel it. This is Gabriel, a battery to the universe, and from this being comes the basis of all vision. The figure nods to you and then turns to face away from you to guard the West for you.

12. With arms still outstretched, you intone the words:

"On my right hand, Michael!"

To your right a column of crystalline red light begins to appear, blazing with all the reds of fire. From it steps a magnificent being, sword upraised. This great archangel handles and purges the unbalanced forces of nature. This being nods to you and then turns away from you to face and guard the South for you.

13. Then tone the words:

"On my left hand, Auriel!"

Visualize a column of crystalline white. From that column of light there steps a giant figure. This being has the primeval light of the Divine and works to manifest it upon the Earth. This being works with the light of all teachings. This magnificent being nods to you and then turns away, facing outward to guard the North for you.

14. Visualize all of the archangels surrounding you within this ring of fire. Feel their protection, their energies and blessings. Then speak clearly the words:

"Before me flame the pentagrams!
In the column of Light that I AM
shines the six-rayed star!"

"In the column of light" refers to the light of the physical body, the column of light you became through the Qabalistic cross. Visualize a six-pointed star shining with brilliance in the heart.

15. Visualize and feel the entire scene. Then seal it all into place by performing the Qabalistic cross once more. It locks the protection upon the ethers for you.

In this exercise, the archangels face away from us to guard against anything false, unhealthy, unbalanced, impure or negative. We are encircled by them - within a ring of fire, studded with flaming pentagrams. We are sealed in with blessing, balance, strength and health!

Chapter Eleven

Validating Your Experiences

"In heaven, learning is seeing; on earth, it is remembering. Happy is he who has gone through the Mysteries; he knows the source and end of life."

- Pindar

There are many lessons and responsibilities upon the spiritual path. In more ancient times, the awakening to higher levels of consciousness and aligning them with day-to-day consciousness was overseen by a master or a teacher. The ancients recognized that opening to higher planes and more subtle energies would stimulate what in the East are called *siddhis* or psychic energies. When activated, these energies require balancing and proper expression on a daily basis.

The siddhis are the energies of our true spiritual essence. They work through our lives whether we are aware of them or not. They bind and flow through our subtle bodies into our physical lives, all from our spiritual essence or higher self. When stimulated or awakened more fully through study, spiritual and occult exploration, meditation, dynamic prayer, psychic development, and a myriad of other ways, our spiritual essence becomes more closely aligned with our physical being. This releases greater amounts of its creative force into our lives - affecting us physically, emotionally, mentally and spiritually.

Remember that we are more than a physical being. We are multidimensional, and we have subtler bands of energy surrounding and interpenetrating our physical vehicle. They comprise part of our auric field, the field of energy surrounding all things. For information on the aura, consult my earlier work *How to See and Read the Aura* (Llewellyn Publications).

When working with the Tree of Life, we are trying to bridge our spiritual essence to our physical being, so that we can access it consciously at any time we desire for any purpose we desire. When we make efforts to "raise our consciousness", we stimulate the release of energy from our spiritual essence to be expressed within the physical life. By working with the Tree of Life we are learning to consciously stimulate the release of energy and to direct its flow and expression into our daily lives. When we work with the Tree of Life, there will *always* be an increased flow of creative forces that will manifest in our lives- with the potential of affecting all levels of our being and all areas of our life.

Ancient masters and teachers recognized this. They knew that concentrated study in the spiritual sciences and leading a spiritually disciplined life possessed greater potential for releasing these forces more tangibly into the physical life. This energy, once released, must find expression. That expression can be beneficial or detrimental because energy is neutral - neither good nor evil. It is only our expression and use of it that determines it.

That expression may become disruptive and destructive, finding inappropriate outlets in the physical life if there is not proper mental, emotional and moral foundations. It will over stimulate the individual in a variety of ways, affecting physical, emotional, and mental health and balance. If not prepared for, it will often find outlet through the person's own weaknesses, augmenting them and bringing them out into the open.

Because of the amount of information and knowledge available today, we do not always need a teacher to open to the more subtle realms of life. Methods and means of doing so can be found everywhere. The problem lies in assuming that the knowledge and information is true and safe. There is a great abundance of information available, but much of it is very irresponsible, and so the spiritual student must be even more discerning and discriminating. This is the spiritual lesson of Malkuth. It is the first thing we must learn and the last thing we will be tested upon on the spiritual path.

Because of the predominance of information, most people will not align themselves with truly qualified teachers, but this more solitary approach requires even greater personal responsibility. The student of the mysteries must still earn the conditions necessary for higher initiation and consciousness. This requires even greater time, care and responsibility in the development process.

There is no fast and easy way. Having done so in a past life does not override the training necessary in this life and those who teach or profess such are living an illusion. We may have learned to read in a previous life or even ten, but we still had to relearn it in this life. We had to learn the alphabet, the phonics, develop a vocabulary and so on. We must be cautious of our assumptions drawn from misinformation, half-truths and incomplete knowledge. This is what makes Daath so important in modern Qabalistic studies.

Spiritual Path in the Modern World

Today, the spiritual path demands a *fully* conscious union with the spiritually creative worlds. This cannot be accomplished by mere clairvoyance or psychism of any kind. Today's path to manifesting a higher destiny requires a genuine search and use of knowledge and truth. It requires a greater depth of study of all spiritual sciences. It requires remembering that information and knowledge is not always truthful and will not always benefit.

Unfortunately, we live in a fast food society. People like to pull up to the drive through window, get their food and drive on. They look for the quick and the easy, even with the spiritual. Many spiritual students want to pull up to the drive through window, get their psychic stuff and then drive on as well. No effort, no work, no problems.

Unfortunately, many spiritual and "new age" aspirants attempt to *be* before they have learned to *become*. It always trips them up through a variety of imbalances. So often people tell me, "You know, I had this great vision and I acted on it, and things started out wonderfully. Then it all changed and everything went wrong."

There is an old Qabalistic adage: *A vision of God is not the same as seeing God face to face.* In other words, a vision is not a promise of what will be. It is a reflection of what can be if there is the proper preparation, knowledge and application of focus, energy and persistence.

Knowledge is impotent unless it can be applied and integrated into one's life and essence in a balanced and creative manner. When it is, it brings understanding (Binah) and wisdom (Chokmah). True wisdom is the proper application of knowledge and understanding to life.

The process of becoming is time consuming, and many people do not wish to put forth the time and energy necessary for the true flow of knowledge, understanding and wisdom within their lives. Assimilating true knowledge is what enables us to manifest the more intense spiritual energies of the universe without short circuiting our lives in the process. Failure to prepare appropriately has the similar effect of running high voltage through low voltage wires. They may handle it at first, but eventually there will be a melt down.

Yes, there are quick ways of "rending the veils" - to open to forces and dimensions more subtle, but if the personal wires cannot carry the load, the current will become distorted or close. It will burn itself up. In the past decade, channeling became very popular, and there are quick methods for learning how to do so, but unless the channels have been cleared, cleaned and properly prepared, the communications eventually will become distorted and misinterpreted. The channel can also become a tool for those who mix the truth with half-truths and even lie to mislead individuals. Such beings, physical and non-physical do exist and so constant vigilance is required.

It is dangerous to enter the spiritual, more subtle realms of life and energy with a thinking that has only been strengthened through meditation, gathering information or mere psychic development. There needs to be an in-depth study and knowledge of the entire path of esoteric schooling in order to truly heal and intensify soul activities and to balance the events of one's life and align it with the universal process. It is to aid in this that Daath reveals its importance in the modern Qabala.

Frequently those with just a little knowledge feel they are constantly in control when in reality they are not. Unfortunately, the true realization of not being in control does not occur until it is usually too late. Even if techniques have been "learned" in previous lives - which many psychics and modern day pseudo-mystics credit for their facility - it still requires proper training to awaken the potentials in the safest most beneficial manner.

Our mind is a gateway to other dimensions. It has been said that we enter the mysteries through the sphere of the mind but only so we can worship at the shrine in the heart. Humans have grown increasingly rational in our thinking processes during this past century, and often this colors our higher feeling aspects. Today we need to link the mind with the heart - Daath with Tiphareth - creating within ourselves intelligence of the heart.

The true spiritual student should be familiar with the spiritual investigations and philosophies of the past. There must be the ability for complete and independent testing of the knowledge. The individual needs to develop the ability to draw correspondences and see relationships - similar and dissimilar. He or she must be able to discern the truth from half-truth and illusions from reality.

Knowledge can upset all previous conditions of the mind and body. Through the temple of Daath, through higher spiritual knowledge, we learn that there is often as much to unlearn as there is to learn. Any lack of control of the knowledge we acquire and how we apply it has the potential to disrupt and unbalance lives, with repercussions on all levels of our being. There are no shortcuts. Through the Tree of Life we learn to open to higher knowledge and to use it to integrate the spiritual forces surrounding us into our daily lives in a balanced fashion.

This doesn't mean it will be easy. It just means that now we have a great tool to help us. It means we can learn to invoke and invite energies into our lives that can bring result. It requires great time and effort, but it also brings great rewards for that time and effort.

The first lesson of knowledge is that nothing is insignificant. Everything has importance and consequence within our lives, helping to shape us. Recognizing this is what working with the Tree of Life is all about. Learning to utilize and incorporate all of our energies at all times - in full consciousness and with full responsibility - is the Great Work. It is *becoming* more than human; it is what makes us a human *being*.

Major Misconceptions and Half-Truths of the Spiritual Path

1. As long as I have my vision, all will be divinely protected.

2. I developed my abilities in a past life, so I don't have to worry about the development stages in my present life.

3. I must follow what my spirit guides (angels, guardians, etc.) say; they know better for me.

4. I have my guides and my psychic insight, which is all I need to keep balanced, grow and evolve.

5. I've developed my psychic ability, so now I am qualified to teach.

6. I have to be working in the metaphysical / spiritual field or I won't be growing or evolving spiritually.

7. If I'm suffering and struggling, I must be growing spiritually.

8. Problems and difficulties are signs of clearing out spiritual obstacles.

9. Others are able to do psychic/spiritual activities because they are more naturally gifted; they are just part of the special few.

10. Once I find my spiritual purpose, everything else in my life will fall into place.

Spiritual Initiation

It is the destiny of humans to conquer matter. This is the quest for the spirit, a search for our innermost part, the point of our greatest reality. It is not a path up to some divine light from which there is no return. Neither is it a path in which our problems and trials are dissolved in a blinding light of spirituality. It is our destiny to bring out the spirit into matter. That is when "the kingdom of heaven" manifests. Part of our life duty is to spiritualize matter, not to escape from it. The spiritual path is the search for a way to bring the spiritual aspects of life into our daily existence.

All of the ancient teachings and scriptures use similar terms to describe this magickal process. Gateways, doors, the outer court, the inner court, temple, the Holy of Holies, the quest, the pilgrimage and many other such words and terms are part of the ancient mystery language that hinted at and veiled the teachings that could assist the individual in manifesting a higher destiny, a more magickal existence. This mystery language often related to stages of development and training. It reflected the unfolding of our spirituality into our daily life.

Every civilization and religion has had its magickal teachings - its spiritual *Mysteries*. The phraseology may have changed and differed, but only to conform to the needs of the time and place. What is extraordinary, however, is that there are more similarities than differences in the methods used by the secret traditions to change the consciousness of their respective students and practitioners.

Today the mystical and magickal teachings are still called Mysteries, as they have been called for eons. In more ancient times the Mystery teachings of life were zealously guarded against outside intrusion to prevent their profaning. It is the profaning that draws the attention of the masses and fuels superstitions, fears and narrow-mindedness about anything occult.

In the Western world this unfoldment of the Mysteries is most often referred to as "The Quest for the Holy Grail". This quest serves two purposes for the modern spiritual student:

1. It is the search to discover and to awaken our true spiritual essence, our innermost self with all of its potentials, and

2. It is the quest for the best manner in which to express our highest potentials, abilities and essence within this life.

The ancient Mysteries have always been available to those willing to put forth the time, energy and patience to find them. For most people, even today, these spiritual Mysteries have assumed a supernormal and supernatural caricature. Occult and magickal teachings have always been referred to as Mysteries. And even today with all of the information available, many of the ideas and teachings are still somewhat unnatural to the average person.

There are a number of reasons for this. For many, the whole idea of an occult life is completely baffling, mysterious, ridiculous, intimidating or any combination of these. For those locked into a strictly mundane perception of life, the procedures for unfolding higher levels of consciousness and inner potentials will always be mysterious. The ancient teachings that lead to a higher destiny or a magickal existence can transcend customary experiences so much that balanced thinking can be disturbed. Unless an individual is well-grounded and has a well-founded base of experience and knowledge of all the spiritual sciences, imbalances will manifest, and unfortunately, these imbalances are what captures the attention and negatively color all spiritual studies.

Be it the mystical Qabala or any other system of unfoldment, certain reminders must be stressed. **All mystery systems, metaphysical philosophies, and religions are nothing more or less than systems of props to support and steady the mind and consciousness while it prepares for higher evolution.** When we set out to consciously bring divine energy into play within our lives more tangibly, we must learn to direct and control it in full consciousness!

The potential to accelerate and awaken our own divinity is within our ability. It is for this reason that above the portals of the ancient mystery schools was the phrase: *"KNOW THYSELF!"* Knowing thyself is the first stage of training in any true system of magick and spirituality. It requires an impersonal approach to all of our desires and beliefs that we have feared facing. It is not always a pleasant task. It often involves purging and stripping away the veils of pretense - those we have placed upon ourselves and those we have allowed society to place upon us.

This process is often repeated. It frequently requires that we retreat from time to time from active study and exploration, but we always return stronger and further along the path than if we had continued to force the growth. In many ways it is similar to the stripping process we go through at death, but only when it occurs while still fulfilling our life obligations in a creative and positive manner do we progress the most.

We can be our own worst enemy in this process. We either can't or won't make the most of our opportunities. We refuse to deal with our obligations and our hardships in a creative manner. We may resort to quick methods that ultimately create tremendously damaging difficulties down the road. These can vary from emotional imbalances to misuse of one's energies by ourselves or others that can hinder the progress of others, preventing them from becoming channels of light. Many just halt because the process is too great or demands too much effort. There are NO shortcuts to true spirituality. Metaphysics and magick are not fast food. It is never quick and easy.

"Do not believe in what you have heard; do not believe in traditions because they have been handed down for many generations; do not believe anything because it is rumored and spoken of by many; do not believe merely because written statements of some old sage are produced; do not believe in conjectures; do not believe in that as a truth to which you have become attached by habit; do not believe merely on the authority of your teachers and elders. After observation and analysis, when it agrees with reason and is

conducive to the good and benefit of one and all, then accept it and live up to it." (Max Muller in Three Lectures on Vedanta Philosophy. London: Longmans, Green and Co., 1984.)

There exists a major misconception today concerning the spiritual path and higher initiation. Many assume wrongly that if they are not actively working in the field of metaphysics (new age, magic, mysticism, psychic, etc.), they cannot truly be making progress. If not ostensibly demonstrating psychic ability or learnings, they wrongly assume they are not growing. As a result there is a preponderance of individuals trying to teach and work in this new economic market place, without the depth of knowledge and experience to do so in the safest and most beneficial manner for all.

Often it is a matter of ego. It is a way for individuals to tell others of their specialness. It is a way for many to make themselves stand out as more unique. Yes, there are many highly qualified individuals in this field, but there are also a tremendous number that are not qualified. The unfortunate part is that the average person entering into this realm is rarely capable of discerning the good from the bad.

It was to prevent such things that the ancient mystery schools required an active life aside from the spiritual studies and work. It is also why many required silence in the first two (and sometimes ten) years of their studies. They recognized that through the fulfillment of daily obligations in a creative manner we are propelled along our spiritual path.

It is not the demonstration of psychic ability or healing or book learning that unfolds our greatest potential. In fact, quite often, it can hinder it, especially in the early years of training. Rather than concentrating and focusing the transformative energy accessed in the learning process, it is dissipated by using it to teach or do psychic work prematurely. The need or desire to be out front, displaying, is part of what ultimately must be purged.

Yes, when we begin to open to these dynamic forces, it is wonderful, and it is natural to want to share that with others. Opening to these universal energies is inspiring. It will stimulate a great desire to share the illumination with others, but there is a proper time and place - one that is beneficial for you and for those with whom you share. Sharing the experience prematurely can dissipate its power and ability to work for you most effectively. Not everyone will be open to your sharing. The raised eyebrows of others can create blocks and raise your own doubts, slowing your progress.

Ultimately, it is through the daily trials and tests that we begin to unfold our sleeping potential, enabling ourselves to identify and then lay down outworn patterns so that the newer can come through. For most people this will involve simply opening the hearts of those they touch on a daily basis through a smile, a kind word or the meeting of an obligation or responsibility. Such individuals may not be demonstrating their knowledge or acquiring the attention that so many others seem to receive, but this does not mean they are less evolved.

This is the Quest for the Holy Grail, and for each person it is different. For some, the form of the quest will involve working and teaching in the metaphysical field as we know it today. For others it will take the form of simply living their daily lives in a creative manner and being a positive influence in the lives of those they touch. The form of the quest does not matter, because the secret of the quest is:

All who go forth,
in whatever manner,
will succeed!

Unfortunately not all have the wisdom or patience
to see this.

Three Tests of Higher Initiation

Today we often hear the term "ascension" being bandied about in metaphysical groups and gatherings. It is just another word for higher initiation, and the process, no matter what it is termed, is still the same. Though some wish to believe it involves a higher force that is taking everyone beyond the mundane into a realm in which troubles and difficulties are dissolved, each must still win for himself or herself the conditions for higher initiation and heightened consciousness.

The modern initiate must be able to take the knowledge, instructions and meditative content of his or her life, judge it independently and then decide what specific steps in esoteric learning and development apply individually. If unable to carry through this necessary self-observation, judgment and the obligation it is based upon, then more preparation is needed.

The process begins by being able to recognize that ultimately no one knows better for you and the divine spark within you. Yes, we all need teachers at times to guide us and help us connect more fully with that divine spark, but regardless of credentials, titles, degrees or abilities, the decisions concerning your life and the ensuing responsibilities and consequences are yours alone! This demands the development of secure perception and cognition - in both the physical world and the supersensible realms as well. This demands careful self-observation, discrimination and judgment, and great control of our own soul processes.

Everyone who intends to work for heightened consciousness and initiation will be tested along three avenues:

Test of Discrimination
Test of the Teacher
Test of Uncontrolled Fancy

1. Test of Discrimination

The test of discrimination is the first thing we encounter

and the last thing we will be tested upon on the spiritual path. We must be able to discriminate and discern reality from illusion, the false from the true, when to act, how best to act, where to focus our energies, when not to focus, whom to believe and whom not to believe. We each must be able to determine half-truths.

In the Tree of Life, discrimination is the test associated with the level of Malkuth, at the base of the Tree. Thus discrimination must be the basis of all our studies in the physical and non-physical world.

Connecting with supersensible states of consciousness and those beings and energies that exist within them does not make us omniscient or omnipotent. It demands even greater testing and discernment because those realms are more fluid, changeable and unfamiliar. The expressions of energy in the more subtle realms of life span the spectrum of positive and negative - as greatly as our own physical world.

2. Test of the Teacher

This is the testing of our ability to discern complete and truthful teachings and to recognize their sources. Today there are many who express a knowledge of how to work with the more subtle energies of life, but it does not mean that the methods are necessarily appropriate or beneficially creative, regardless of the momentary effectiveness. I have met a great number of individuals who have read a book or two and immediately set themselves up as a teacher.

Any time greater knowledge becomes more accessible, there is the opportunity to use it for greater benefit. There is also ample opportunity for it to be misused - sometimes consciously and sometimes unknowingly. Test and discriminate what comes to you - whether through a book or a person. Remember that no one knows better for you than YOU. When we do this, then our teachers and the teaching we encounter become mediators and assistants for our own bridge building to higher consciousness.

3. Test of Uncontrolled Fancy

This is the test of our ability to discern the maya and illusions that affect us when we begin to open to the more ethereal realms. Visions, channelings, insights can be nothing more than uncontrolled fancy, a manifestation of our own imaginings to stroke the ego. What may come through as spiritual insight may be little more than a fanciful manufacturing to verify what we already know or to justify our viewpoint.

Imagination is important to unfolding our higher potential, but it must be controlled. Sometimes the difference is difficult to detect, which is why continual self-observation is essential in all of the spiritual practices. Not delving deeply enough, accepting blindly and failing to be objective can all lead to uncontrolled fancy.

Today more than ever, there is a much greater need to test and validate all of our experiences. The difficulty for most people is figuring out how. There are not always clear signals. Sometimes, the determining is trial and error, but that helps us to learn and grow.

What we can do though is begin with simple questions about our experiences. Do they help us to resolve situations? Do they make us more productive and creative in all areas of our life? Do they have practical applications within our life? Do they blend the rational with the intuitive, the practical with the imaginative, the scientific with the philosophical and the physical with the spiritual?

And if our experiences accomplish these things, then we are truly opening to higher initiation. Then we are truly preparing for the Holy of Holies.

The Holy of Holies

Our individual quest for our true essence is one that can lead down many paths. Each of these paths become like a polishing stone that cuts and facets our rawness into a priceless gem.

In more ancient times, the spiritual student underwent symbolic faceting. Each phase of the training brought the student to a new temple which reflected energies and manifestations of the divine within the physical world. And each time the student had to synthesize and integrate this with the past. Temple by temple, the student grew until he or she was led into the last of the temples, the Holy of Holies.

This consisted of an empty chamber. No symbols. No altars. No tools. Just an empty chamber. Here the student is left to find the divine that exists within the temple's emptiness. Here the student learns to rely on his or her own higher self and the knowledge of the innate union between humans and the Supreme Being.

Here in the darkness of the last temple, we learn that only we can bring light and illumination to this temple. Only we can light the lamp within the sanctuary that brings brilliance out of darkness. Here we cease to look for a light to down but rather for the light that shines within us to shine out from us.

Here in this temple is the lesson of the divine within. Here we learn that only we can truly initiate ourselves into the mysteries. Here we understand the words of the ancient masters who all said in their own ways, "At that day ye shall know that I am in the father and ye in me and I in you!"

Appendix A

Pronunciation Guide

The guide that follows is to help provide a basis of correct pronunciation for the Hebrew words and names used most frequently with the Qabala. For our purposes, we will focus on the pronunciations for the sephiroth, their corresponding divine names and the archangelic names as well.

There are, of course, dialectical differences that do exist, but it is important not to become hung up on that aspect. If one is close in pronunciation, and focuses upon its correlations, the energies will be activated.

The names are spelled out phonetically, using the more common phonetic pronunciations found within any American dictionary. For the most part, several points should be kept in mind. (If some of these seem too obvious, and I imagine some people may roll their eyes at parts of this guideline, please be patient. I receive a great deal of mail and I am frequently asked questions about the proper pronunciations, in spite of phonetic spellings provided in my earlier texts.)

1. There are no vowels in the Hebrew alphabet. Vowel sounds are designated by diacritical marks. I have provided English phonetics for these sounds that are as close to the Hebrew pronunciations as possible.

2. In general, our consonant sounds are very similar or identical to the Hebrew, and so the consonant sounds should be pronounced as you would in English.

3. There are, of course, always exceptions. For example, the English language has no sound that is equivalent to the Hebrew "cheth" or "ch" sound. For those with a familiarity with the German language, the "ch" is pronounced a lot like the German words "nicht" or "ich". (Some people compare this to a soft clearing of the throat.) Until you become practiced in the more guttural pronunciation, pronouncing it as our traditional "k" sound will work quite well.

4. Long vowel sounds (where the vowel speaks its own name) are reflected through being written in capital letters. Thus an "E" is pronounced as in the word *bee.*

5. For vowels that are pronounced like the long sound of another vowel, it will be spelled out in capitals of the vowel whose sound it has. For example, for the sephira Binah the "i" has a long E (as in bee) sound. Thus it is spelled out phonetically as "bE - nah".

6. Short vowel sounds, are spelled phonetically, and with the key provided, there should be little confusion.

7. Although, most Hebrew words have an accent on the last syllable, for the basis of our work with the Qabala, give each syllable equal length and accent.

In the guide that follows, the information is in no way complete. Generalizations are made, and some of the more subtle distinctions in pronunciation have been eliminated. For example, the difference in pronunciation between the "t" of tau and the "t" of teth" is not distinguished and is rarely recognized by anyone other than those who are extremely familiar with the Hebrew tongue and language. These generalizations will not diminish your effectiveness and power when intoning these names.

Vowel Pronunciation

(REMEMBER: The long sounding vowels are designated and written with a capital letter. The short sounding vowels are spelled phonetically and will not be capitalized throughout this guide.)

a	"ah" sound as in *father* "uh" sound as in *sofa*
e	"eh" sound as in *bet* "E" sound as in *bee* "A" sound as in hay
i	"ih" sound as in *bit* "E" sound as in *bee* "I" sound as in *bite*
o	"ah" sound as in *not* "O" sound as in *opal*
u	"uh" sound as in *but* "U" sound as in *you*
ai	"I" as in *bite*

Sephiroth Pronunciation

Malkuth	mahl - kUth
Yesod	yeh-sahd
Hod	hOd
Netzach	neht-zahk
Tiphareth	tih-fah-rehth
Geburah	geh-bU-rah
Chesed	heh-sehd
Binah	bE-nah
Chokmah	hahk-mah
Kether	keh-thehr

Divine Name Pronunciation

Malkuth	Adonai ha Aretz	ah-DO-nI-hah-ah-rehtz
Yesod	Shaddai El Chai	shah-dI-ehl-kI
Hod	Elohim Tzabaoth	eh-lO-hEm-tzah-bah-Oth
Netzach	Jehovah Tzabaoth	yah-hO-vah-tzah-bah-Oth
Tiphareth	Jehovah Aloah va Daath	yah-hO-vah-A-lO-ah-vuh-dahth
Geburah	Elohim Gibor	A-lO-hEm-gih-bOr
Chesed	El	ehl
Binah	Jehovah Elohim	yah-hO-vah-A-lO-hEm
Chokmah	Jah	yah
Kether	Eheieh	A-huh-yAh

Archangel Pronunciation

Malkuth	Sandalphon	sahn-dahl-fOn
Yesod	Gabriel	gah-brE-ehl
Hod	Michael	mE-kah-ehl
Netzach	Haniel	hah-nI-ehl
Tiphareth	Raphael	rah-fah-ehl
Geburah	Kamael	kah-mah-ehl
Chesed	Tzadkiel	zahd-kI-ehl
Binah	Tzaphkiel	zahf-kI-ehl
Chokmah	Ratziel	raht-zI-ehl
Kether	Metatron	meh-tuh-trOn

Appendix B

Toning the Divine Names

The use of divine names in prayers, rituals, and affirmations has been practiced by all societies and traditions. All names and words have their own magic if we know how to use them. Frequently, I receive inquiries about specific words and phrases to uses for specific purposes, as if magic words have been hidden away in some secret cave to which only a few of us have access.

It is not the ancient words or divine names that have been kept secret. The real mystery of the power of words and names lies in the proper use of them. The steps to their use have been phenomenally consistent among all traditions:

1. Learn as much about the name, its meanings, and its correspondences as you can before using it.

The more you understand a name's significance and symbology, the more you can fully manifest the name's power when using it properly.

2. Use the correct pronunciation.

Do not get hung up on this aspect. If you are close and focus upon its meaning and significance, you will still activate the name's energies.

3. Try to tone the names syllable by syllable, giving each syllable a single breath.

4. Use directed esoteric toning techniques which has a two-step process.

First, inhale, sounding the name silently. Then, exhale, sounding it audibly. Inhale, exhale. Inner, out. Silent, audible. Spiritual, physical. As you perform the toning process, focus on the significance of the name and its energies. (Give equal emphasis to each part. Hold each tone as long as possible, pronouncing the entire name within a single breath. Refer to my earlier works, *Sacred Sounds* and *Music Therapy for Non-Musicians* for variations of this technique.)

The silent sounding or toning of the name on inhaling is most important. We are activating the name of the inner level; when we exhale, we bring the name forth audibly and substantially, releasing its energies into the outer world.

5. Keep the tones even and steady.

Volume does not make it any more effective. Allow yourself to find your own rhythm. The names can also be sung in specific tones to further amplify the effects. On the following page is a chart of the divine name of the Tree of Life with their corresponding energies.

Tones Associated with Each Sephira

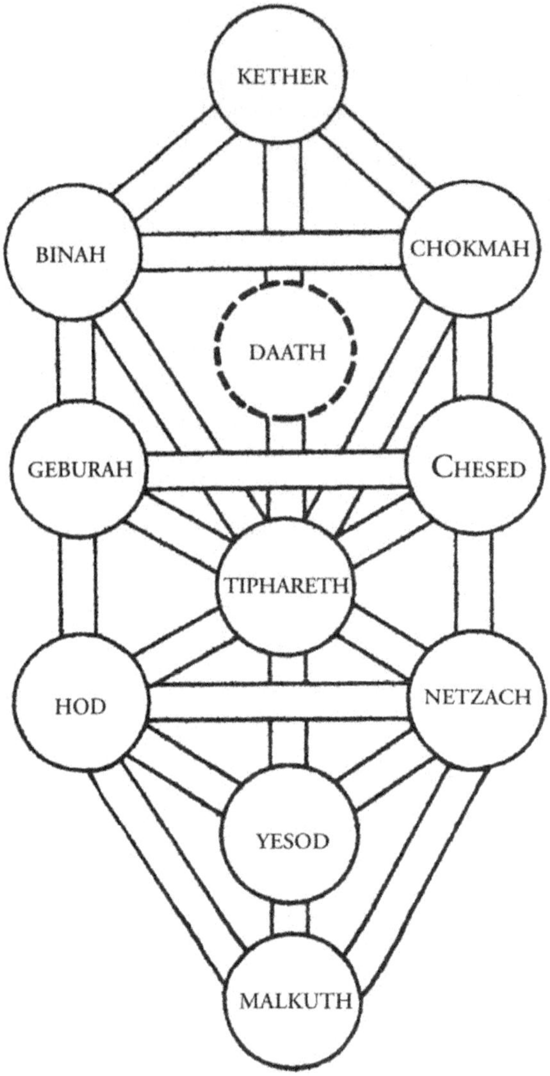

Malkuth
Adonai ha Aretz

Yesod
Shaddai el Chai

Hod
Elohim Tzabaoth

Netzach
Jehovah Tzabaoth

Tiphareth
Jehovah Aloah va Daath

Geburah
Elohim Gebor

Chesed
El

Binah
Jehovah Elohim

Daath
Jehovah Elohim

Chokmah
Jah (Jehovah)

Kether
Eheieh

Tones and Corresponding Energies

God Names and Tone Names	Energies within Consciousness Affected by Names
EHEIEH tone of B	Greater creativity; any final ending information; inner spiritual quest and its causes and attainment.
JAH/JEHOVAH tone of A#	Greater personal initiative; a source of energy which puts things in motion; father-type information; realization of one's abilities.
JEHOVAH ELOHIM tone of A	Greater understanding of sorrows and burdens; mother-type information; understanding on its deepest level; for strength through silence; understanding anything secretive.
EL tone of G	Greater sense of obedience to the Higher; financial gains, opportunities; building the new; justice; abundance; prosperity; hearing the inner call.
ELOHIM GEBOR tone of F#	Greater energy and courage; for tearing down of old forms; for change of any kind; critical judgment; information on enemies and discord.
JEHOVAH ALOAH va DAATH tone of F	Greater and higher sense of devotion; all matters of healing, life, and success; for harmony on any level and any matter; awakening of Christ consciousness; glory and fame.

Tones and Corresponding Energies (cont.)

God Names and Tone Names	Energies within Consciousness Affected by Names
JEHOVAH TZABAOTH TONE OF E	Greater unselfishness; understanding and power in relationships; sexuality and elements of nature; creativity and the arts; love and idealism.
ELOHIM TZABAOTH tone of D	Greater truthfulness; revealing of falsehood and deception around us; greater ability in communications, learning, magic, wheeling and dealings.
SHADDAI EL CHAI tone of middle C	Greater sense of true independence and confidence; greater intuition and psychic ability; mental and emotional health; dream work; understanding and recognition of the tides of change.
ADONAI HA ARETZ tone of F	Greater ability to discriminate in your life; to overcome a sense of inertia in life; physical health problems of self and others; affairs of home; greater self-discovers; elemental life.

Appendix C

Magickal Images & Gifts Quick Reference

This appendix contains an alphabetical listing of the magickal images and/or magickal gifts encountered when working with the Tree of Life. Additional information concerning the magickal images and magickal gifts can be found in the temple references located in chapter one and in the path references located in chapter five.

Magickal Image/Gift	Temple	Path
all seeing eye		12 Binah to Kether
apple		28 Yesod to Netzach
armor and weapons	Geburah	
ass		26 Hod to Tiphareth
basket of grain	Malkuth	
bear		27 Hod to Netzach
beetle (scarab)		29 Malkuth to Netzach
boat		24 Netzach to Tiphareth
Book of Knowledge	Daath	
bow and arrow		13 Tiphareth to Kether 25 Yesod to Tiphareth
bridge		25 Yesod to Tiphareth
bull		16 Chesod to Chokmah
caduceus	Hod	12 Binah to Kether
cauldron and the girdle		32 Malkuth to Yesod
chalice		15 Tiphareth to Chokmah
chariot		18 Geburah to Binah
child	Tiphareth	

Magickal Image/Gift	Temple	Path
clay pots		23 Hod to Geburah
cloak of concealment	Binah	
corn (basket of grain)	Malkuth	
Cornucopia	Chesed	
crescent	Daath	
crone (mature woman)	Binah	
crown that is too large	Tiphareth	
cup		12 Binah to Kether
cup and sacramental wine		23 Hod to Geburah
cup of bitters		19 Geburah to Chesed
cup of a king	Chesed	
dog		13 Tiphareth to Kether
dolphin		29 Malkuth to Netzach
dove		14 Binah to Chokmah 16 Chesod to Chokmah
eagle		24 Netzach to Tiphareth 28 Yesod to Netzach

Magickal Image/Gift	Temple	Path
egg		14 Binah to Chokmah
elephant		22 Tipareth to Geburah
equal armed cross		14 Binah to Chokmah
Eucharist host		20 Tiphareth to Chesed
fan		11 Chokmah to Kether
feather		22 Tipareth to Geburah
flint		31 Malkuth to Hod
full moon		14 Binah to Chokmah
girdle		17 Tiphareth to Binah
god (sacrificed)	Tiphareth	
golden fleece		21 Netzach to Chesed
Grail		21 Netzach to Chesed 28 Yesod to Netzach
hat with one feather		11 Chokmah to Kether
hawk		15 Tiphareth to Chokmah
Hermaphrodite	Hod	
Ibis		12 Binah to Kether
Isis figure	Daath	
Janus type figure	Daath	

Magickal Image/Gift	Temple	Path
jewels & gems of the earth	Malkuth	
king's cup	Chesed	
king (ancient, bearded seen only in profile)	Kether	
king (majestic)	Tiphareth	
king (mighty, crowned, throned)	Chesed	
lamp		20 Tiphareth to Chesed
lightning		27 Hod to Netzach
lion		19 Geburah to Chesed 30 Yesod to Hod
maiden (young) crowned and thorned	Malkuth	
male figure (older, bearded)	Chokmah	
man—beautiful, naked, strong	Yesod	
matron or a mature woman (crone)	Binah	

Magickal Image/Gift	Temple	Path
mirror	YESOD	
moon		13 Tiphareth to Kether
pentacle	DAATH	12 Binah to Kether
phallus	CHOKMAH	16 Chesod to Chokmah
phoenix		24 Netzach to Tiphareth
queen (mighty, crowned, throned)	CHESED	
rainbow		25 Yesod to Tiphareth
robe of many colors	BINAH	
rose	NETZACH	
rubies		27 Hod to Netzach
ruler (mighty, crowned, throned)	CHESED	
scales		22 Tipareth to Geburah
scarab (beetle)		29 Malkuth to Netzach
scared oils	MALKUTH	